1066

ANDREW BRIDGEFORD

1066

The Hidden History in the
Bayeux Tapestry

Walker & Company
New York

Published in 2006 by Walker Publishing Company Inc.
Distributed to the trade by Holtzbrinck Publishers

All papers used by Walker & Company are natural, recyclable products
made from wood grown in well-managed forests. The manufacturing
processes conform to the environmental regulations of the country of origin.

The Library of Congress has cataloged the hardback edition of
this book under LCCN: 2004381071

Paperback ISBN-10: 0-8027-7742-2
ISBN-13: 978-0-8027-7742-3

Originally published in Great Britain in 2004 by Fourth Estate
First published in the United States in 2005 by Walker & Company
This paperback edition published by Walker & Company in 2006

Visit Walker & Company's Web site at www.walkerbooks.com

Printed in the United States of America by Quebecor World Fairfield

2 4 6 8 10 9 7 5 3 1

Eventually
All things decline
Everything falters, dies and ends
Towers cave in, walls collapse
Roses wither, horses stumble
Cloth grows old, men expire
Iron rusts and timber rots away
Nothing made by hand will last
I understand the truth
That all must die, both clerk and lay
And the fame of men now dead
Will quickly be forgotten
Unless the clerk takes up his pen
And brings their deeds to life again

Wace, *Roman de Rou*, III, ll. 131–142
(*c.* 1170)

Contents

Map of Northern France and England · ix
Genealogical chart: England · x
Genealogical chart: Normandy · xi
Genealogical chart: Charlemagne/
    Boulogne/Jerusalem · xii
Genealogical chart: Ponthieu · xiv

1 *In Search of the Bayeux Tapestry* · 1
2 *A Tale of Consequence: The Impact of
    Conquest* · 11
3 *Sources* · 19
4 *Stitches in Time* · 26
5 *The Strange Journey of Harold
    Godwinson* · 48
6 *The Fox and the Crow* · 66
7 *The English Decision* · 98
8 *Invasion* · 118
9 *The Battle of Hastings* · 136

10 English Art and Embroidery 155
11 A Connection with Bishop Odo
of Bayeux 162
12 The Bayeux Tapestry and the
Babylonian Conquest of the Jews 166
13 The Tanner's Grandsons 173
14 The Scion of Charlemagne 181
15 Count Eustace and the Death of
King Harold 191
16 Eustace and the Attack on Dover 200
17 The Downfall of Bishop Odo 209
18 Turold the Dwarf 225
19 The Scandal of Ælfgyva 246
20 Wadard and Vital 272
21 Bayeux Cathedral and the Mystery of
Survival 295
22 The Patronage of the Bayeux Tapestry 304

Notes 311
Bibliography 333
Index 343
Acknowledgements 353

References to scene numbers in the book refer to scenes in the first plate section. References to plates correspond to images in the second plate section.

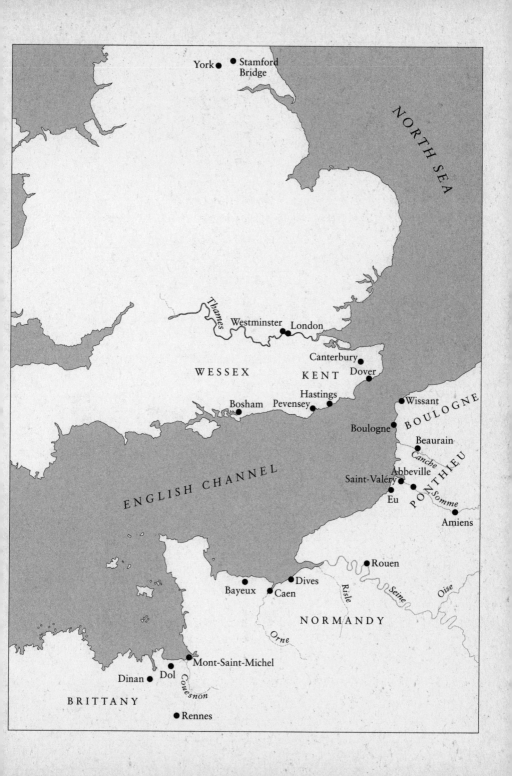

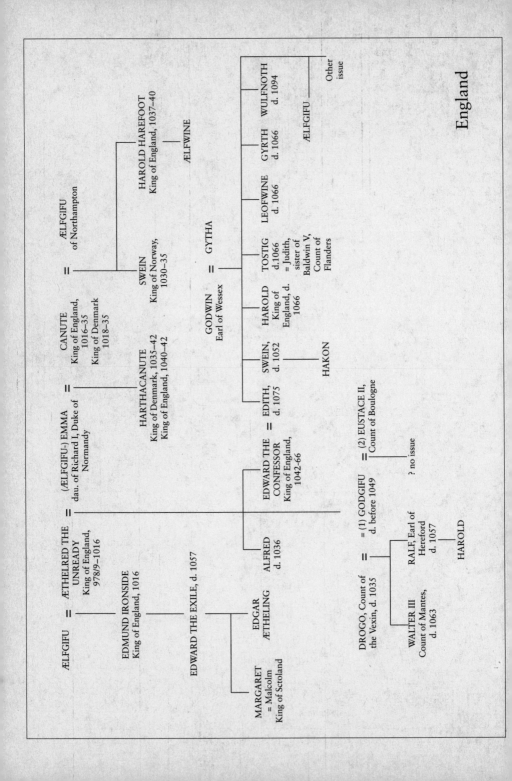

England

Normandy

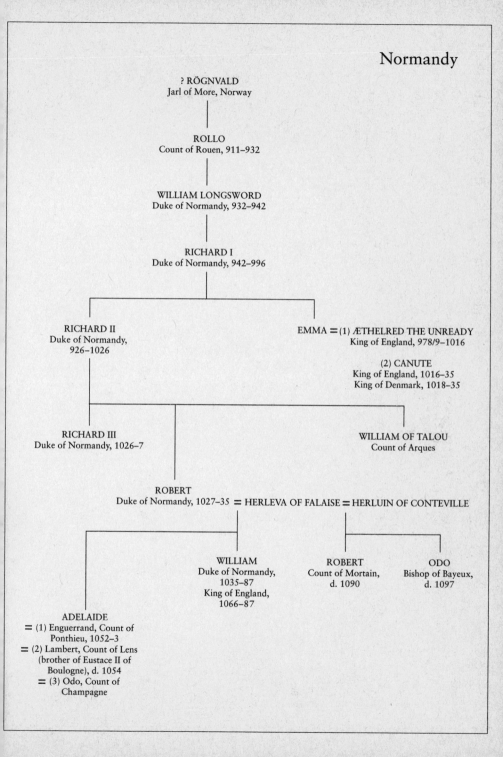

? RÖGNVALD
Jarl of More, Norway

ROLLO
Count of Rouen, 911–932

WILLIAM LONGSWORD
Duke of Normandy, 932–942

RICHARD I
Duke of Normandy, 942–996

RICHARD II
Duke of Normandy,
926–1026

EMMA = (1) **ÆTHELRED THE UNREADY**
King of England, 978/9–1016

(2) **CANUTE**
King of England, 1016–35
King of Denmark, 1018–35

RICHARD III
Duke of Normandy, 1026–7

WILLIAM OF TALOU
Count of Arques

ROBERT
Duke of Normandy, 1027–35 = **HERLEVA OF FALAISE** = **HERLUIN OF CONTEVILLE**

WILLIAM
Duke of Normandy,
1035–87
King of England,
1066–87

ROBERT
Count of Mortain,
d. 1090

ODO
Bishop of Bayeux,
d. 1097

ADELAIDE
= (1) Enguerrand, Count of
Ponthieu, 1052–3
= (2) Lambert, Count of Lens
(brother of Eustace II of
Boulogne), d. 1054
= (3) Odo, Count of
Champagne

Charlemagne / Boulogne / Jerusalem

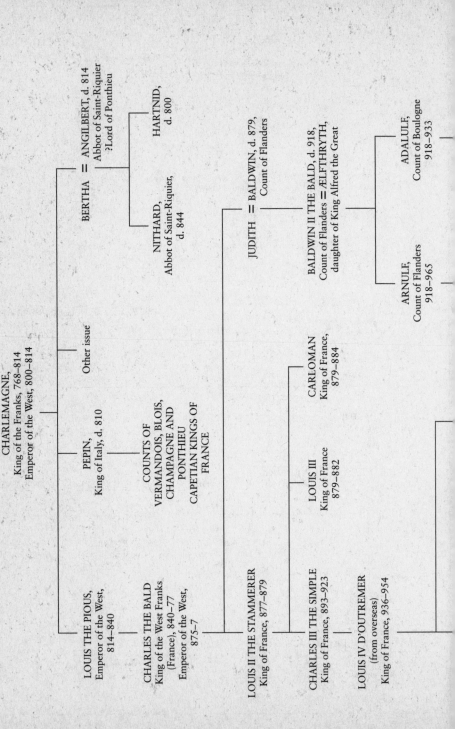

CHARLEMAGNE,
King of the Franks, 768–814
Emperor of the West, 800–814

BERTHA = ANGILBERT, d. 814
Abbot of Saint-Riquier
?Lord of Ponthieu

NITHARD,
Abbot of Saint-Riquier,
d. 844

HARTNID,
d. 800

PEPIN,
King of Italy, d. 810

Other issue

COUNTS OF
VERMANDOIS, BLOIS,
CHAMPAGNE AND
PONTHIEU
CAPETIAN KINGS OF
FRANCE

JUDITH = BALDWIN, d. 879,
Count of Flanders

BALDWIN II THE BALD, d. 918,
Count of Flanders = ÆLFTHRYTH,
daughter of King Alfred the Great

ARNULF,
Count of Flanders
918–965

ADALULF,
Count of Boulogne
918–933

LOUIS THE PIOUS,
Emperor of the West,
814–840

CHARLES THE BALD,
King of the West Franks
(France), 840–77
Emperor of the West,
875–7

LOUIS II THE STAMMERER,
King of France, 877–879

LOUIS III
King of France
879–882

CARLOMAN
King of France,
879–884

CHARLES III THE SIMPLE
King of France, 893–923

LOUIS IV D'OUTREMER
(from overseas)
King of France, 936–954

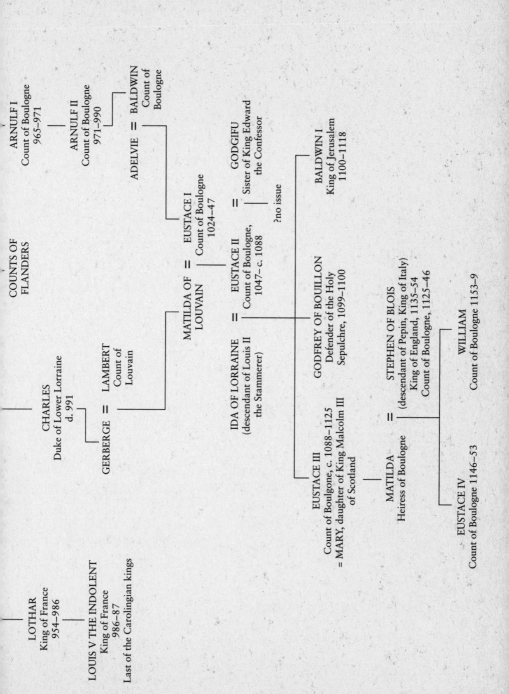

Ponthieu

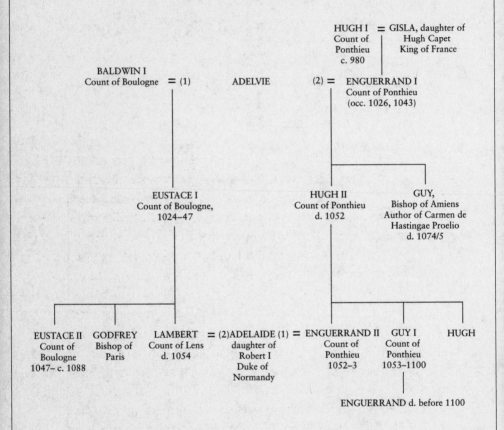

HUGH I = GISLA, daughter of
Count of   Hugh Capet
Ponthieu   King of France
c. 980

BALDWIN I
Count of Boulogne = (1)   ADELVIE   (2) = ENGUERRAND I
                                             Count of Ponthieu
                                             (occ. 1026, 1043)

EUSTACE I
Count of Boulogne,   HUGH II   GUY,
1024–47   Count of Ponthieu   Bishop of Amiens
                      d. 1052   Author of Carmen de
                                           Hastingae Proelio
                                           d. 1074/5

EUSTACE II   GODFREY   LAMBERT   = (2)ADELAIDE (1) =   ENGUERRAND II   GUY I   HUGH
Count of   Bishop of   Count of Lens   daughter of   Count of   Count of
Boulogne   Paris   d. 1054   Robert I   Ponthieu   Ponthieu
1047– c. 1088   Duke of   1052–3   1053–1100
                                            Normandy

ENGUERRAND d. before 1100

1

In Search of the Bayeux Tapestry

Five miles from the coast at Arromanches, in the gently shelving valley of the River Aure, lies the historic Norman town of Bayeux. From a distance the medieval cathedral emerges first into view, a faint impression of towers and spires, which gradually falls into sharper perspective as you approach the fringes of the town. War has touched Bayeux, but not scarred it. A ring road circumscribes the old centre, like a protective wall, and within its confines lies a network of shadowy streets and old stone buildings; and here and there the late-medieval frontage of a half-timbered house protrudes into the sunlight, as if it had emerged unwittingly out of the past into the present. At the centre of the town rises the enormous cathedral, a Gothic masterpiece built upon a Romanesque shell, its stark western towers, completed in the days of William the Conqueror, still soaring above the family of little houses gathered closely around its base. But it is not the cathedral, remarkable as it is, that every year draws half a million visitors to Bayeux. They come to see one of the most famous, intricate and mysterious works of art that has ever been made. Signs directing you to this masterpiece are dotted around the centre of the town. They are marked with a single descriptive word, in French and in English: '*Tapisserie.* Tapestry'. Here, in Bayeux, anything else would be redundant.

The route marked 'Tapestry' takes you along these narrow streets, under the eves of ancient houses and beneath the angular shadows of the cathedral. It passes by shops selling every item that can possibly be embossed with images of the Bayeux Tapestry, from mugs to mouse pads, tea towels to T-shirts. You may pause to recall the conquering exploits of Duke William of Normandy under the pale green awning of the Restaurant Le Guillaume or remember his wife, Queen Matilda, at the Hôtel de la Reine Mathilde. Not far away a crêpe may be consumed at the somewhat more alarmingly branded Crêperie Le Domesday. The journey takes you past these establishments and along the Rue de Nesmond until you reach a sizeable seventeenth-century building that was turned into a museum in the early 1980s. During the course of its long and dangerous history, the Bayeux Tapestry has been kept, and sometimes concealed, in several places in and around the town of Bayeux. This building is its modern home. Your eyes narrow at the museum's gate. Rain puddles scattered around the courtyard reflect the sun's fresh glare like so many broken panes of glass. A party of English schoolchildren has gathered in front of the door, a posse of noisy chatter, scuffed heels and clipboard assignments gripped with an innocent disregard. Two hundred yards away, Bayeux Cathedral is a silent witness to your journey, a stone silhouette imposed on a bright and changing sky.

You open the museum door, blinking as you enter. Inside it is quiet. You must buy a ticket. You follow a broad flight of stairs and then you emerge into a series of introductory rooms, like antechambers taking you step by step into the inner sanctum of a medieval mystery. At length you arrive in the longest of all the rooms, a long, windowless, narrow corridor with an unexpected bend in the middle. It is here that the Bayeux Tapestry is displayed, carefully illuminated in the darkness behind a thick glass case. It is stretched out in front of you like an enormous strip of film, a great colourful frieze of the Middle Ages, bright and lively, receding narrower and narrower into a dim and uncertain distance. Although barely half a metre wide, the work is astonishingly long, incredibly long for something that is so old and that ought to be so fragile that if you picked it up it might collapse into shreds. It runs for as far as can be seen along the wall of this narrow gallery, and then it rounds a bend and continues for as long again. It is, in total, about seventy metres in length; and it would have been perhaps ten metres longer had the final scenes not been lost at some distant point in the past. Even as it is, the surviving tapestry would outstretch Nelson's Column by more than a third of its height.

The dramatic story of the Norman invasion of England in 1066 is set out in these threads, stitched by contemporaries and preserved and displayed here, in the very heart of victorious Normandy. Despite its great age and fragility, the work is uniquely well preserved. Most of what we see today is entirely original, and in those places where it has been repaired, the marks left by the original stitches seem, with certain exceptions, to have been followed with care, and such restorations as have been made to the tapestry do not generally interfere with the thrust of its interpretation.[1] Embroidered on to a plain linen background in wools of red, yellow, grey, two greens and three shades of blue, the tapestry remains, against all expectation, as bright and captivating as if it had been made yesterday rather than nearly a thousand years ago. As you step along the dimly lit gallery, the extraordinary story unfolds. The linen stage fills up quickly with busy figures, in castles and halls, on ships and on horseback, urgently looking here, pointing there, full of meaning, their voices straining through the centuries to tell us something secret and important. This is a medieval tale of intrigue, danger and war. It begins with the mysterious events that occurred a year or two before 1066 – the crucial background to what followed – before building to a climax with the events that made 1066 the most decisive year in English history. Amidst all the high drama, everyday details, recorded incidentally and without pretension by the artist, vividly bring his world to life: here some men are feasting on spitted birds; there they are drinking wine from ivory horns; others hunt, sow or go to church; men wade through the shallow water with their tunics hitched high or struggle, bent forward, to load heavy provisions on to a waiting ship. Each time you look, it seems that some further beguiling detail, previously missed, becomes apparent. The work is at once accessible and straightforward and yet at the same time deeply mysterious and arcane. A Latin commentary running along the top of the main frieze by turns illuminates and then infuriates us by its very terseness and ambiguity. Above and below the main frieze, two narrow borders are filled with strange designs: creatures, real and mythical, ancient fables drawn from Classical authors, astrological symbols, scenes of everyday life, the odd erotic incident.

Despite all the signs saying 'Tapestry' the Bayeux Tapestry is not a tapestry at all. It is, to be more accurate, an embroidery, for the images are stitched on to the fabric, rather than woven in the true manner of tapestry-making. That said, the work is probably the most famous 'tapestry' in the world and it would be unnecessarily pedantic to insist on calling it

4

anything else. It stands alone. We have no equivalent wall hanging from its time to hold up for comparison, nor do we have any document which describes when, why and by whom it was made. What can be known about the Bayeux Tapestry can only be deduced by historical detective work. Likewise, how it came to be in Bayeux, where it only appears in the surviving records in 1476, must be surmised, if at all, from evidence.

Even after you have seen the Bayeux Tapestry many times, the detail, length and complexity of the work remain astonishing and beguiling. Depicted along its length are 626 human figures, 202 horses, 55 dogs, 505 other animals, 49 trees, 37 buildings and 41 ships. It is a man's tale: of 626 human figures only three in the main frieze, and two in the borders, are female. There are a few intriguing instances where the identity of a person, although not named, can be deciphered; but to identify individuals we are generally reliant on the running Latin inscription.

The inscription singles out by name a mere fifteen of the woollen actors; clearly, these are the key players in any quest to understand the true origin and meaning of the work. The named characters belong, for the most part, to the higher echelons of medieval society and they include famous men who would appear in any account of 1066; men such as Edward the Confessor, the old English king, and the two main rivals for his throne, Earl Harold of Wessex and Duke William of Normandy. In addition, however, four very obscure characters are also identified: a dwarf called Turold, depicted in the role of a groom [plate 1]; an English lady identified as Ælfgyva, seemingly embroiled in illicit liaison with a priest [plate 3]; and two minor Norman knights of no obvious significance, Wadard and Vital [plates 8 and 9]. The little dwarf, the elegant but scandalous lady and the two lesser-ranking Norman knights share the limelight with kings, dukes, counts, earls and bishops, teasing us to rediscover from other sources who they were and what strange significance they had in the artist's vision of 1066. We must attempt to turn these curious characters into more rounded individuals. Amongst those who are better known is Bishop Odo of Bayeux [plate 10]. Odo was William's greedy and ambitious half-brother. A key supporter of Duke William, he became, thanks to the Conquest, one of the richest men ever to have lived in England. Compared to other contemporary accounts, the Bayeux Tapestry gives Odo a surprising degree of prominence in the story of 1066. Studies of the tapestry have devoted much attention to the flattering way in which Bishop Odo is portrayed, but the focus on Odo has eclipsed the emphasis which is more subtly placed on others and it has obscured some of the more astonishing layers of hidden meaning in the work.

The popular conception of the Bayeux Tapestry is that it is a work of Norman triumphalism, of immense historical interest, no doubt, but ultimately a straightforward work produced by the Normans in order to celebrate and justify the conquest of England. Read any one of the many popular accounts and you will be told a similar story. It is said that we can see, in these threads, the childless English king, Edward the Confessor, near the end of his life, sending his foremost earl, Harold of Wessex, on a mission to Normandy; that Harold's mission is to confirm to Edward's distant cousin, Duke William of Normandy, that the old king has chosen him to be his heir; that after a misadventure in another part of France, from which Duke William obligingly rescues him, Earl Harold duly swears a solemn oath to be William's man. Back in England, however, when Edward dies in January 1066, Harold treacherously seizes the throne for himself. Duke William has been cruelly wronged by the greedy Englishman and so he assembles a large Norman army and invades England in order to claim his rightful inheritance; and in the end, of course, he defeats the perfidious English at the Battle of Hastings (though not without a little help from his half-brother Odo) and Harold gets his come-uppance thanks to the famous arrow in the eye. The story is told 'strictly from the Norman point of view.' 'It is all presented from a Norman perspective.' 'The story told in the tapestry is told from the Norman point of view.' Such is the view of the Bayeux Tapestry reiterated time and time again in travel guides, brochures and popular history books.

The truth is very different, and it is much more extraordinary. It has emerged only slowly over the last fifty years half-hidden in the dry journals and dusty tomes of academia. Much remains mysterious, and not all specialists are in agreement, but there are very good reasons to believe that the Bayeux Tapestry was not made in Normandy at all but in conquered England, probably within about a decade of 1066, and that the ingenious master artist, who drew the designs for a team of English embroiderers, produced a dangerously many-layered masterpiece. The result is brilliantly conceived, and full of hidden meaning. Only superficially does it support the Norman story. It is a testament to the ingenuity of the artist that so many ensuing generations have failed to notice that his agenda was in reality subversive. Working under the domination of the Normans, he designed the embroidery in a way that, super-ficially, would not displease the conquerors; however, at the deeper level he tells us a very different story. At a time when it was not possible to record the English view in writing the artist did so pictorially. What could not be said could at least be shown, subtly and ingeniously; and a work of art that the

Normans could accept and admire was in reality a Trojan horse within which the English viewpoint was ingeniously preserved. There is thus another story stitched in these pictures, a story that we must rediscover. It is a subversive account in which the Norman claim to the English throne, and much of the propaganda that the Normans were circulating, is systematically contradicted.[2] Far from being Norman propaganda, the Bayeux Tapestry is more like a long-lost version of the *Anglo-Saxon Chronicle*. At last we can begin to unravel this hidden story and in the process astonishing new light can be shed on the dark background to Duke William's pretension to the English throne in 1066.

In the same vein, it is often assumed that since the Bayeux Tapestry shows the Norman victory, it must be a Norman work. Mention *la Tapisserie de Bayeux* to a French person and you will often encounter a look of complete bewilderment. Mention *la Tapisserie de la Reine Mathilde* (Queen Matilda's Tapestry) and you are much more likely to be greeted with a smile of recognition. Old legends can be very enduring. There was once a romantic notion, first recorded in the eighteenth century, that the Bayeux Tapestry owes its origin to William's proud and admiring wife, Queen Matilda. She and her busy handmaidens, so it was said, embroidered the work in order to celebrate William's recent achievement in conquering the English. This notion has long been abandoned by historians (in France as much as anywhere else) but the old name has proved uncommonly difficult to displace in the popular French mind. A plaque bearing the words *La Tapisserie de la Reine Mathilde* is still fixed to the wall outside the museum in Bayeux where the tapestry is kept, presumably because numerous French visitors continue to arrive at its gates in the full expectation of seeing Queen Matilda's handiwork.

It is undeniable that the Bayeux Tapestry shows the Norman victory; the victory itself could not be denied. We shall see how the master artist set about subtly recording the English version of events that led up to the Norman Conquest, but more than that he sought to understand the Conquest in terms of the deeply held religious and metaphysical beliefs of his time. It was a tenet of eleventh-century Christianity that all great events were caused by the will of God. Thus, in seeking to explain how England came to be conquered by the Normans, the artist looked for guidance to the Old Testament scriptures and in the final analysis he sought to rationalise the subjugation of England as a divine punishment for sin. This was how the helpless, conquered people attempted to understand what had happened to them; the Normans, too, claimed God on their side. Yet there is a twist to all this; and the full implications of this twist have never truly been grasped. The artist appears to have been a supporter of Count Eustace II of Boulogne, a French count who, though he joined Duke William's invasion in 1066, was in other respects a rival to the Normans in the power games of northern France. He may even have had his own claim to the English throne. Generally misunderstood and wrongly called a 'Norman' in almost all popular accounts, Count Eustace of Boulogne was merely a lukewarm ally of Normandy and he was on the whole deeply distrusted by Duke William. Yet in the tapestry only three persons, Bishop Odo of Bayeux, Duke William of Normandy and Count Eustace of Boulogne, are named on the Norman side as being present at Hastings, and of these three Count Eustace, of all people, seems to be given the starring role [plate 11]. Particularly close attention must be paid to the career of this ambitious and powerful Frenchman. The perspective of Boulogne, too long forgotten, ignored or misunderstood, holds some of the Bayeux Tapestry's most beguiling secrets. The quest of this book is to attempt to unravel these and other millennial mysteries of the work.

2

A Tale of Consequence: The Impact of Conquest

Today the walls of eleventh-century buildings, such as survive, are cold and bare and they give nothing away of the brightness and luxuriance that once clothed them within. Were we to be transported back in time, however, and to step inside some of the great churches or secular palaces of the day, it would not be long before we encountered bright and colourful hangings draped around interior walls, as well as painted murals and other decoration on the stonework itself. Thus in the great Anglo-Saxon poem *Beowulf* a secular hall is described as resplendent with drapes, 'embroidered with gold' and picturing 'many a sight of wonder for those that delight to gaze on them'.[1] The widow of the Anglo-Saxon warrior Byrhtnoth, who died in 991 at the Battle of Maldon, is known to have produced an important stitchwork hanging to commemorate her husband's death and to have given it to the church at Ely.[2] Nothing of this survives; its size, design and technique are simply matters of guesswork. The Bayeux Tapestry is the unique survivor of a fragile genre. Even in the eleventh century it probably stood out as exceptional, for few persons would

11

have had the space to display a work so long and so vast, let alone the resources to commission it. That so many textile decorations, large or small, have perished in the interim is hardly surprising. What is extraordinary is that even one has survived. It is doubly fortunate that the sole surviving work of its kind is the one that recounts the single most important event in English history.

Nowadays it is more fashionable to have been a conquered people, rather than a nation of all-conquering warriors. It is more correct to bask in the innocent glories of defeat than to trumpet the more tainted achievements of conquest. Although England is often portrayed in the latter pose, the invasion and conquest of the country by the Normans must rank as among the most complete and ruthless that any nation has had the misfortune to suffer.[3] The Normans and other Frenchmen who settled in England formed only a small part of the overall population of between one and a half and two million, but they seized almost all the key positions of power. Within a few years, virtually all of the country's Anglo-Saxon aristocracy had been summarily ousted and replaced by a new French-speaking elite. One by one the leading bishops and abbots were also replaced by Normans or Norman appointees. Wealth beyond dreams, the spoils of conquest, now flowed into the coffers of the most important of these foreign invaders. By 1086, when King William took stock of land ownership in the country with his famous Domesday inquest, a quarter of England was held by just eleven of his closest followers. Of the 200 or so other aristocrats and adventurers who held another quarter of the country, only four were English. The great bulk of England's Anglo-Saxon ruling class had either perished in 1066 or had been reduced to second-class citizenry in their own land, or had fled to a hasty exile. Most of the new men were Normans but an important minority were allies of the Normans from other parts of France and from Flanders.

A network of castles, at first in wood, later in stone, was constructed around the country in order to enforce the new Norman order. Few castles had been built in England before 1066. Now the motte-and-bailey castle – a square fortress built on a man-made mound – became a familiar feature of the English shires. The death of King Harold at Hastings had removed the one man who was remotely capable of uniting the country in opposition. Henceforth resistance was never more than sporadic, and it was ultimately futile. If castles dashed any hope of rebellion, the nation's soul cowered under the shadow of magnificent new churches and cathedrals, confidently built by the invaders in a frenzy of construction in the latest continental style. Elegant, soaring cathedrals, such as those at Winchester, Ely and Durham, are outstanding artistic legacies of the Norman Conquest. The famous White Tower of London is a reminder of the military might which actually brought it about.

No one held a monopoly of violence in these violent times, but it is impossible to ignore the particularly brutal side to William the Conqueror's character. It was this that made the Conquest possible. He was a man of rigid will. If he thought that he was right he did not flinch from acting with all the terrifying force at his disposal, and with little regard for the innocent. The invasion of 1066, so vividly recorded in the Bayeux Tapestry, is a testament to the single-minded strength of purpose of the man. Less well known, though no less revealing, is William's crushing of a revolt in the north of England in 1069 and 1070 with a severity which touched all levels of society. Dividing his army into small units, he ordered his men to ravage the countryside wherever they went. Crops were burnt, English peasants slaughtered at will and the implements of farming everywhere broken and destroyed. It was a policy of deliberate terror: great swaths of land remained unproductive for at least a generation and there was widespread starvation – but of revolt we hear nothing more. Thousands must have died. Simeon of Durham recorded that corpses were left to rot in the streets and houses and that the surviving English citizens were reduced to eating horses, dogs and cats or else sold themselves into slavery. Every village between Durham and York was left deserted and lifeless.[4] Fifty years later Orderic Vitalis, a monk of dual English and Norman parentage, poignantly recalled all the 'helpless children, young men in the prime of their life and hoary greybeards' who had perished as a result of William's harrying of the north.[5] It was his reputation for this kind of brutality that enabled William to impose his rule on England. Few dared to speak out against such a man, still less to rebel.

If the immediate human cost of the Norman Conquest was large, the longer-term impact was in its own way just as dramatic, and in some measure it can still be felt today. The events of 1066 profoundly influenced the subsequent development of British, and indeed European, history. The country was summarily dragged from a niche in the Scandinavian world and with a jolt its face was turned firmly towards France. In the centuries that followed England was led by a French-speaking elite whose interests, or at least ambitions, lay on both sides of the Channel. As time went by England became more, not less, entangled in the regional and dynastic affairs of France. When the Norman dynasty came to an end, with the death of King Stephen in 1154, it was replaced by another French dynasty under Henry Plantagenet, a great-grandson of

William the Conqueror. The conflict known as the Hundred Years War, which finally came to a close in 1453, was the most prominent example of the long and often violent entanglement of Anglo-French relations whose ultimate cause can be traced back to a single event – the victory of Duke William of Normandy at Hastings in 1066.

The administration of England under the Anglo-Saxons had been sophisticated for its time and in their own interest the Normans took over the existing machinery of English government. The Normans retained, for example, the old Anglo-Saxon shires or counties as administrative units, and the division of England into counties survives to this day often with similar boundaries. Schoolchildren are taught that the Normans introduced 'feudalism' to England but historians are no longer certain whether this was so, or indeed whether the word 'feudalism' is useful at all. If nothing else, the need to hold down and subdue a conquered land with relatively few numbers enhanced the personal authority of the king and his powers of patronage. More susceptible of definition, and perhaps more enduring, were the cultural and linguistic changes. At a stroke, the old English language became the tongue of powerless underlings and it ceased largely, though not entirely, to be written down, and the development of English literature, hitherto represented by Anglo-Saxon poems such as *Beowulf* and *The Battle of Maldon*, was quite simply stalled in its tracks. *Beowulf*, a tale of the old Scandinavian lore, has recently found a wider audience with the acclaimed modern version of the poet Seamus Heaney. If some French speakers scoffed at Anglo-Saxon poetry, which to them probably sounded incomprehensible and uncouth, they, in turn, contributed impressively, both as patrons and authors, to the flourishing of a new culture. French epic poetry, exciting histories and didactic fables, written and recited to entertain french-speaking lords and ladies in their new English castles, all represent important staging posts in the history of French literature itself. Some even believe that the first great work that was composed in the French language, the *Chanson de Roland* (the *Song of Roland*), was actually written in conquered England.[6] Whether or not this is so, the earliest surviving version of the *Song of Roland* is certainly a copy that was written down in twelfth-century England.[7]

For hundreds of years the two languages existed side by side, French for the richer classes, English for those of middling status and the poor. As Sir Walter Scott observed in his novel *Ivanhoe*, echoes of this social and linguistic division can still be heard in modern English. Many living animals continue to be called by their old English names (sheep, cow, ox, deer) whereas once cooked and served up on the tables of the gentry they acquired names derived from the French (mutton, beef, veal, bacon, venison). Only in 1362 did French cease to be the language of the English parliament. When in 1399 Henry IV succeeded to the throne, he became the first English king since Harold Godwinson whose mother tongue was English rather than French. Even as late as the seventeenth century, English lawyers were using a degenerate form of French in order to report cases in the law courts. The Normans never sought to eradicate English. William the Conqueror is said to have tried to learn the language, but he found it too difficult and quickly gave up. Inevitably, because of the overwhelming preponderance of people speaking English, and endemic wars with France, French slowly died out as a spoken tongue, and by the fifteenth century modern English emerged as the common vernacular of the nation. By this time the French of the Normans and Plantagenets had enriched the language with thousands of new words. The vast number of synonyms in modern English is largely the result of this grafting of French, in the wake of the Norman Conquest, on to older Saxon and Norse roots. If Harold had won the Battle of Hastings, the language this book is written in would have been very different, a much more Germanic tongue.

Travelling around northern France today one can still find echoes of 1066. There are, of course, great Romanesque buildings erected, in part, thanks to money that poured in from conquered England – the completion of Bayeux Cathedral in the 1070s was probably financed by confiscated English wealth. Other reminders are less tangible but no less noticeable. From the hedged-in pastures of the Cherbourg peninsula in the west to the flat expanse of Flanders in the north-east there are many sleepy towns and villages whose names are poignantly redolent of some of the most famous British families. Each place is quintessentially French, each may have its café-bar, its boulangerie, its shuttered houses, its old ladies in blue cardigans who shuffle quietly down the street. It is from places such as these, with names like Cuinchy, Montbrai, Mortemer, La Pommeraye, Sequeville and Ver, that the eponymous aristocratic families of Britain sprang – de Quincy, Mowbray, Mortimer, Pomeroy, Sackville and de Vere.[8] It is a testament of the lasting social impact of the Norman Conquest that to British ears these names still bring to mind a succession of plummy-voiced aristocrats. The ancestors of these families (and many others could be cited) were powerful men who settled in England as a result of the Norman Conquest, if not immediately, then in the second and subsequent waves of immigration.

In these varying ways the events depicted in the Bayeux Tapestry had an impact that can still be felt today, like distant ripples in a pond long after the surface has been disturbed by the violent splash of a rock. That more than nine centuries later we can still perceive these effects is not simply a consequence of the Conquest itself. Since then the waters have remained largely undisturbed, for the Norman invasion in 1066 was the last time that England was conquered by a foreign power. No other unwanted invader – neither Philip II of Spain in 1580s, nor the Napoleon in the early 1800s, nor Adolf Hitler in the 1940s – has been able to match the extraordinary achievement of William the Conqueror.

3

Sources

Our quest is to investigate the true origin and meaning of the Bayeux Tapestry, to understand more about the characters who are named in it and with this to gain new insight into some of the darkest events of the Norman Conquest. This, of course, will require the story told in the tapestry's threads to be closely examined, but we will also need to compare it with the other contemporary accounts of the same events. There are a handful of these. Each has its own limitations; none has any inherent right to be regarded as inviolable truth.[1] On the English side of the Channel, two versions of the annals known as the *Anglo-Saxon Chronicle* have accounts of the Norman invasion, whilst a third comes to an abrupt end in 1066 shortly before it took place.[2] The fragile surviving manuscripts of the *Anglo-Saxon Chronicle* are themselves national treasures. The monks who wrote the *Chronicle* attempted to distil the important events of each year, as they saw them, into single short paragraphs. Sometimes this can provide us with important information. The treatment of the events of the Conquest is pervaded by a memorable sense of sadness, but as a source for its key events and causes, the *Anglo-Saxon Chronicle* is disappointingly brief and superficial. It passes over in complete silence the crucial episode that opens the story in the Bayeux Tapestry: the strange journey that Earl Harold made to the continent in 1064 or 1065. It seems that the authors of the *Chronicle* either did not know or were unable to reveal the truth behind Harold's mission.

The *Vita Ædwardi Regis* (the *Life of King Edward*) is a work which King Edward's queen Edith commissioned in the 1060s from a Flemish monk residing at the royal court and it is therefore usually treated as another English source.[3] Edith, who died in 1075, was Earl Harold's sister. She is seen (though not named) in the Bayeux Tapestry as a dutiful wife at King Edward's deathbed in January 1066 [plate 6]. The *Life of King Edward* survives in one near-contemporary manuscript copy, written out around 1100 in the small, neat handwriting of a single scribe. The work itself, though begun before 1066, seems to have been mostly written during King Harold's short reign. The author's original plan had been to celebrate the deeds of Edith's family, notably her father Earl Godwin and her brothers King Harold and Earl Tostig. The events of 1066, however, completely overtook this plan. The anonymous scribe, having optimistically begun his work in order to extol Harold's family, now had to make sense of the disaster that had overcome it. He turned to console the widowed and saddened queen by presenting her late husband Edward as a saint in heaven, and the *Life of King Edward* thenceforth dissolves into hagiography. Its contemporary character gives it many points of interest, including a dramatic account of Edward's final hours, but the *Life of King Edward* is often obscure and the work as a whole seems to provide little that truly enlightens the reader about the key events that led up to the Norman

Conquest. Here, too, Harold's strange journey to the continent is ignored. Even more surprising is the fact that Duke William of Normandy receives not a single direct mention.

In the written sources emanating from the Norman side of the Channel, Duke William cuts, as might be expected, a much larger figure. A Norman monk called William, working at the monastery of Jumièges, covered the period of the Conquest down to about 1070 in a Latin prose history known as the *Gesta Normannorum Ducem* (the *Deeds of the Norman Dukes*).[4] More detailed is the biography of William the Conqueror written in the 1070s by one of his chaplains, William of Poitiers. His work, the *Gesta Guillelmi Ducis* (the *Deeds of Duke William*), survives only through an incomplete version that was printed in the sixteenth century, for the only known manuscript perished in a disastrous fire in 1731.[5] It is by far the most detailed contemporary account of the events that concern us and its author was clearly well informed. As such the *Deeds of Duke William* will always be invaluable; but it is also biased. William of Poitiers was a Norman patriot. At each opportunity he loads praise upon Duke William and odium upon the evil and usurping Harold. His aim was to justify the Norman invasion, after it had happened; few doubt that he embellished the truth, and even knowingly lied, in what is quite patently a one-sided quest to make the Conquest appear lawful and justified. There are times when consulting William of Poitiers seems as useful as asking the editor of the Soviet *Pravda* about the inner dealings of the Kremlin, but in the absence of any similarly detailed English account of the same events it is William of Poitiers' story which has been widely accepted as history. He provides us, crucially, with the Norman interpretation of Harold's journey in 1064/5. He tells us that King Edward, nearing the end of his life, sent Earl

Harold to Normandy with specific orders to confirm that he had chosen the Norman duke to be his successor as king of England. The Bayeux Tapestry is often interpreted as telling exactly the same Norman story. We shall uncover the clues in the tapestry that subtly tell a very different, and much more plausible, version of Harold's mission.

The earliest written account of the Battle of Hastings is neither English nor Norman. It was written in another part of northern France. What we call France today was then a patchwork of regions over which the French king, beyond his own limited domain, exercised little more than nominal authority, and sometimes none at all. Normandy was a largely autonomous region. It had been founded in 911 when King Charles the Simple, despairing of ever seeing an end to Viking incursions, agreed to sue for peace by ceding land around Rouen to the Viking leader Rollo. Duke William of Normandy was Rollo's great-great-great-grandson. By 1066 the Normans had consolidated their rule over a large territory stretching from the Cherbourg peninsula almost as far as the mouth of the River Somme. To outsiders they appeared thoroughly French in language, custom and religion. They nevertheless retained a distinctive sense of identity, aloof, as Norman rather than 'French' in a more limited sense. The French neighbours of Normandy, on the other hand, had much to fear from the growing power of the duchy and in no sense should they ever be called 'Normans'. To the north and east of Normandy lay the counties of important non-Norman magnates such as Count Guy of Ponthieu and his kinsman Count Eustace II of Boulogne. Both had been enemies of Normandy in the 1050s and in lending support to Duke William's invasion of 1066 they were moved only by their own concerns. It is, therefore, of considerable interest that the earliest surviving account of

the Battle of Hastings was written by a non-Norman Frenchman, Bishop Guy of Amiens, who was the uncle of Count Guy
of Ponthieu and an uncle or step-uncle of Count Eustace of
Boulogne.

Bishop Guy's work is a substantial Latin poem called *Carmen de Hastingae Proelio* (the *Song of the Battle of Hastings*).[6]
Although long known to have existed, his account of the battle
was not rediscovered until 1826, when the archivist to the king
of Hanover happened to stumble across two twelfth-century
copies while researching in the Royal Library in Brussels. It
was a fortuitous find. The *Carmen* was possibly written as
early as 1067 and certainly before Bishop Guy died in 1074
or 1075. It gives us a distinctively French, but non-Norman,
perspective on the events of 1066, a continental counterpoint
to the Norman biases of William of Poitiers. Unlike the Norman sources, but intriguingly like the tapestry, the author of
the *Carmen* portrays Count Eustace II of Boulogne as the hero
at Hastings.

As the years went by further writers added their own
accounts. An English monk named Eadmer, working at the
abbey of Christ Church in Canterbury, wrote the *Historia
Novorum in Anglia* (the *History of Recent Events in England*)
between about 1095 and 1123.[7] Usually disregarded in favour
of earlier sources, Eadmer's brief account of the Norman Conquest in his *History* flatly contradicts the Norman background
to 1066 and it deserves much greater attention than it has
conventionally been given. Other twelfth-century writers followed Eadmer's lead and showed a marked degree of sym-
pathy for the conquered English, although they still justified
the Norman victory as leading to improvements in standards
of monasticism and morals in the country. In England there
were John of Worcester, Henry of Huntingdon and William

of Malmesbury; in Normandy there were Orderic Vitalis in the first half of the twelfth century and in the second the Jersey-born poet Wace.[8]

Orderic Vitalis was familiar with the complete version of William of Poitiers' *Gesta*, which he used extensively, though not without discretion, and he provides us with the most detailed and useful of the twelfth-century accounts of the Norman Conquest. Born near Shrewsbury in 1075 to an English mother and a Norman father, Orderic was placed by his parents in the Norman monastery of Saint-Evroul at the age of ten, 'a weeping child', he tells us, 'unknown to all, knowing no one'. He spent his whole life as a monk there, devoting himself to researching and writing. He wrote a continuation of the history of William of Jumièges, and then, between 1115 and 1141, he threw himself into a much larger project, a history of the Normans, which he called his *Ecclesiastical History*. Orderic's own beautifully neat copy of this work survives in the Bibliothèque Nationale in Paris. Divided in his sympathies between the England of his boyhood and the Normandy of his education and adult years, Orderic justified the Conquest of 1066 as bringing Church reform to England, but at the same time he did not flinch, where necessary, from criticising the brutality of the conquerors. He even makes William the Conqueror refer to himself as a 'cruel murderer' as he lies dying in 1087 and has him make the following rather uncharacteristic (and unlikely) admission: 'I treated the native inhabitants [of England] with unreasonable severity, cruelly, oppressed high and low, unjustly disinherited many, and caused the death of thousands by starvation and war, especially in Yorkshire.'[9]

Written sources such as these are the bedrock of historical investigation. The story told in these black-letter records is exciting and revealing and puzzling. Yet when you close these books and pass to the Bayeux Tapestry your imagination still feels as if it has emerged out of the darkness of a cave into a world of sunlit colours. These busy little figures are not just eleventh-century cartoon characters stitched on to linen. They stand for real people, real people whose lives were changed, and in some cases ended, by the greatest of all events in English history. More than that, recorded in these threads are forgotten stories yet to be retold.

4

Stitches in Time

How is it that so fragile an object has survived for so many centuries? What accident of fate decreed that it should endure, when so much else that is inherently more durable has perished? This, in itself, is a remarkable story.[1] The earliest evidence of the tapestry's existence appears at the turn of the eleventh and twelfth centuries. Some time between 1099 and 1102 a French poet named Baudri, abbot of the monastery of Bourgeuil, composed a poem for Countess Adela of Blois, a daughter of William the Conqueror.[2] Part of this poem describes, in elaborate and flowing detail, a brilliant tapestry that was apparently draped around the walls of Countess Adela's bedchamber. This tapestry, so Baudri tells us, was made out of gold, silver and silk, and among other things it depicted the famous conquest of England by Adela's late father. The poet proceeds to describe the work, scene by scene, and it slowly becomes apparent that what he is describing mirrors closely a large part of what we now know as the Bayeux Tapestry. Yet it cannot possibly be the Bayeux Tapestry. The work that Baudri describes is much smaller in scale;

the technique is different and the materials are altogether richer. Did Countess Adela's tapestry – a sort of exquisite, miniature version of the real thing – really exist on the walls of her luxuriant bedchamber? If it did, it has long been lost. Or was her tapestry, as Baudri seems to imply and as most scholars believe, purely imaginary, a literary conceit based upon his having seen the real embroidery at some unknown time and place before 1102? For he says that:

> This hanging contains ships and leaders and names of
>   leaders,
> if, however, this hanging ever existed
>   . . .
> If you could believe that this weaving really existed
> you would read true things on it.

This glimpse of the Bayeux Tapestry, through the mirror of a poet's imagination, is all that we have in any surviving record until well into the fifteenth century. Only in 1476 – over 400 years after the events depicted – do we find the first unequivocal mention of the work. This is also the earliest time that the tapestry can be proved to have been situated in Bayeux. An inventory of Bayeux Cathedral in the year 1476 tells us that the cathedral possessed 'a very long and narrow hanging of linen, on which are embroidered figures and inscriptions comprising a representation of the Conquest of England'.[3] Each summer, the document informs us, this old embroidery was hung around the nave of the Cathedral for a few days in the religious calendar.

How so fragile an artwork had survived since the 1070s, through the long and dangerous medieval age, has never been discovered. Even for a long time after 1476 the tapestry remains unrecorded in any surviving document. Always vulnerable to fire and vermin, and to the whims of changing fashion, it was especially at risk in times of war. It might easily have been destroyed during the bloody religious conflicts of the sixteenth century, for in 1562 Bayeux Cathedral was broken into and sacked by Huguenots. They went on a rampage through the building, burning letters and charters and destroying most of the items listed in the inventory of 1476. These included a great gilded crown that had been a gift of William the Conqueror and at least one extremely valuable, though unnamed, tapestry. The local clergy had warning of the attack and they had managed to transfer some of their most precious possessions to the care of the municipal authorities. Perhaps the Bayeux Tapestry was amongst the items secreted away; perhaps it was just overlooked by the frenzied attackers; somehow, at any rate, it escaped this near-disaster.

Other vicissitudes came and went; more peaceable times returned. The practice of exhibiting the work around the cathedral for a few days each year seems to have continued. We can, therefore, imagine the good citizens of Bayeux filing along the nave of their cathedral with the rhythm of each passing summer, admiring this antique embroidery on those few days when it was displayed to them. Apart from the changing fashions from the fourteenth to the eighteenth centuries, from flowing robes and pointed hats to tight breeches and coiffured wigs, the scene would have remained much the same – men and women, young and old, shuffling quietly along the smooth grey flagstones of their cathedral, peering intently at the work, some of their faces filled with pride at what seemed to be a simple chronicle of Norman achievement, others furrowing with perplexity at one of its more curious details. It was only in the eighteenth century that the Bayeux Tapestry came to the attention of the outside scholarly world. From this point its perilous journey down to the present day can be traced with greater certainty.

The chain of events that led to the 'discovery' of the Bayeux Tapestry is known in broad outline. The story begins with Nicolas-Joseph Foucault, who had been intendant of Normandy from 1689 to 1694. He was a learned man who spent much of his spare time in study. When he died in 1721 he bequeathed his collection of papers to the Bibliothèque du Roi in Paris. Among those papers was a skilful, if rather stylised, drawing of the first part of the Bayeux Tapestry. The antiquaries of Paris were intrigued by this mysterious drawing. Nothing in the drawing indicated where the original was, or indeed what it was. Nor was there any indication who the artist of the reproduction had been. The identity of the artist remains a mystery although it is possible that it was Foucault's own daughter Anne, who is known to have had a talent for drawing. In 1724 a scholar named Antoine Lancelot (1675–1740) brought the curious drawing to the attention of the Académie Royale des Inscriptions et Belles-Lettres. The Foucault sketch was reproduced in an article Lancelot wrote in the Académie's journal. This was the first time that any image of the Bayeux Tapestry would appear in print, but as yet nobody had the slightest idea what the thing was. Lancelot realised that the drawing was of an important work of art but in other respects he confessed his bewilderment. He had, he said, 'been unable to discover whether this sketch represents a bas-relief or the sculpture round the choir of a church or a tomb; whether it is a fresco or a painting on the glass of several windows or' (and here he hazarded a last guess) 'possibly a tapestry'.[4] He could see that the Foucault sketch only represented part of some larger work. He concluded that 'there must be a continuation'; though he can hardly have imagined how extraordinarily far the continuation ran.

The credit for tracking down the original goes to the Benedictine historian Bernard de Montfaucon (1655–1741). Having been alerted to the matter by Lancelot, he commenced his own quest to find the mysterious and intriguing artwork. By October 1728 his network of contacts had put him in touch with the prior of the abbey of Saint-Vigor in Bayeux. The prior was a local and he was able to tell Montfaucon that what was depicted in the Foucault drawing was an old band of embroidery which was exhibited in Bayeux Cathedral on certain days of the year. At last the enigma of the Foucault drawing had been solved and the Bayeux Tapestry became known to the outside world.

There is no surviving evidence that Montfaucon himself visited the embroidery, although it is difficult to imagine that he did not, having taken such pains to track it down. In 1729 he published the Foucault drawing on a slightly reduced scale in the first volume of his *Monuments de la monarchie française*. He then sent Antoine Benoît, one of the foremost draftsmen of the period, orders to produce an accurate sketch of the rest of the tapestry and to change nothing. In 1732 Benoît's sketch of the remainder of the tapestry was reproduced in the second volume of Montfaucon's *Monuments*. The whole of the surviving tapestry had now appeared in print. The early drawings are important: they provide evidence of the condition of the tapestry in the first half of the eighteenth century. Already the last section must have been missing for the work peters out in Benoît's drawing much as it does now. In his commentary Montfaucon reported that there was a local tradition that ascribed the tapestry to William's wife, Queen Matilda. Montfaucon thought that this theory was entirely reasonable. So began the unfortunate and pervasive myth of 'Queen Matilda's Tapestry'.[5]

A trickle of visitors arrived from England. One early English visitor was a learned antiquary called Andrew Ducarel (1713–85), who visited the tapestry in 1752.[6] He found that gaining access to it was surprisingly difficult. Ducarel had heard of the Bayeux embroidery and he was keen to see it at first hand but when he arrived he found that the priests at the cathedral resolutely denied all knowledge of it. Surely this could not be right, he insisted. He had read about the tapestry. He had travelled from England in order to see it. It depicted the conquest of England by William the Conqueror and they must know about it. No, they replied, he was mistaken. They had never heard of such a thing. Ducarel was not one to give up easily. He reiterated what he knew and then added the further information that the embroidery was displayed yearly around the nave of the very cathedral in which they were standing. At last, this appeared to jog the memories of the priests. It seems strange, but it was not the content of the tapestry but rather the circumstances of its exhibition that were familiar to them; but perhaps they were simply unwilling to unroll it for some passing traveller. At any rate, Ducarel's persistence paid off and he was at last led to one of the small lateral chapels on the south side of the cathedral, one dedicated to Thomas Becket. It was here that the Bayeux Tapestry was kept, rolled up in a strong wainscot press. Inch by inch it was unravelled for him in all its vivid colourful detail. Ducarel must have been one of the first Englishmen to see the Bayeux Tapestry since the eleventh century. He later wrote of his great satisfaction at seeing this 'immensely valuable' work; though he lamented its 'barbarous needlework'. The general difficulty in locating the tapestry was not helped when no less a thinker than the great philosopher David Hume incorrectly reported that 'this very curious and authentic monument' had been lately discovered in 'Rouen'.[7] At any rate, the celebrity of the Bayeux Tapestry on both sides of the Channel was slowly increasing; but dangerous times were ahead. Having survived seven centuries of obscurity in astonishingly good condition, the fragile embroidery was now to embark on some of its most perilous adventures.

The storming of the Bastille prison on 14 July 1789 ushered in the overthrow of the monarchy and the violent upheavals of the French Revolution. The old world of religion, aristocracy and monarchy stood for everything that the revolutionaries were against. In 1792 the revolutionary government of France declared that everything that reflected the history or 'vanity' of the monarchy was to be destroyed. In a frenzy of iconoclasm, buildings were damaged, sculptures were torn down and the priceless stained-glass windows of many French cathedrals were smashed to pieces. In 1793 a bonfire took place in Paris in which 347 volumes and 39 chests of historical documents were summarily consigned to the flames. Other precious historical papers were used to make cannon cartridges. The atmosphere of destructive paranoia soon reached Bayeux. In 1792 a local contingent was called up to fight in the French Revolutionary Wars. In all the haste, it was forgotten that one of the equipment wagons needed a protective covering. As soon as this was realised, someone helpfully suggested that there was an old stretch of vainglorious embroidery made by Queen Matilda and kept in the cathedral. It seemed that this would suffice admirably for the purpose. The agreement of the local administration was obtained and a motley crowd of soldiers marched into the cathedral. They perfunctorily seized the tapestry and placed it on their wagon. The local commissary of police, a Bayeux lawyer called Lambert Léonard-Leforestier, was informed of the matter only at the last moment. Knowing all too well the incredible artistic and historical value of the town's tapestry, he immediately issued an order for its return. Then, showing remarkable courage, Léonard-Leforestier rushed to where the tapestry was being held and personally harangued the crowd until they agreed to hand it over in return for a stout piece of canvas. It was a close escape. Evidently, however, there were still some revolutionaries who nursed an ongoing desire to destroy the Bayeux Tapestry. In 1794 there was a proposal to cut the tapestry into shreds in order to decorate a carnival float in honour of the 'Goddess of Reason'. By this time, however, the tapestry was in the hands of a local art commission and they were fortunately able to take steps to prevent its destruction.

From Baudri onwards, no one seems to have guessed that there was an English viewpoint ingeniously stitched into this ostensibly Norman work. No one even dreamt that the Norman story was being subtly undermined at every turn. On the contrary, it seemed to Frenchmen and Englishmen alike that the Bayeux Tapestry was a primitive celebration of the defeat of Anglo-Saxon England, happily embroidered by the wife of the victorious conqueror. Predictably Napoleon Bonaparte looked upon the tapestry as useful propaganda. In 1803 he was planning his own invasion of England and in order to drum up further enthusiasm for this enterprise he issued an order that the *Tapisserie de la Reine Mathilde* should be brought to Paris for public exhibition at the Louvre (or Musée Napoléon as it was then called). The tapestry had been kept at Bayeux Cathedral for as far back as written records could attest. Grave concerns were expressed by the townspeople at the prospect of seeing the work depart, perhaps never to return. In spite of their misgivings, the local authorities felt constrained to comply with First Consul's directive and so it was that for the first time in hundreds of years the Bayeux Tapestry left the small town of Bayeux and was taken to Paris.

The Paris exhibition was a great success. Crowds flocked to see this curious exhibit and it quickly became a topic of conversation in fashionable society. A play was even written about the tapestry, during the course of which the eponymous Queen Matilda is seen busy at work and a fictitious boy called Raymond complains to her that he, too, wants become a soldier-hero and to be depicted in embroidery.[8] Whether Napoleon saw this play is not recorded, but the First Consul is said to have brooded over the embroidery itself for some time. Like William the Conqueror, he was making vast and detailed preparations to invade England. His forces were formidable. At this moment Britain stood more gravely exposed to invasion from northern France than at any time since 1066. Napoleon's fleet of 2,000 ships lay assembled between Brest and Antwerp and his *grande armée* of between 150,000 and 200,000 soldiers was encamped at Boulogne. The historical parallels became even more apposite when, in late November 1803, a comet-like object was seen passing across the skies of northern France and southern England; the parallel with the ominous appearance of Halley's Comet in April 1066, itself vividly depicted in the Bayeux Tapestry [scene 29], did not pass without mention. Was this another portent of the defeat of England? A description of the 1803 'comet' was hastily printed and inserted into the brochure of the Paris exhibition. Yet despite the nicely timed appearance of another passing celestial body, Napoleon Bonaparte was not to repeat the success of William the Conqueror. This time Britain stood prepared; the invasion never came. Napoleon could not risk the Channel crossing without control of the sea, and an indomitable navy stood guarding the southern coast. Napoleon's invasion plans were in due course abandoned in 1805. By this time the tapestry was once more back in Bayeux. Contrary to the fears of many townspeople, the work was duly returned to Bayeux in early 1804, but this time it was passed into the hands of the town's secular, rather than religious, authorities. Never again has it been displayed in the great edifice of Bayeux Cathedral.

With peace restored between Britain and France by 1815, the Bayeux Tapestry ceased to be of interest to propagandists and it returned to the more genial province of international scholars and artists. As people began to appreciate just how narrowly it had escaped destruction, attention turned to the question of the tapestry's continued preservation. There was concern that the contemporary method of exhibition – which involved repeatedly coiling and uncoiling the tapestry with a machine – was itself causing damage, though the authorities were lamentably slow to respond to this concern. It was in this context that the Society of Antiquaries of London commissioned Charles Stothard, an eminent draughtsman, to produce a set of drawings in order to record the complete embroidery. Stothard worked on the project for the two years between 1816 and 1818. His drawings in particular, as well as those of previous artists, have been immensely valuable to researchers in tracking the appearance of the tapestry down the years. Stothard was not only a fine artist. He wrote a short commentary on the tapestry that was learned and perceptive, one of the best that had yet been written.[9] Moreover, by closely examining the surviving evidence where the tapestry had deteriorated, Stothard was able, here and there, to reproduce in art what he believed to have been the tapestry's original appearance. In due course his work helped to guide the hands of subsequent restorers. To his great credit, Stothard realised the urgency of making such a record. 'Within a few years,' he noted, 'the means of accomplishing it will no longer exist.'

And yet the endnote of Charles Stothard's involvement with the Bayeux Tapestry turns out to be one of human frailty. Working for long periods alone with this unique work of art, so vividly redolent of the greatest event of his nation's past, Stothard succumbed to the temptation to remove a small piece of the upper border for himself, approximately 2½ by 3 inches in size. In December 1816 he managed to return to England with his souvenir undiscovered. Five years later, before it had become known what he had done, Stothard tragically fell from a scaffold at the church of Bere Ferrers in Devon and was killed. Through Stothard's heirs, the little fragment found its way to what is now known as the Victoria and Albert Museum in London, where it was exhibited, quite openly, as 'A Piece of the Bayeux Tapestry'. In 1871 the museum decided that it ought, in all propriety, to return the stray piece to Bayeux. The missing fragment was gratefully received but by then the damage had been done and repairs effected. It was decided that Stothard's souvenir should remain in the little glass case in which it had arrived from London, complete with its English description, but that it should be displayed adjacent to the place where the fragment had originally been cut away. This was all well and fine, except that hardly a day would pass without a visitor accosting the keeper and asking him about the fragment and its curious English label. Eventually the keeper became so exasperated that Stothard's piece was removed from display and it was placed for safe keeping in the municipal archives, where it still remains.[10] A story also circulated that Mrs Stothard had been the culprit – on account, some said, of 'the weakness of the feminine character'; but no one now doubts that Charles Stothard himself had been the thief. He was not alone in wanting to depart with a memento. A thief on a lesser scale was the Rev. Thomas Frognall Dibdin – and it would be naive to assume that there were no others. Dibdin visited the tapestry shortly after Stothard departed in 1818. In a book of his travels he reported, with an air of perfect normality, that having gained access to the tapestry with some difficulty, he managed to obtain for himself 'a few straggling shreds of the worsted with which it is worked'.[11] What became of these scraps is unknown. In 1842, when the tapestry was removed to a new home in the town, it was finally placed beyond the reach of souvenir hunters on permanent display in a long glass case.

The fame of the tapestry continued to spread, aided no doubt by the photographic reproductions that became possible in the second half of the nineteenth century. To Mrs Elizabeth Wardle, however, this was not enough. The wife of a wealthy silk merchant, she decided that England ought to have a record of the Bayeux Tapestry that was more tangible and enduring than a mere coloured photograph. In the mid-1880s she gathered a group of Victorian ladies of like mind and together they set to the task of embroidering a life-sized replica. So it was that the whole of the Bayeux Tapestry was made again, once more in England, 800 years after the original embroiderers had laboured over the selfsame task. The Victorian copy took two years to complete; the result was in most respects a brilliant and accurate likeness. Half close your eyes and walk around this replica today and you can easily believe that you are standing in front of the original itself. There were, however, limits to what these ladies could bring themselves to portray. When it came to depicting the male genitalia, which appear, on occasion, with noticeable prominence in the original, a strictly accurate rendering had to be forsaken in order to spare the blushes of all concerned. In their copy, the Victorian embroideresses decided to deprive one naked male character of his manhood entirely; another, they thoughtfully provided with a pair of underpants. Perversely, what they modestly sought to censor now draws attention to itself by its concealment. Completed in 1886, the facsimile was taken on a triumphant tour of England and thence on visits to the United States and Germany. In 1895 the replica was donated to the town of Reading by Arthur Hill, a former mayor. Britain's own version of the Bayeux Tapestry now has pride of place in Reading Museum.

The Franco-Prussian War of 1870–71 and the First World War passed without mishap to the Bayeux Tapestry. It was during the Second World War that it was to undergo some of its greatest adventures.[12] On 1 September 1939, just as German troops were attacking Poland in a manoeuvre that was to plunge the continent into five and a half years of war, the tapestry was carefully removed from its exhibition case, rolled on to the spool, sprayed with insecticide powder and locked for safe keeping in a concrete shelter within the basement of the bishop's palace at Bayeux. There it remained for a year, except for the odd occasion when it was checked and the insecticide renewed. In June 1940 France fell. It was not long before the tapestry came to the attention of the occupying forces. Between September 1940 and June 1941 the tapestry had to be retrieved and exhibited to eager German visitors at least a dozen times. Like Napoleon before them, the Nazis were hoping to repeat William the Conqueror's invasion of England. They, too, regarded the tapestry as a potent source of propaganda and inspiration, never suspecting for the slightest moment the subversive undercurrent that runs through the work. The German invasion, like that of Napoleon, was postponed in 1940. Churchill's Britain was also better prepared than Harold's England. Britain narrowly won the battle of the skies and, though the bombing of its people continued, Hitler's thoughts turned to the invasion of the Soviet Union.

Even so, German interest in the tapestry was not to be assuaged and a more sinister group soon began to take an abiding interest in the work. This was the *Ahnenerbe* (Ancestral Heritage), the research and teaching branch of Heinrich Himmler's SS which had been set up to provide 'scientific' evidence of the superiority of the Aryan race. The *Ahnenerbe* attracted a significant number of German historians and scientists who enthusiastically moulded their scholarly careers to the advancement of Nazi ideology. As an organisation, it remains notorious for its role in the inhuman medical experiments that were perpetrated on concentration camp victims, but history and archaeology continued to be a focus of its attentions. Even at the height of war, the SS devoted considerable resources to the study of Germanic history and archaeology, to Himmler's occult interests, and to the plundering of art and artefacts of Aryan origin from occupied territories.

What commended the Bayeux Tapestry to the *Ahnenerbe* was not only its depiction of a successful invasion of England. It was a work of art that seemed to celebrate the fighting prowess of Nordic peoples – the Normans, descendants of the Vikings, and the Anglo-Saxons, descendants of the Angles and Saxons. Amid the terrible conflagration of world war, amid the seismic clash of army with army, the 'intellectuals' of the SS devised an ambitious project of study of the Bayeux Tapestry, including its complete photography, with an artist copying the images and publishing of the results. The French authorities had little choice but to comply. The most that could be done was to make representations concerning the safety of the work and to ensure that no one could say that it had passed into ownership of the occupying forces.

For the purposes of study, the tapestry was transferred under military guard to the nearby abbey of Juaye-Mondaye in June 1941. The head of the study team was Dr Herbert Jankuhn. Professor of archaeology at Kiel, he was an active and enthusiastic member of the *Ahnenerbe*. Jankuhn gave a lecture on the Bayeux Tapestry to Himmler's Circle of Friends on 14 April 1941 and he talked on the same subject to a regional meeting of the German Academy at Stettin in August 1943. After the war, Jankuhn, although implicated in the Nazi plundering of artwork from occupied territories, resumed his academic career. He published widely on Dark Age history; many students and scholars must have read and quoted his works without ever knowing of his more dubious past. In due course Jankuhn became an emeritus professor at Göttingen. He died in 1990. His papers on the Bayeux Tapestry have recently been donated by his son to the Bayeux Tapestry museum, where they will form an important part of its archives.

At length, at the suggestion of the French authorities, the Germans agreed that the tapestry should be moved for safe keeping to the art depot that had been created at the Château de Sources, near Le Mans. This was a sensible idea, as the château, a vast eighteenth-century mansion set in 200 hectares of parkland, was situated at a safe distance from any vulnerable conurbation. Unfortunately, however, no facilities were provided to assist the French make the journey, and this, there and back, was a good 220 miles. The mayor of Bayeux, Monsieur Dodeman, a distinguished-looking old man with a pointy beard as white as Edward the Confessor's, did his best to find some suitable form of transport for the famous embroidery. Despite much searching, the only vehicle that he was able to obtain was a singularly unreliable and potentially dangerous lorry which ran on charcoal, a Delahaye 10-horsepower *camionnette à gazogène*. So it was, early in the morning of 19 August 1941, that the Bayeux Tapestry began one of its most improbable journeys. The great work, together with its unrolling mechanism and twelve bags of charcoal, was loaded on board. The prefect of police, Monsieur Cervotti, and the keeper of the tapestry, Monsieur Falue, followed their driver on to the vehicle, and the spluttering *camionnette* departed with its priceless cargo in the direction of Sourches. The journey had already begun two hours late, on account of difficulties in starting the engine, but it was with earnest hearts and eager minds that the three gentlemen entrusted with the Bayeux Tapestry set off on a route that was to take them through the undulating countryside known as 'Swiss' Normandy.

At first things appeared to be going rather well. Not having eaten since early morning, the custodians of the tapestry stopped for lunch in the small town of Flers; the driver tuned off the ignition and the engine came to a halt with a shudder. The repast was presumably enjoyed; but when it came to recommencing the journey the engine refused to start. For twenty minutes the driver poked and twisted and shoved with his tools, and when at last the motor spluttered into life he re-emerged from a puff of smoke with his face black with soot and his features glistening with sweat. Cervotti and Falue hastily regained their places, but any further optimism was again misplaced. The engine faltered on the very first incline, just outside the town. Fearing that the motor would give out completely, the middle-aged keeper of the tapestry and the prefect of police jumped off the lorry and by dint of their considerable efforts managed to push the vehicle and its precious cargo to the brow of the hill. At this point, however, it proceeded to get away from the men pushing it and only came to rest when it reached level ground, the breathless Cervotti and Falue running behind as fast as they could in order to catch up with the runaway tapestry. The exercise of pushing the lorry uphill had to be repeated many times. It took ten hours, in all, to accomplish the distance of little more than 100 miles which separates Bayeux from Sourches.

Once at their destination, our exhausted heroes had no time to rest, or even eat. As soon as the Bayeux Tapestry and its mechanism were unloaded, the return journey had to be commenced, for the Germans enforced a strict curfew at 10 p.m. and it was hoped to regain Bayeux that night. Although the *camionnette* was now considerably lighter, it proved no more adept at surmounting the rolling hills of Normandy. Cervotti and Falue were obliged to dismount and push many more times. By 9 p.m. they had only reached Alençon, not even halfway back to Bayeux. It was getting dark and drizzling coldly; they had no choice but to break the journey. The Germans, however, had recently evacuated the coastal regions and Alençon was overflowing with refugees. Our heroes began a quest of biblical proportion to find somewhere to stay. There was absolutely no room at any hostelry, nor could any restaurant or café provide them with the slightest sustenance. Eventually the concierge at the town hall, having heard of their plight, took pity and offered them an attic room, which doubled as a prison cell for black marketeers. All that he had in the way of food was eggs and cheese, but this modest meal was accepted and consumed with relish. The next day, by dint of another four and a half hours of sweaty toil, the three gentlemen arrived back at Bayeux. Cervotti and Falue immediately reported to the mayor, who had been anxiously waiting for news ever since the previous evening. Despite all the vicissitudes of the journey, they were able to report that the Bayeux Tapestry had been transported across occupied Normandy, safe and intact, and that it was now in storage at the art depot at the Château de Sourches.

The tapestry remained practically undisturbed at Sourches for another three years. It was not until 1944 that it faced renewed danger. On 6 June 1944 the great seaborne Allied landings on the coast of Normandy, years in preparation, finally took place. It was as if history had held up a great mirror to the events of 1066: a vast fleet of ships, packed with warriors, was crossing the Channel but this time in the opposite direction, from England to France, and it was intent upon a mission of liberation rather than conquest. Despite intense fighting, the Allies found it difficult to break free of their initial bridgehead. Sourches was over 100 miles inland, but evidently it was still too close for comfort, for on 18 June 1944 orders were given by the German authorities, with the agreement of the French minister of education, for the Tapestry to be taken for its own safety to Paris. It appears that the leader of the SS himself, Heinrich Himmler, was the impetus behind this latest move. Alone among the priceless artworks which were deposited at Château de Sourches, it was the Bayeux Tapestry that he insisted should be taken to Paris.[13] On 27 June 1944 it duly arrived, this time under SS guard, and it was placed in a dry cellar at the Louvre.

Ironically, long before the tapestry arrived in Paris, Bayeux had already been liberated. It was taken by the 56th British infantry division on 7 June 1944, the day after the Allied landings. Bayeux was the first town in mainland France to be freed from the Nazi yoke and, unlike so many other old towns in Normandy, its historic houses and monumental cathedral emerged unscathed from the war. The British War Cemetery, just outside the town, now bears a fitting Latin inscription recording that those whom William conquered returned to liberate the land of the conqueror. Had the famous tapestry depicting William the Conqueror's invasion remained at Bayeux it would have fallen into the safety of the liberators' hands sooner than it eventually did. Now in Paris, however, it was to suffer another knife-edge encounter with disaster.

By August 1944 the Allies had at last advanced to the outskirts of Paris. Eisenhower, the supreme commander of the Allied forces, had been keen to bypass the city and push on towards Germany, but the leader of the Free French, General de Gaulle, feared that Paris would fall into the hands of the Communist resistance and insisted that the French capital be liberated as a priority. Eisenhower eventually agreed and the Allies were now moving in on the city. Sporadic street fighting was already taking place between the Germans and disparate resistance groups. General von Choltitz, the overall German commander of the city, had received orders from Hitler that if Paris were not defended it was to be utterly razed to the ground, an act of wanton vandalism that would, if carried out, have been unsurpassed by any in history. To this end, the principal bridges and buildings of Paris had been mined, and a tunnel under the city had been filled with U-boat torpedoes capable of causing tremendous explosions. Von Choltitz came from an old Prussian military family. To disobey orders ran against every fibre of his being, but he now realised that Hitler was a madman, or at least that Germany was going to lose the war, and he sought, during those tense August days, to play for as much time as possible in order to find a way to surrender Paris to the advancing Allies without either wanton destruction or loss of face.[14] Under these circumstances, on Monday, 21 August 1944, two SS men suddenly presented themselves at his office at the palatial Hôtel Meurice.

The two men, elegantly attired in smart new SS uniforms, gave the customary 'Heil Hitler' salute. Von Choltitz may well have thought that his time was up, that they had come to arrest him for disobeying Hitler's orders, but what they actually wanted was rather more bizarre. They said that they had orders from Himmler to seize the Bayeux Tapestry and to take it to Berlin. In the curious logic of the Nazis, the city of Paris with all its monuments was to be destroyed but the Bayeux Tapestry was to be saved. What was to become of it in Berlin is not known. It would be naive to assume that it would have ever found its way back to Bayeux. The ultimate intention may have been to house it, along with other Nordic relics, at some quasi-religious shrine for the scrutiny and instruction of the elite of the SS.

Von Choltitz took the two SS officers to his balcony and gesturing towards the Louvre told them that the tapestry was being kept in a basement there. Events were moving fast. It was clear that the Louvre was by now in the hands of the street fighters of the French Resistance. At that very moment stuttering machine-gun fire could be heard emanating from the portals of the museum. Von Choltitz suggested that five or six of his own men could provide covering fire, so as to enable the SS officers to storm the Louvre and seize the precious tapestry. The two SS officers withdrew for a moment to consider their position. One of them thought that he had found an honourable way out. Surely, he said, the French authorities must have evacuated the tapestry long ago and the assault would turn out to be pointless. Von Choltitz replied that he believed the tapestry to be still there. He asked for his artistic adviser to come into his office; the adviser duly confirmed that the tapestry remained at the Louvre. The two SS men reflected for a further moment before deciding that it would be better to depart empty-handed, for, as von Choltitz later remarked, the courage of their hearts did not quite live up to the brilliance of their uniforms. According to von Choltitz, the SS men had two lorries at their disposal and enough petrol for the return trip to Berlin. At a time when large amounts of fuel were almost impossible to come by, and the resources of the German army were in every way stretched, the length to which Heinrich Himmler was prepared to go in order to safeguard the Bayeux Tapestry for his own nefarious purposes is quite remarkable. Four days after this incident, on 25 August 1944, Hitler, holed up in his headquarters in the forests of east Prussia, finally lost his patience and snarled at his generals, 'Is Paris burning?'[15] Fortunately, on that very day von Choltitz surrendered, Paris was safe in Allied hands and the wartime dangers faced by the Bayeux Tapestry were effectively over.

The old mayor of Bayeux, Monsieur Dodeman, had received not a breath of news about the tapestry's fate since November 1943. He assumed, as did many, that the embroidery was still at the Château de Sourches, well out of harm's way; and he had no idea just how narrowly it had escaped the threatened destruction of Paris and the clutches of Himmler's SS. Likewise the first 'monuments' officer of the Allied force to arrive on Norman soil, a New York architect named Bancel LaFarge, notwithstanding that he was based in Bayeux, was at first unaware of the tapestry's precise location. It was only at the end of August 1944 that LaFarge was able to inform the mayor that the tapestry was not at Sourches at all, but in liberated Paris. Overjoyed to learn that the precious treasure was still intact, Monsieur Dodeman at once requested the authorities in Paris to return the tapestry to Bayeux, where, no doubt, British troops and Norman civilians alike would appreciate viewing a relic so redolent of their shared past. The roads of northern France were still vulnerable to air attack, and the Parisian public had not had the opportunity of seeing the tapestry in their own city since the days of Napoleon. The mayor was therefore persuaded to allow it to be placed on public exhibition for a few months at the end of 1944 at the Louvre, a repeat in rather different circumstances of the exhibition of 1803.

Finally, in March 1945, on the eve of peace in Europe, and following a successful showing in Paris, the Bayeux Tapestry was returned to Bayeux after an absence of almost four years – the longest known period that it has ever been absent from the town. The Tapestry was at last able to resume a more tranquil existence. The post-war years saw an enormous increase in tourism, and with the number of visitors increasing each year, it became evident in the 1970s that the building it then occupied in Bayeux was no longer adequate. A Bayeux seminary, built in 1653, was chosen as the tapestry's new museum. In 1983 the conversion of the building – renamed as the Centre Guillaume le Conquérant – was completed and Bayeux's great embroidery is now fittingly displayed there. Visitors of every nationality arrive each year in their thousands at the gates of this fine museum. Few know of the tapestry's own eventful past. They come to admire this precious and unique survivor of the distant age of the eleventh century and to recall the deadly rivalry of Earl Harold of Wessex and Duke William of Normandy – a rivalry that shook their world, and still, in some ways, affects ours.

5

The Strange Journey of Harold Godwinson

The year is 1064 or early 1065 [scene 1]. The elderly king of England, seated on his finely made chair, is in a secret conference with two men. One of them is his brother-in-law, Earl Harold of Wessex; the other is unknown. The pale, full-bearded old king, known to history as Edward 'the Confessor', is a large, stooping figure in a long green robe. Now in his sixties, he has reigned over England for more than twenty years. The country is prosperous; its government, for the times, is sophisticated and efficient. The ability of the Anglo-Saxon monarchy to collect a nationwide tax is elsewhere unparalleled, and no doubt envied, in the other halls of European power. All, however, is not well. In twenty years of marriage Edward has failed to produce a single heir and this failure has inevitably caused an aura of uncertainty to hang over the delicate matter of the succession.

The low and muffled talk at that meeting would have proceeded against a very different background had Edward ever fathered a son; but his marriage with Edith, Earl Harold's sister, had been completely barren.[1] It was one of those political unions which kings are often constrained to make. In this case the political imperative in the 1040s had dictated an alliance with the powerful Godwin family, without whose support he would have found it difficult to rule England. We cannot know the true cause of Edward's childlessness – the secrets of the royal bed remain discreetly curtained off to history – but it is certainly not difficult to identify strains which may have affected the conjugal life of the royal couple. Long before they were married, before Edward was even king, a terrible crime had taken place which had touched Edward deeply. In 1036 his younger brother Alfred had been kidnapped, tortured and murdered by a rival faction during a period of uncertainty that had followed the death of King Canute – when, as now, there had been no single indisputable heir to the throne. Edward long suspected that Queen Edith's father, Earl Godwin, had been a party to the crime, but Godwin was the most powerful man in the nation and the case against him had never been proved. On Edward's accession in 1042 he had had little choice but to work with Godwin, to accept Godwin's oily hand of friendship and to harness his power as best he could for the governance of the country. He may even have married Earl Godwin's daughter on an optimistic note. The marriage was, after all, a potent alliance of blue blood and raw power; but it was not an amorous success and Edward soon regretted it.

He had made one abortive attempt to break free of the bonds, both political and matrimonial, that bound him to the Godwin family. In 1051 he acted with unexpected resolve and contrived to send Godwin and his sons into exile, and his unloved queen to a nunnery. The following year the Godwins returned. They were armed, angry and amply supported. The king's soldiers, fearing outright civil war, were reluctant to fight and Edward backed down. Godwin was restored to power; Edith returned to the royal household; and from that moment the king's authority was fatally weakened. Against this political and familial background, it is not entirely surprising that no children were ever born to Edward and Edith. When Earl Godwin died in 1053, having collapsed at an Easter feast given in the king's own hall, his mantle as England's leading earl was inherited by the queen's senior brother, Earl Harold of Wessex.

Now, as they meet in that secret huddled gathering that opens the story of the Bayeux Tapestry, more than ten years have passed, ten years since Harold first stepped into his father's shoes. In those ten years he has consolidated his position as by far the most important nobleman in the nation. Neither before nor since has any one noble ever been quite so predominant. With his brothers Tostig, Gyrth and Leofwine also holding key earldoms, and his sister Edith as queen, Harold's family appears, at least while it remains united, a more formidable entity than ever. Harold, then, is a man of stature, a sprightly, moustachioed figure in his forties, elegant of physique, noble in his bearing and enormously wealthy. To his friends he is handsome, open-hearted and clever. To his enemies he is beginning to be feared for his battle-hardened qualities as a war leader. Recently he has been campaigning on the king's behalf in Wales where King Gruffydd had been a thorn in England's side. Aided by Welsh rebels, Harold returned to England in triumph at the end of 1063, presenting the unfortunate Gruffydd's head to King Edward in person.[2] Earl Harold has proved himself a worthy successor to his father's legacy and he has formed what, at the very least, seems to be a satisfactory working relationship with the king. From cool beginnings, the two men seem to have warmed to each other over the years.

The old king stoops forward as if speaking to Harold in a low voice; their forefingers touch. It is almost as if we are there, in this wispy opening scene, eavesdropping on history at one of its pivotal moments. Frustratingly, the inscription above tells us no more than that this is King Edward – EDWARD REX – and the woollen figures meet in enigmatic silence. We must also remember that the Bayeux Tapestry was made ten or so years later. Like all historical sources, it has its own perspective and the temptation must be resisted of assuming that the events were recorded as they happened, like a film on a camcorder. What remains certain is that this meeting took place and its outcome set in motion a chain of events that changed history.

At the time when Harold and Edward met there were several men who potentially had an interest in the English throne. Royal succession in Anglo-Saxon England did not solely depend on who had the closest blood kinship to the king, though this was undoubtedly a persuasive factor. The king retained discretion during his life to nominate an heir from among his eligible relatives; and it was also the custom that the heir should be approved by the Witan, a council of the great and powerful in the land.[3] The question of inheritance was thus inherently fluid; and sometimes legal theory, such as it was, went entirely out of the window, and 'might' counted more than 'right', as when earlier in the century the country was conquered by the Danes under Swein Fork-Beard and was ruled, most famously, by his son King Canute (1016–35).

The Danish conquest had lasted little longer than Canute's lifetime; but it had shown foreigners what was possible: England was vulnerable. Nowhere was Danish success more envied than in the kindred land of Norway. King Harald of Norway's claim to the English throne was little more than a slender pretext based on an ambiguous treaty in the 1030s, but this mattered not to a man whose very *raison d'être* was war and the warrior's way.[4] The story of his life was already the stuff of saga.[5] The nickname they gave him – 'Hardrada', the Hard Ruler – was an advertisement indeed, considering that it distinguished him as noteworthy even among the Vikings themselves. In his youth Harald had left Norway to fight as an axe-wielding mercenary in the Mediterranean lands for the army of the Byzantine empire. He quickly gained the reputation of being the most formidable warrior of his age. A coin was even minted in his honour. Then, one night in 1043, Harald of Norway hoodwinked the emperor and slipped out of Constantinople in a fleet of ships laden with an enormous treasure. He muscled his way back into Norway and by 1047 he had succeeded his nephew Magnus as the sole king of the country. He would have turned his attentions to England earlier had he not been embroiled in a long war with Denmark. In 1062 he defeated the Danes in battle and in 1064 he finally made peace with them at Gota. This last intelligence may not yet have reached England but its importance was paramount. Now that the Hard Ruler had a free hand it would take little to encourage him to turn his attentions to England where the incumbent king had failed to produce an heir of his own loins and men looked to the future with uncertain eyes.

Across the more even waters of the English Channel lay another potential claimant, Duke William of Normandy, a more unlikely one, perhaps, and something of an unknown quantity.[6] The Danish invasion of England fifty years earlier had forced Edward and his siblings into exile in Normandy, the homeland of their mother Emma. Edward's exile was long and listless. He spent almost half his life in Normandy, becoming in the process as much Norman as English, before peaceably, and somewhat unexpectedly, being invited to return and ascend the English throne in 1042 on the death of Harthacanute, Canute's last surviving son. It was out of gratitude for his long Norman asylum that Edward chose to nominate Duke William, a distant cousin, as his own successor to the crown of England. That, at least, is what the Norman sources tell us; the English sources are entirely silent on the matter. Although the Norman accounts were written after the Conquest, and contain several untrustworthy embellishments, it is very probable that at some stage Edward did dangle the prospect of the English crown in front of William. The subsequent course of history is scarcely understandable if that were not the case. Edward may have dropped hints to this effect while still in exile, when Duke William was no more than a boy, and if the matter was ever taken up with greater formality after he became king, it was probably during that brief year in 1051–2 when Edward broke free of Earl Godwin. There is evidence in the *Anglo-Saxon Chronicle* that in 1051 'Earl William' paid a visit to England 'from beyond the sea', though for what purpose it is not stated.[7] The problem for William was that in 1052 the Godwins had been restored to power and they were implacably opposed to a Norman succession. Moreover at various times Edward seems to have made similar promises, or half-promises, to others; how seriously they were meant to be taken was a moot point. By the early 1060s Englishmen could be forgiven for regarding Duke William of Normandy to be the least of their worries. The real danger of invasion had always come from Scandinavia. Although the Normans were the descendants of Vikings, they had, for the most part, dismantled their warships 150 years earlier. By 1064 the prospect of a seaborne invasion from the duchy of Normandy seemed on the whole rather remote.

There had been another development, too. Following the restoration of the Godwins, King Edward was prevailed upon to prefer an authentic prince of the Anglo-Saxon line, a prince who, unlike that Norman duke, could command general support among the people. According to English custom, the king was perfectly entitled to do this. He was entitled to revoke whatever promise he had made to William, or to anyone else. What mattered was his last wish before dying. It must have been clear by the 1050s that the marriage with Edith was going to be barren but far away in eastern Europe there was, so it was said, a half-nephew of the king who was still alive and who might be persuaded to return. The same Danish whirlwind that in 1016 had forced Edward into his Norman exile had propelled a second branch of the family to distant Hungary in equal fear for their lives. That branch was now represented by another Edward, known to the English as Edward the Exile. The Exile was indeed still alive; he had grown up in Hungary, married a local princess and, better still, he was now a father. The quest to find him began in the year 1054. It took three years of diplomatic soundings, patient negotiation and perilous journeys across the face of Europe but finally, in the spring of 1057, the difficult project to bring the Exile home came to fruition. When his longship docked on the southern coast, the exiled prince gingerly placed his first foot on England's shore. Behind him followed his exotic wife Agatha and three little children, and strong men carrying his great chests of Hungarian treasure. The England he stepped on to was a strange land and it was inhabited by a people he did not understand; for he had been no more than a babe in arms when hastily carried away from these same shores forty years earlier. His return had been long, slow and reluctant. It was duty, more than enthusiasm, that brought him back; but what mattered was that he had arrived at last, and there was now a new optimism in the air that the problem of the English succession could peaceably and lawfully be resolved. A few days later Edward the Exile dropped dead.

'We do not know for what cause it was arranged that he might not see his relative King Edward. Alas! that was a cruel fate, and harmful to this nation, that he so quickly ended his life.'[8] In these sad words, the writer of the *Anglo-Saxon Chronicle* for 1057 laments the tragic turn of events, hinting darkly at foul play – poison slipped, perhaps, into Edward the Exile's food or drinking cup, even before he had met with his older namesake. The circumstances of this sudden death are undeniably suspicious but it is impossible to discern on whose behalf the murderer (if murder it was) was working. With the Exile dead, the hope of many now rested on the immature shoulders of his son Edgar, a toddler recently carried across a continent and now inextricably caught up in the vicious power games of the adult world. It was decided that Edgar should be taken into the care of the royal household. Such fostering of children in the household of a superior lord was not unusual; but in this case it was also hoped, no doubt, that it would protect the little princeling from further danger. Edgar was brought up under the direction of Queen Edith and he was given the title of *Ætheling* showing that he was considered to be throneworthy.

To the improbable trio of Harald of Norway, William of Normandy and little Edgar of England could be added the name of a fourth contender for the English throne: Harold Godwinson himself. Though related by marriage to the Danish royals through his mother Gytha, Earl Harold had no blood link to his brother-in-law the king. What he had in abundance, however, was wealth, power and supporters. An uncharitable view would take Harold as scheming to seize the main prize all along, for he must have realised that it might one day fall within his grasp. That view would probably be wrong. It is not supported in the threads of the tapestry, where, if we observe closely, we see a more sympathetic portrait of the man. The Bayeux Tapestry is far from a work of Norman propaganda and in its threads it is often silently more revealing than the slippery post-Conquest apologetics of William of Poitiers. Harold comes across as essentially well meaning, a man racked by dilemma, one who, when he does become king, only does so at the behest of others and in a procedure that is depicted, in its fundamentals, as scrupulously legal. At the time of his meeting with Edward, Harold's policy must have been to favour the succession of young Edgar. Harold seems to have been involved in, and may even have been one of the prime movers of, the project to bring the Exile home.[9] The Exile was dead; but his line continued. If little Edgar succeeded to the throne whilst still a minor, Harold was well placed to rule as regent. In that capacity he could further consolidate himself as the real power behind the throne. What is more, in the longer term, another chance beckoned to ally the blood of the Godwins to England's royal line. Earl Harold, though well known for having an eye for the ladies, was not yet married. His father's scheme had drawn a blank but if Harold were able, in due course, to marry off a lawful daughter to Edgar, success might at last be achieved. All this he may have planned; events were to take a different and more rapid course.

Others were watching and waiting too. No one, at this stage, could rule out a challenge from King Swein Estrithsson of Denmark. He was a kinsman of Canute, as well as a cousin of Earl Harold. Like Duke William of Normandy he claimed that Edward had promised him the throne.[10] Across the Straits of Dover, a mysterious and neglected figure, Count Eustace II of Boulogne, was also biding his time. Eustace is the shadowy Frenchman whom the tapestry depicts as a hero by William's side at the Battle of Hastings.

The meeting has concluded. It seems that a decision has been made and the conferees have departed in a swirl of tunics. Few know exactly what has been said. At once a tight-lipped Harold rides to the southern coast whence he will put to sea. In the turbulent years that followed men speculated about what had really been said. To William of Poitiers and the Normans it was simple: Edward had not wavered for a moment in his choice of William and he was now sending Earl Harold on a formal embassy to Normandy to confirm to the worthy duke his happy status as the next king of England.[11] This story, of course, suited the Normans; but it contains much that is questionable. Since contrary winds drove Harold on to unexpected shores and, as we shall see, into another adventure entirely, his original purpose remains mysterious. Several factors undermine the Norman case. It is highly improbable that Edward had the ability to order Harold to support the Norman succession. Harold was simply too powerful and the whole course of events, ever since the restoration of the Godwins in 1052, strongly suggests that Harold and his family were opposed to William succeeding. Nor is there any independent evidence that Edward himself continued to favour William. On the contrary, he seems to have changed his mind. A very great deal of time and effort had been expended in persuading the exiled branch of the family to return and there was now in England a young prince who was being brought up at the royal court and who had an undeniably superior blood-claim to the throne.

What is more, King Edward had, or at least had until recently, a French nephew whose blood-claim was also superior to William's. Edward's late sister Godgifu, exiled like him in France, had entered into a first marriage with Drogo, the count of the Vexin (she later married Eustace of Boulogne). In the 1060s their son Walter, Edward's full nephew, was count of Maine, a territory lying on the southern borders of Normandy. Walter could have considered himself a prime contender for the English throne but he did not fare well at the hands of Duke William. In 1063 the Norman duke took advantage of a slender pretext, marched into Maine and conquered it. Not long afterwards Walter and his wife Biota died in Norman custody; it was widely rumoured (according to Orderic Vitalis) that they were poisoned.[12] These events were alarming. They would hardly have endeared Duke William of Normandy any further in King Edward's world-weary heart.

If the Norman account is rejected, what really did happen at that secret meeting between Harold and Edward in 1064 or early 1065? Some forty or fifty years later an English monk named Eadmer, working in the serenity of his turn-of-the-century cloister at Canterbury, wrote his own *History of Recent Events in England* (*Historia Novorum Anglia*). Eadmer's work is an unjustly neglected source. He tells a quite different story from that told by the Normans, and it is one that would have been too dangerous to record in any explicit way earlier. According to Eadmer, in 1052 a brother and nephew of Harold, Wulfnoth and Hakon by name, had been handed over to Edward by Earl Godwin as hostages for his future good conduct; this, apparently, was part of the settlement reached between Godwin and Edward when the former returned from his brief exile in the years 1051–2. Shortly afterwards Edward had the hostages transported to his cousin Duke William of Normandy for safe custody.[13] Godwin died the following year and it could well be said that the purpose of Wulfnoth and Hakon's detention had long expired. But they were still there, more than ten years later, wasting away their lives as captives in a foreign land. Their plight must have touched Earl Harold's heart, for Eadmer tells us that Harold wanted to go to Normandy in order to meet with Duke William and negotiate the release of his brother and nephew. Before leaving, Harold quite properly came to King Edward to tell him of his plans, and it would be this precise meeting that we can see in the tapestry's opening scene. Edward was not impressed by what he heard. Far from sending Harold to Normandy, Eadmer tell us that the king positively warned him not to go. 'I will have no part in this,' he is supposed to have said, 'but not to give the impression of wishing to hinder you, I give you leave to go where you will and to see what you can do. But I have a feeling that you will only succeed in bringing misfortune on yourself and the whole Kingdom. For I know that the Duke is not so simple as to be at all inclined to give [Wulfnoth and Hakon] up . . . unless he foresees that in doing so he will gain some great advantage for himself.'[14]

There is nothing in the tapestry's opening scene which is in contradiction to this radically different account. It seems that the master artist has audaciously designed an image that could please both sides. Puffing Normans, gorged on the spoils of conquest, could pass up and down the tapestry and see what they expected to see – that Edward, of course, favoured William all along and that near the end of his life he was sending perfidious Harold to Normandy to confirm just this. The English, or those who knew, would see a different tale – they would be reminded by the silent meeting of those little woollen figures that in his old age King Edward did not think much of Duke William at all; that on that fateful day he was, in fact, advising Harold to stay away from Normandy; but that Harold nevertheless chose to make the journey at considerable risk to himself, in the hope of obtaining the release of his captive kinsmen.[15]

All that the tapestry explicitly shows is that Harold left the secret meeting and rode with his men to the southern coast. The old village of Bosham makes a secluded harbour; it lies within the safety of an inlet, where the sea has poked itself like a fat finger into the underbelly of Sussex, and it is from here that many a Channel crossing leaves from the safe edge of land. We see Harold riding there, at the head of his men; a pack of collared hunting dogs runs ahead of the party in pursuit of two hares. Perched on Harold's left hand, as he rides, is a handsome hawk, colourfully embroidered out of red, yellow and green yarn. Hunting was the favourite pastime of the nobility and one of Harold's great passions was to hunt with trained birds; it is attested by a later source that he possessed several manuscript books on falconry.[16]

Harold and a companion now arrive at the door of Bosham church [scene 3]. Here they will pray before crossing the sea, as was the custom when ships were insecure and the weather far from predictable. The artist provides us with a view of the church that, at first sight, we might ignore for its lack of proportion and apparently childlike qualities, but it merits closer inspection. It is in fact a composite view that encompasses the building's internal and external features in one and the same picture. The parish church of Bosham is the first touchable link between the tapestry's story and the present day. It still stands where it did, almost 1,000 years later, scarcely beyond the lick of waves and overcircled by the calling gulls. Generations of seafarers have come and gone. The church has been extended and altered many times but the eleventh-century interior arch, which divides the nave from the chancel, is still to be seen; it is, in the words of a recent observer, 'one of the noblest spans in early English architecture'.[17] The Anglo-Saxon church at Bosham was not on a par with the great architectural marvels that were being built on the continent of Europe but it nevertheless impressed our artist. This, to him, was modern architecture and he included the great horseshoe of an arch at the centre of his composition, giving it the same proportions in wool as it has in real stone.[18]

Harold stepped under this arch. He stood by these stones; he saw them as we can see them; and his cheeks were touched by the same chill air. Forty years earlier Bosham may have been the scene of a tragedy touching the family of King Canute, an accident if the story is true, though the medieval mind would have discerned the hand of providence in all such matters. Canute had a home in Bosham (it may have been here that he tried to command the incoming tide to turn, but that is another, and possibly apocryphal, story[19]). One day it is said that Canute's little daughter, aged about eight, fell into the mill stream behind the church and was drowned. It was long said by local people that she lay buried in the church. The truth of this tradition was dramatically supported in 1865 when excavations by the right foot of the chancel arch unearthed a stone coffin dating from the time of Canute.[20] They broke open the lid and inside they found the remains of a female child of about eight years. If there is any truth in the story, Canute's poor little daughter could easily have been a contemporary of Harold; perhaps he knew and played with her as a child, for Bosham had been one of the principal residences of his father Godwin, and Godwin was a protégé and friend of

Canute. As Harold stood there that day, it would not have been inappropriate for him to muse on his own mortality.

Now we see Harold and his men feasting in the upper storey of his Bosham manor [scene 4]. Drinking cups and horns are brought to lips; there is animated conversation. Standing on the steps outside, a man informs the party that the ship is ready. It is a dragon-headed ship, typical of its time; and like the familiar Viking longship, it may be propelled by oars or a large rectangular sail. Harold wades out to the vessel, his tunic hitched up to his waist, his bare feet and legs exposed to the cold sea. Once more his favoured hawk sits on his raised left hand; the hunting animals are brought on board. Another barelegged man wades through the shallows, carrying a large dog in his arms; a third makes his way with oars or poles. A party of some dozen men are now aboard. The mast is raised, the anchor pulled in and the men, singing perhaps, row the ship into deeper waters. Thus begins the secret journey of Harold Godwinson, the first of four journeys back and forth across the woollen sea stitched by our embroiderers.

It is not long before the wind picks up. Sheltered from the spray behind closely packed shields, the men on board begin to cast anxious glances. The hours progress; the ship must have rocked and creaked. The wind has become stronger and it is not clear that it is taking them in the right direction. ET VELIS VENTO PLENIS VENIT IN TERRA WIDONIS COMITIS (and with the wind full in his sails he came to the land of Count Guy). In these enigmatic words the tapestry tells us that Harold's ship was being driven towards the French county of Ponthieu, sandwiched between Normandy to the south and Boulogne and Flanders to the north. Ponthieu is decidedly not where Harold intended to go; for like many medieval nobles Guy, the youthful count of Ponthieu, had a penchant for taking captives and holding them for ransom. At this point an Englishman has climbed to the top of the mast and, with his hand cupped over his eyes he spots the line of land ahead; a man on deck is holding a great anchor at the ready. They make landfall, possibly at the mouth of the River Maye, and Harold steps out into the shallow waters of Ponthieu.[21] He must be ignorant of the danger, or else he would have quickly departed to a less hostile strand.

According to a much later account, a fisherman of Ponthieu, who had been to England, saw Harold step ashore and immediately recognised him. He then rushed breathlessly to Count Guy, knowing that Earl Harold's unexpected arrival would be of interest to his avaricious lord.[22] Something like this must have happened; but the tapestry, for its part, tele-scopes events by showing the English party confronted by Guy and his men immediately as they land [scene 6]. Either way, Harold is about to fall into the unwelcoming hands of Count Guy of Ponthieu. Earl Harold now sees the danger. From somewhere he draws a dagger but he is quickly overpowered by one of Guy's men. The count himself now approaches with the rest of his soldiers. They are on horseback and all have swords, lances and kite-shaped shields. Harold's mission was peaceful and he is accompanied by only a handful of men. They have few arms and no horses, only hawks and hunting hounds. There is no escape.

It was the harsh custom in Ponthieu, dating from the time of Emperor Charlemagne, that the count was entitled to hold as captive any person driven on to his shores, as well as ships and chattels.[23] A shipwrecked noble could be ransomed for a large sum; ransom was good business. When you are the count of Ponthieu, idly wondering what to do next, and the richest man in England is suddenly tossed upon your shores, as lost and helpless as a piece of wreckage, it is like winning the lottery ten times over. The Norman writer William of Poitiers hinted that the people of Ponthieu were wreckers. 'Certain Gallic peoples,' he interjected into his own version of the story, 'have been led through avarice to adopt a cunning practice, which is barbarous and utterly removed from Christian justice. They lay ambushes for the powerful and wealthy, thrust them into prison, and torture and humiliate them. When they have reduced them almost to the point of death, they turn them out, usually ransomed at a very high price.'[24] It is unlikely that Harold was deliberately lured to Ponthieu. As the tapestry implies, it was the strong wind that landed him there. What is clear is that he was now at the mercy of Count Guy, a man notorious for his greed. At best, Harold might be treated well but ransomed for an enormous sum, and it might take months, or even years, to raise. At worst, he could be the victim of the kind of sadistic excess that William of Poitiers described, and he would be bound and shackled, and thrown into a dark prison.

The Harold that we see in the tapestry's threads is no doubt confused and angry. His mission has gone disastrously wrong even before it has started. In the eleventh-century view, the invisible hand of God was everywhere controlling events and, like all men of his time, he would have taken his misfortune to be divine punishment and racked his conscience to remember quite what he had done wrong. Had he neglected his God? Surely he had prayed before the journey, as any good Christian should, and in his time he had given profusely to the Church. Some of his dealings had been a little shady, and some of the churches and abbeys of England had complaints against him, but no more than they might have against any great noble; and besides, in the eyes of the Almighty this was as nothing, he would have thought, when compared to the magnificence of his benefactions to Waltham.[25] At Waltham's Holy Cross he was once cured of an illness and in gratitude he had transformed the modest church built by Tofig the Proud into a splendid college for canons. He had lavished vast sums on the building; he had donated as many as sixty priceless relics. Brilliant gold furnishings shone brightly through the haze of incense in every corner of the candlelit edifice; the altar he provided was itself a sight to behold, made of marble and supported in front by golden statues of the twelve apostles, and at the back by radiant golden lions; and the gold that decorated one chasuble alone weighed seventeen pounds. Were these gifts not enough in the eyes of the Lord? How could such glittering piety be rewarded thus? How could it be that the greatest living Englishman, whose estates stretched from Cornwall to Yorkshire, who could hunt and roam almost as freely as he pleased, who prided himself on his understanding of the strategies of foreign princes, how could it be that he, Earl Harold, was now held as a miserable captive in this foreign place?

He was far from the love of his life, Edith the Fair; far from his sister Edith the Queen; far from his brothers, loyal Gyrth and Leofwine and the hot-headed Tostig and the lesser earls who might take advantage of his absence; far from old King Edward and the little Ætheling and all the people in England who depended on his protection; far from England itself at this uncertain time; and if he had come with the intention of rescuing his long-lost kinsmen, Wulfnoth and Hakon, he was just as far from finding them as well. Harold of Wessex was the helpless prisoner of an obscure French count. Somehow he would have to get away – and fast.

6

The Fox and the Crow

There appears in the tapestry's lower border, at the point where Harold and his men were embarking aboard their ship at Bosham, a seemingly irrelevant illustration of a fox, a crow and a piece of cheese. This is an old fable. Sitting on a branch, there was once a foolish crow with some cheese in his mouth, which he had just carried off from a window. The crow was about to eat the tasty morsel when a fox, fancying it for himself, looked up and spoke the following artful words: 'My dear crow, how shiny and beautiful your feathers are! And your face and figure, how graceful they are too! If only you had a voice, you would be the finest of all birds.' Pleased by this flattery but taken aback by the insinuation that he could not sing, the crow opened his mouth to prove otherwise. The cheese, of course, dropped to the ground and was promptly snapped up by the cunning fox. The moral of the tale: he who takes delight in treacherous flattery will usually end up paying a hefty price.

The fable of the fox and the crow is as old as Aesop, the celebrated teller of animal tales in ancient Greece; it was known in classical Latin times through adaptations by Phaedrus and Babrius; and in Anglo-Saxon England the Aesop fables had become popular through translations from the Latin made, so it was said, by King Alfred the Great. The artist of the tapestry included several animal fables in the borders, touching on themes of deceit, dishonesty and possession, but this one he seems to have considered particularly apt, for he included it three times.[1] There is surely art in this. It is hard to believe that the fable of the fox and the crow was not deliberately included as an ironic commentary on the unfolding drama, but the crucial question is this: who is the fox and who the crow? Once more the artist courts danger by teasing his public with double meaning. Norman observers, in the aftermath of the Conquest, would immediately see Harold as the fox, scheming with cunning words to take the crown of England from under the nose of its rightful heir, Duke William of Normandy. Yet if the threaded drama is more closely observed it becomes increasingly possible to interpret the fable in exactly the opposite way, with Harold the cheated one and the treacherous and deceitful fox William of Normandy. It is in the crafty guise of a rescuer, a knight, in brightly stitched chain mail, that William of Normandy will make a dramatic entrance on to the linen stage.

Harold is a prisoner on that strand of Ponthieu, but his nerves must shortly have begun to calm. It has become clear that Count Guy will treat him honourably. 'By the ancient law of my land, you are now my captive, Earl Harold, but rest assured – I will not treat you badly.' Some such words were presumably spoken to the Englishman, for they are implied by the tapestry's pictures. In this, once more, the woven story differs markedly from the written account of William of Poitiers. It seems that the latter's evocation of the dire imprisonment that awaited Harold in Ponthieu was an exaggeration, designed, no doubt, to cast Duke William's impending intervention in the most favourable light. For its part the tapestry ennobles Guy with a certain nascent chivalry. He is intent on getting what he can from Harold, but this is an honourable captivity. Harold is neither shackled nor bound; he sits proudly on his horse as together he and Guy ride along the country paths of Picardy to one of Guy's castles [scene 7]. At the rear of the party two hunting dogs, dodging the gnarled tree which separates this scene from the last, run after their English lord, panting with canine enthusiasm, and both Harold and Guy ride with hawks at hand. Were it not for the armed guard, which discreetly follows, one might think this the picture of a friendly day's chase. There can be no doubt, however, that Harold is effectively a prisoner. The inescapable truth is underlined by a prosaic inscription. HIC APPREHENDIT WIDO HAROLDUM ET DUXIT EUM AD BELREM ET IBI EUM TENUIT (Here Guy seized Harold and led him to Beaurain and held him there).

Beaurain lies by the mellow, slow-flowing River Canche, nine miles from the Channel coast. Today it is an inconspicuous hamlet, lost amidst the fields of Picardy half way between Montreuil and Hesdin, but in those days Guy's castle at Beaurain must have been an impressive fortress. It is represented three times in the tapestry (which is more than any other structure) and if we pause to observe closely, and not ignore what is often taken to be another child-like or conventional representation, we can see how cleverly its essentials were tricked out of the threads [scene 13].[2] They must have taken Harold first to an outer stone wall, with battlements and towers, and then through a great arched gate to the large enclosure (the bailey) within. Dominating the enclosure, at the back, was a steeply-sided earthen mound (the motte), rising perhaps seventy feet into the air. Now within the bailey Harold would have creaked up his neck at the impregnable centre-piece, a gleaming stone keep standing proudly on top of the mound and itself crowned by a remarkable domed roof. Today a little village still bears the name Château-Beaurain; but nothing is left of the eponymous motte-and-bailey castle or even of any later stronghold on the same site. The last of its stones were whistled away by masons in 1822 in order to be recycled in the construction of a new watercourse. Only an overgrown hillock, obscured by trees, stands where the motte once stood. There is now nothing in this windswept place that we can touch, nothing tangible to remind us of the clank of armour, the rustle of hoofs, the shouts of men or the squeaky pulling of gates as Harold and Guy arrived that day. Only their woollen counterparts live on to re-enact the tale.

Now Harold is taken to the door of Guy's hall; he is surrounded by no less than six guards, one of whom holds his confiscated sword [scene 7]. Harold enters, slowly, and with trepidation. A fellow Englishman from his party encourages him forward with a push in the back. Under the domed roof, captive and captor now converse, man to man, eye to eye, noble to noble, sizing each other up with sly glances, but just as in the tapestry's opening scene, when Harold met Edward, we do not know exactly what passes between them. UBI HAROLD ET WIDO PARABOLANT (Where Harold and Guy confer) is all that the inscription says. Do the discussions range over Harold's wealth? Are they talking of how much gold Harold is willing to hand over for his freedom? For the moment (for the picture, as it were) Harold has been handed back his unbelted sword. He stands throughout the meeting, whereas Guy makes a point of sitting on his comital throne, raised higher than Harold; the seated position is always indicative of authority in the tapestry. It is a dapper, ambitious young Frenchman, still in his twenties, whom Harold can see before him, now with his arm raised, pointing directly at his captive – 'I have you under my complete custody and control,' he seems to be saying. Guy's sword is held upright by the blade, like a sceptre, and his feet are resting on a cushioned footstool. His face is clean-shaven and his hair is worn in the northern French style, which is to say shorn very short at the back. This contrasts with the English who, like Harold, are in the habit of wearing their fair locks thick and long around the nape of the neck and a little stitch of a moustache underlining the nose. The count's dark cape lies over his shoulders like the wings of a mantling hawk; it is neatly buttoned in front with a large brooch. Guy's tunic is something like a long, unbelted dress, with folds and creases forming around his waist and uplifted knees; he wears a fine hose that has been carefully embroidered in horizontal black and brown stripes. His throne, scarcely less noble than a king's, has carved claw feet and its arms are made into sculptured animal heads. This is a man with a taste for luxury, but clearly someone who must be taken seriously within the boundaries of his own county. A contemporary monk at the monastery of Saint-Riquier, the chief monastic centre in Ponthieu, described him as pitiless, haughty and corrupted by greed: 'only gold would satisfy him', he said.[3] In the next century William of Malmesbury wrote that Count Guy was effeminate.[4]

If Guy seemed vaguely familiar to Harold, it was because he had met him, or at least seen him, once before. Harold had not often travelled to the continent but during a visit to Flanders, some eight years earlier, he had been called upon by Count Baldwin of Flanders to lend his name as a witness to a local charter.[5] It was the practice for nobles and officials to attest legal transactions in order to give them greater authority, and Harold duly obliged. The young Guy was presumably visiting Baldwin's court too, for the two names 'Duke Harold' and 'Count Guy' appear side by side in the same document, among twenty-eight other witnesses. The surviving diploma, subscribed at the Flemish town of St-Omer, bears the date 13 November 1056. To what extent they conversed in 1056 is unknown, but there was presumably ample opportunity for the assembled nobles gathered at Baldwin's court to mingle and to indulge in feasting and entertainment. Under the late autumnal skies Harold and Guy would have been able to partake in their shared passion for falconry.

To those who were there at that noble Flemish gathering in 1056, Count Guy probably seemed a bitter and resentful youth. He had himself only recently emerged from two years' imprisonment and his jailer was none other than his powerful enemy Duke William of Normandy. Guy knew what it was like to be a helpless prisoner; and he had personal experience of the wrath of the Norman duke. It is one of the ironies of history that nowadays Guy of Ponthieu, like his cousin Count Eustace II of Boulogne, is often erroneously referred to as a 'Norman'. Ponthieu (still less Boulogne) had never been part of the lands ceded to the Vikings in 911 and it had never been part of Normandy. Its culture, history and ruling class were all quite separate from the much larger land of Normandy, lying just to the south and west. The people of Ponthieu were proud of their past. They sang heroic tales of how they had once resisted the pagans and they would have considered themselves as belonging to an older Gallic culture, one which was Christian hundreds of years before any Norseman had abandoned the religion of Odin and Thor.[6] Guy of Ponthieu and

Eustace of Boulogne were French, but on no account were they Normans.[7]

These were not merely matters of abstract nuance; they reflected a real hostility on the ground. The smaller territories of northern France had much to fear from the growing power of Normandy under its indomitable and headstrong duke. William had inherited the duchy of Normandy in 1035 while only a boy, but he outlived those who had idly scoffed at him and he had grown into a powerful and violent man. In Norman accounts 'France' is often distinguished from Normandy and the 'French' are portrayed as the natural enemies of the Normans. Together with lands such as Boulogne and Mantes, great Anjou to the south, and for much of the 1050s the French king himself, Ponthieu formed a block of powers hostile to Normandy. Duke William was a strong and fearless opponent; he also had luck on his side. He survived all attempts to depose him, both from within and without his duchy, and emerged with his authority not only intact but enhanced. In October 1053 Guy's elder brother, Count Enguerrand of Ponthieu, famous for his nobility and beauty, was killed fighting the Normans at Saint-Aubin-sur-Scie. Guy, as yet still in his teens, inherited the county but was himself captured by Normans in February 1054 when engaged in a similar venture at the town of Mortemer. It was in these circumstances that Count Guy of Ponthieu became Duke William's prisoner.

William did not kill Count Guy: instead he wanted to teach him a lesson, and in the process reduce Ponthieu to the status of a client state. For two years he held Guy in captivity at Bayeux.[8] At long last he was released, in 1056, but only after he had sworn a humiliating oath of loyalty to his Norman enemy and in particular to provide the annual service of 100 knights. This did not make Guy a Norman; but it certainly curtailed his freedom of action. The oath was a primary bond in the society in which these men lived. It bound the swearer both in sanctity and honour. To break such an oath was to incur the wrath of God and, which was no less certain, though possibly more immediate, the wrath of William. Now more than eight years had passed, eight years during which Guy had kept out of harm's way and had been able once again to enjoy the kind of luxury that befitted the ruler of a small but prosperous French county. He stood to gain much from capturing Earl Harold, but if there was one person in the world that he feared, one person that he did not want to see flexing his muscles just now, one person that he would rather not pay him a visit at his castle at this particular, rather delicate juncture, it was Duke William of Normandy.

Guy feels a little tap at his elbow. One of his soldiers, standing by his throne, alerts him to the fact that two Norman knights have just arrived at the castle gate and wish to speak to him as a matter of urgency in the next scene. What can they know? What on earth do they want? What has brought them in such haste to the northerly castle of Beaurain, which is just about as far from Normandy as Guy could have taken Harold within his own territory? In an obscure corner of the hall, hiding behind a pillar, a sly fellow in a jagged-edged tunic has been watching the proceedings all along – a jester perhaps, or a spy, or both.

The meeting with Harold is over. Guy has moved outside his castle in order to speak with the two Norman knights [scene 9]. They have dismounted their horses and are standing upright. Tall, lanky, aggressive men, each is armed with a lance and sword. What they lack in number is more than compensated by their unquestioned authority as the emissaries of the Duke of Normandy. UBI NUNTII WILLELMI

DUCIS VENERUNT AD WIDONE[M], says the inscription (Where Duke William's messengers came to Guy). 'It is no use trying to be clever,' they seem to be saying. 'Our lord William knows very well that you are holding the Englishman Harold here. He requires you to hand him over forthwith and without question.' As this tense scene unfolds, Guy's dwarf 'TUR-OLD' grips the reins of the Normans' horses, an incongruous little figure holding the two hot animals, freshly ridden across the border from Normandy and through the forests of Pon-thieu to the riverside castle [scene 10; plate 1]. A mere fifteen people are named in the tapestry; most of them are more or less familiar players on the stage of history. Turold the dwarf is the first of four highly obscure figures whose names have been stitched in for us. Although the dwarf is often passed over without comment, his identity and significance will be of the highest interest.

Guy hears what William's henchmen are saying. His dark hair, though shaved at the back, is combed across his forehead so that it almost flops into his eyes. On this occasion he wears an extravagant knee-length tunic, represented in embroidery in a manner that suggests overlapping leaves of leather; his over-cloak is long and buttoned at the side. His right hand rests quaintly on his hip, while gripped firmly in his left is an upright axe, a great English-style fighting axe with a handle almost as tall as himself. This last gesture is nicely symbolic of the fact that he currently holds in his custody England's foremost earl. But for how much longer? This is an uncomfort-able encounter, more confrontation than meeting. Guy does not sit authoritatively on his throne; he cannot lean back comfortably on the seat of his power while those who speak with him are lorded over and left shuffling foot to foot in embarrassment. These Normans are the emissaries of Duke

William, the man to whom he had been forced to swear his allegiance, so Guy must meet them standing upright, on his own two feet.

Perhaps Guy is thinking now, biting his lip, wondering whether he might just be able to defy Duke William and get away with it. He remembers his long captivity at Bayeux. He remembers the oath of allegiance he has sworn. He remembers that God is his witness and that William has a fiery temper, which no one in their right mind would wish to rekindle. If he disobeyed now, the Norman duke might invade Ponthieu and have him killed, and then take over the whole of the county, as he had done only recently in Maine. Other accounts (though not the tapestry) reveal that William sweetened the pill with promises. In particular, it is said that William offered Guy a stretch of land by the River Aulne if he would cooperate in handing over Harold.[9] Threatened and bribed, the choice turns out to be surprisingly easy. It is agreed. Harold is to be passed, like a football, from one to the other, from Ponthieu to Normandy – from a covetous jailer to a duplicitous rescuer.

At this moment in the story the Bayeux Tapestry clarifies (up to a point) how Duke William discovered so quickly that Harold had been taken prisoner in Ponthieu. This intriguing sub-plot unfolds like a flashback, in a right-to-left direction; the thread of history is momentarily reversed. The two Norman knights, whom we have already seen at Beaurain, are now riding towards there [scene 11]. Their mission, as we suspected, was urgent for the horses gallop at full tilt. Hoofs rumble past us at great speed; the hair of the riders flows like streamers in the wind. Each carries his couched lance in the latest military style and a wing-shaped shield embroidered with a dragon motif. Evidently there was no time to be lost; William desperately wanted to ensnare Harold before he escaped. It is a strange thought, but had these two knights been riding slower, and Earl Harold been able to negotiate his release, the whole history of England might have been different. But there are many such moments in the Bayeux Tapestry, such is the pivotal nature of each passing episode in its story. Now we venture further back in time. We are shown where the two Normans have come from. This must be outside William's ducal palace at Rouen [scene 12]. Here, in flashback, we catch our first glimpse of the majestic Duke of Normandy, a large, imposing figure, sword in hand, seated on his carved throne. It has been estimated, on the basis of the surviving bones found in his grave at Caen, that William was about 5 feet 10 inches tall, which would have made him impressively tall for the eleventh century.[10] Here he is being pleaded with by an Englishman who is on the point of falling to his knees. The giveaway is the thick mop of hair and the pencil-thin moustache: this man is certainly English. Somehow a member of Harold's party must have escaped or evaded capture in Ponthieu, secretly crossed into Normandy and hurried to Duke William in order to plead for his help in rescuing Harold. The tapestry does not tell us how. The reverse order of these scenes distracts us from pondering the question too long. Perhaps the furtive fellow whom, a little while ago, we saw hiding behind a pillar at Guy's castle had some clandestine hand in the plot.

Harold has evidently turned to Duke William of Normandy for help. This might seem to support the Norman case – that Harold had been sent to the continent specifically to give William news that he would be the next king of England. It is certainly consistent with the Norman story, but the Canterbury monk Eadmer, like the tapestry, tells us that Harold implored William's help in a bid to evade further detention in

Ponthieu. Eadmer, it will be recalled, reported that Harold's purpose in crossing the Channel had nothing to do with the English succession but rather it was to secure the release of his nephew and brother from Duke William's custody. In Eadmer's version it was one of the common folk of Ponthieu (not an Englishman) who, having been bribed by Earl Harold, carried the secret call for help to William.[11] Whether the messenger was English or French, Harold must have weighed matters in the balance and concluded that incurring a debt of honour to William was preferable to remaining shamefully in the custody of Count Guy. This was not a wise move. In fact, it was one of the gravest political miscalculations ever made. Earl Harold, it seems, was still blissfully unaware quite how seriously the Norman duke took his claim to the English throne.

The flashback over, we pick up again the thread of the embroidered story. We are shown the formal handover of Harold as it takes place on open ground at a prearranged spot [scene 14]. HIC WIDO ADDUXIT HAROLDUM AD WILGELMUM NORRMANORUM DUCEM (Here Guy brought Harold to William, Duke of the Normans); this is all that the tapestry says on the matter, but the place of rendezvous is independently identified in the chronicle of William of Poitiers as the Norman border castle at Eu. Guy approaches from the left. He is riding a smaller, prick-eared mount rather than a warhorse, this in order, presumably, to symbolise his submission to Duke William. He is closely followed by Harold who is seated on a more worthy steed; each of them still has a hawk on his wrist. Behind them we see a group of Guy's knights. Now the Norman side rides in from the right. The duke appears first, wearing a great red cloak, two tassels trailing from his neck; behind him follows a handful of his own mounted knights. These Normans are aggressive, bent-forward soldiers, much more eager than Guy's, but at least they hold their lances pointing backwards in an effort to offset the impression of immediate hostility. One of them carries a shield threaded with the same dragon motif that we saw borne by the knights who rode to Ponthieu. The Norman at the back of the party points to the next embroidered scene, into the heart of Normandy, where Harold must be taken.

Harold now accompanies Duke William into Norman territory. They are heading for William's great ducal palace – HIC DUX WILGELM CUM HAROLDO VENIT AD PALATIU[M] SUU[M] (Here Duke William comes to his palace with Harold). The English earl rides at the head of the party; he has no weapon and the Normans at his back keep him under constant watch. Evidently he is told to ride first so that he cannot turn tail and escape. His hawk has gone too; William has it on his wrist. The party arrives at what is probably Duke William's palace at Rouen, where a guard manning the watchtower greeets them with a smile. We are now inside the hall, a long and impressive stone building, with an arcaded upper level, like the clerestory of a church, consisting of eighteen embroidered arches [plate 2; scene 16]. William and Harold are deep in animated conversation. It is the first formal meeting of the two men and if, as we hear so often, the Bayeux Tapestry tells the story 'strictly from the Norman point of view', it is surely here that we would expect the inscription to make clear, beyond any measure of doubt, that Harold is fulfilling the supposed purpose of his journey – that he is confirming to Duke William his status as the next king of England. Instead the meeting is depicted in total silence; there is no inscription at all. It thus behoves us to look closely at what the embroidered picture itself reveals, what it covertly tells us of that distant meeting of the two men who, within as many years, would be the most famous of mortal enemies on the battlefield of Hastings. Each detail at this meeting is potentially telling. There are secrets here.

William, as we would expect, is seated authoritatively on his throne, with its dragon-headed arms, fine cushion and attendant blue footstool; for he is the Duke of Normandy and this is his palace. Harold stands, but unlike each previous encounter with a figure of authority, where the standing person is drawn artificially small, Harold is depicted as sufficiently large to look William straight in the eye [scene 16]. The artist, it seems, wishes to portray these two men as equals; there is no sense in which Harold is belittled, as he is so often by William of Poitiers. Observe, now, how Harold, while busy talking to William, points at the armed and bearded man standing to his left, and how this man reciprocates the gesture. Evidently this man is the subject of Harold's conversation with William. Behind him are three Norman knights. Each listens eagerly to the proceedings; each is also armed with a lance and shield; but closer inspection reveals two curious and unexplained anomalies: the three Norman knights have *four* shields between them and only *five* legs. Whatever the reason for that, it is clear that the mysterious man to whom Harold is pointing is different from the three Normans. Crucially, his hair is long at the back; he also has a thick growth of beard;[12] his posture and bearing are quite distinct, too. In the iconography of the tapestry, long or facial hair is the trademark of the English. The man's shield also bears a design that is very similar to the one later borne by Harold at Hastings. The bearded man in William's hall is clearly English, but who can he be? Why does he bear arms in the incongruous company

of these Norman knights within the close confines of William's
ducal palace?

There is only one obvious answer. He is one of Harold's
kinsmen who had been detained in Normandy since the early
1050s and whose return to England, according to Eadmer's
later story, Harold had come specifically to secure.[13] In the
circumstances the artist has probably chosen to depict the
more senior of the two, Harold's brother Wulfnoth. This
would carry a certain poignancy, for Wulfnoth remained a
hostage even when the tapestry was made, indeed he was never
freed, and the woollen Harold would thus still be pleading for
his brother's release long after Harold himself had died. Since
William and Harold are not yet at war the hostage has evidently been allowed a measure of freedom and serves as a
soldier in the Norman army. The implication of the tapestry's
imagery is profound. At the first opportunity, Harold is portrayed seeking Wulfnoth's and Hakon's release, not conveying
any supposed message about the English succession at all.
Edward, it seems, had not sent Harold to Normandy as his
ambassador; and he had changed his mind about William
succeeding him. If this mysterious Englishman is Wulfnoth,
he is not the only brother of Harold to be seen in the Tapestry.
Later we will see his named brothers Gyrth and Leofwine
fighting loyally by his side at Hastings. Harold's sister Queen
Edith, though unnamed, also appears in the work.

This deftly drawn, wordless meeting of William and Harold
is usually passed over with little comment, and the bearded
Englishman is unnoticed or forgotten, but the silent allusion
in these threads to the Canterbury tale later told by Eadmer, far
from supporting the Norman case, substantially undermines it.
It is an allusion which the artist must have made at considerable risk to himself, perhaps to his life, certainly to his career,

and we should pause and listen to his brave witness, at a time when all others were drowned out by the noise of Norman propaganda.

Immediately after this meeting, there occurs an even more intriguing scene, one of the most curious in the whole tapestry, for it seems to bear no relation to what comes before or after. There is this mysterious lady called ÆLFGYVA, which is an aristocratic Anglo-Saxon name; she is the only named woman in the whole work [scene 17; plate 3]. Ælfgyva is standing in an ornate wooden doorway, elaborately carved in apparently Norse style; the doorposts are topped by dragons' heads that sprout long, flicking tongues. Into this scene intrudes a tonsured priest wearing a green cloak; he leans across from an adjacent tower, thrusts his hand into the doorway and touches or caresses Ælfgyva on the cheek. The meaning of this gesture is obscure. It is certainly not elucidated by the inscription, which is teasingly short, omits any verb and leaves us still wondering exactly what the lady and the priest are up to. UBI UNUS CLERICUS ET ÆLFGYVA (Where a priest and Ælfgyva) is all that it says. Many have read a hint of sexual scandal into the mock coyness of this brief and abruptly curtailed sentence. The tower and the doorway are themselves erotically suggestive, at least in our post-Freudian age. So, too, is the appearance of the naked man in the lower border; he seems lewdly to be mimicking the priest and gesturing up Ælfgyva's skirt. Was there, perhaps, a scandalous liaison between a lady and a priest, well known at the time, and that had some bearing on what we see in the tapestry? Does this scene reflect an aspect of William and Harold's discussions at Rouen? Like Turold the dwarf, the Lady Ælfgyva is one of the four mysterious figures named in the Bayeux Tapestry. We must return later to the enigma of Ælfgyva.

Harold's attempt to secure the release of his kinsmen is not going well. This is hardly surprising for in truth the whole idea had been unwise from the start. King Edward, in his dotage, had much the clearer picture of William. Cunning, implacable, supremely ambitious, with a cruel edge, he was the last person to bow down and release such valuable hostages without gaining something extraordinarily important in return. William knows that Earl Harold holds the keys to England; he can hardly believe how foolish the Earl of Wessex has been in allowing himself to fall uninvited into his grasp. For the moment, however, the Duke of Normandy is keeping his plans to himself. According to the written sources, he received Harold in Normandy as an honoured guest.[14] The English party were fed and clothed and given every Norman hospitality; we can imagine them hunting by day and passing torch-lit evenings entertained by the likes of musicians, dancers, jugglers and acrobats in a lively ducal household. Harold should simply be grateful, the Norman sources imply, that William has taken such pains to rescue him from Ponthieu. By now, of course, he may realise that William's display of friendship is entirely false and that he has merely exchanged one kind of imprisonment for another, but he must wait and see what fate William has in store for him. There is no question that he can return to England yet. The coastline of Normandy might as well be enclosed behind iron bars.

It so happens, at this time, that there is trouble brewing in Brittany. We learn from William of Poitiers that Duke Conan of Brittany had presumptuously announced a date on which he intended to invade Normandy and it seems he was already threatening to attack one of William's Breton allies, Rivallon of Dol. In response to this provocation, William decided to take his army into Brittany and to subdue Conan once and for all. He has asked Earl Harold to accompany him, an offer that Harold, of course, could hardly refuse, for a warrior such as he has his honour at stake. For William it meant something more; a war in Brittany would incidentally provide a chance to test Harold's mettle, to kit him out in the best of Norman arms and armour and then see if he is half the warrior men say he is. Slyly he could observe the Englishman, and overawe him with a display of Norman fighting prowess.

So it is that we leave behind the strange enigma of Ælfgyva and see Duke William and his army passing into Breton territory at the mouth of the River Couesnon [scene 18; plate 4]. There they are: men and horses making steady progress across the open-mouthed estuary at low tide. In the distance, a mile offshore, the island abbey of Mont-Saint-Michel rises dreamily into an empty sky. In these parts the tidal range is vast, and each day the sea draws itself like a great curtain across the bay, sweeping across miles of hazardous sand, curling and swirling its way around the island-hill on which the famous abbey stands. William and his men are crossing here, within sight of the semi-diurnal island; now they are wading towards Brittany through limpid shallows, shields lifted above heads in order to protect the metal from the salty water. Today the abbey of Mont-Saint-Michel is famous for its pyramidal shape; each level rises taller and narrower than the last, until it reaches its apex with a skyward spire surmounted by a golden statue of St Michael himself. It is almost as if the whole assemblage of buildings was once entirely flat but was then pulled up by the spire and stretched reluctantly out of the sand. In the 1060s Mont-Saint-Michel had a different aspect, one which gives the lie to any such fantasy. Stripped of its Gothic and later accretions, the church that Harold can make out in the hazy distance is a long, cruciform, roof-tiled building, poised upon the rocky island 75 yards above the visiting sea, stranded there, at the very top of the mount, as if it were some great ship that had been left behind by an exceptionally high tide.

It must have been an awesome sight. It must have drawn the gaze from far across the sands just as magnetically as it does today. Only the point where the nave crosses the transept actually touches the summit; the sloping shoulders of the mount were built up in order to support the rest of the church, a structural feat which is clearly symbolised in the tapestry. The abbey of the Archangel Michael, whose legend is often associated with the highest promontories, had been founded on the island in 708 by one Aubert, in response to his strange thoughts and dreams. In 966 Duke Richard I of Normandy established a colony of Benedictine monks at the place. A new spate of building began in 1023 under the patronage Duke Richard II, William's uncle; it was now continuing apace under the direction of Abbot Ranulphe, a former monk from Bayeux. Nothing in the tapestry, or any other source, indicates that William and Harold halted their travels that day, crossed by ferry or foot to the island and ascended the rocky mount in order to pray at the church of St Michael, although it would not be surprising if they did. It was a popular place of pilgrimage and St Michael himself had become a favoured saint among the Normans. In 1066 Duke William's half-brother, Robert of Mortain, fought at Hastings (and no doubt shed much blood) while dutifully holding aloft a banner embroidered with an emblem of the saintly Michael.[15]

In the upper border adjacent to Mont-Saint-Michel there appears quite unexpectedly, out of thin air as it were, a small, seated man pointing at the abbey. Over the years many guesses have been made as to who he is, this mysterious 'Norman' gesturing at the abbey of Mont-Saint-Michel. The visionary

Aubert, perhaps, Duke Richard I, Duke Richard II, Abbot Ranulphe from Bayeux, or Abbot Scollandus, a former monk here, promoted by William to be the head of St Augustine's Abbey in Canterbury after the Conquest.[16] None of these guesses has found universal favour. There is another more intriguing possibility; and it is one which accentuates the growing sense of Englishness about the tapestry. As we have seen, the seated position always represents high rank and authority; thus far, the seats in the tapestry have been reserved for a king, a count and a duke. Clearly observable, too, though rarely noticed, is the fact that the seated figure has long hair at the back of his neck, a hallmark of the English. Evidently, this is a high-ranking *Englishman*, not a Frenchman. From the picture he is not an old man; he is probably an adult in the prime of his life. Equally it should not be overlooked how cleverly (and uniquely) the abbey is drawn. It is both a picture in the main frieze and simultaneously a device in the upper border; the floor of the church is identical to the line which separates the main frieze from the border. Moreover, the seated figure's connection with Mont-Saint-Michel must truly be a remarkable one for he has the privilege of sharing the same border compartment as the fabulous abbey itself.

It so happens that one man, a secular figure, fits all these clues rather well. In the early 1030s Edward the Confessor, while still exiled in Normandy, appears to have made a formal gift of certain English lands to Mont-Saint-Michel.[17] The gift included the eerily similar island off the Cornish coast known as St Michael's Mount where Edward hoped would be established a subordinate house of Benedictine monks. Intriguingly, Prince Edward describes himself in this charter as 'I, Edward, by the grace of God King of the English . . .' King he was not; it was the best part of another ten years before the exiled prince returned to England and became king. The gift was made more in hope than reality; but it shows that, even then, at the height of Canute's power, Edward's hopes of returning to rule over his native land had not entirely died – and neither were they discouraged by his Norman hosts. In due course (by the grace of God and St Michael, it would have seemed) he did return and peaceably ascend the English throne. Could it be that his munificence towards the abbey of Mont-Saint-Michel was now being remembered by the artist of the tapestry?

Suddenly two men, their backs turned to the distant abbey, have become mired in quicksand and they are in danger of sinking within minutes to a wet death [scene 18; plate 4]. A horse has also stumbled into a gully. Did they not tell Harold that this is a dangerous place? The exposed bay is awash with hidden pools of quicksand, quicksand that will open up like a toothless mouth and suck a man up with pursed lips into a terrible, slippery grave. What is more, when the tide rises it bears down on the unwary (so men say) with all the speed and venom of a charging horse. Cries of alarm must have shot into the air. Arms must have waved in panic and fear. Harold has leant down and grabbed one of the men by the wrist; the second has managed to climb on to his back. The first is Norman, the second English. Still holding his shield, Harold drags both of them to safety using all his remarkable strength. HIC HAROLD DUX TRAHEBAT EOS DE ARENA (Here Duke Harold pulled them out of the sand). This episode, recorded in the tapestry though omitted in every other source, does Harold much credit. Not only is he brave and strong, he has also shown himself to be selfless and noble towards Norman and Englishman alike.

William's army has now penetrated deep into the coastal

plains of eastern Brittany. Intelligence has apparently been received that Duke Conan is holed up within the wooden fortress at the town of Dol. There is little time to prepare. As quickly as possible a group of mounted Norman knights launches a surprise attack [scene 19]. It has caught the Normans, as much as the Bretons, unawares, for none of the attackers has had the time to put on his chain mail and only one has a helmet. As they attack one side of the castle, Conan makes a hurried escape – he is slipping down a rope at the back in order to disappear out of sight. Now the Norman knights have advanced deeper into Breton territory. For some reason they have reached the hilltop castle at Rennes [scene 20]. There is no sign of Conan here; so they backtrack northwards, 35 miles to Dinan. Conan has already reached Dinan. He is determined to hold out, but William's knights have prepared themselves for a full-scale assault. They have put on their chain mail and conical helmets. They have placed silvery swords in hilts. They have mounted their warhorses and kicked them with spurs. They are charging the castle at speed. Fingers of the left hand tightly grip the strap of a kite-shaped shield as well as the horse's reins, fingers of the right are curled around a vicious lance held at the ready.

The Bretons have gathered at the highest point of the castle. Protected by similar armour, they defend the place on foot as vigorously as it is attacked and they return as many spears as arrive. It is a hard-fought battle. What they do not know is that two Normans, bearing flaming torches, have scurried to the base of the wooden structure [scene 21]. At this very moment they are setting it ablaze with dancing, menacing flames. Smoke must have risen around Conan's eyes and curled into his throat, and choked his desire to continue; for he has signalled his surrender. From the top of the motte he proffers the keys to Dinan at the end of a long lance. He holds the lance outstretched with both hands. The Normans proffer one of their own lances and now the great iron keys to the town are slipping from one lance to the other. Evidently the two sides are still keeping a safe distance, but evidently, too, the victory is William's.

The noise of action has abated. Away from any residual smoke, Duke William has strutted over to Harold [scene 22]. The Earl of Wessex is standing there; he is clothed in full Norman armour and the great lance he has planted in the ground is topped with a fluttering Norman banner, or gonfanon. The slithery iron rings of chain mail that he can feel against his body were forged in Normandy and he can smell Norman leather on the inside of his helmet.[18] Although his armour is much the same as English armour, there is still something incongruous about this little picture of Harold, the most famous of Anglo-Saxon kings, standing there in Norman garb, dressed like a little schoolboy in the wrong uniform. He is an awkward, out-of-place figure, this Harold, as his eyes look downwards in an attempt to avoid William's gaze.

Harold may have thought that William had strutted up to him in order to offer his congratulations at the end of the Battle of Dinan. But the Duke of Normandy is now placing one hand on Harold's helmet and with the other he is fixing something symbolic to his chest. HIC WILLELM DEDIT HAROLDO ARMA (Here William gave arms to Harold). The giving of arms, a sort of knighthood, was a redolent gesture. It carried with it heavy, if indefinite, overtones of vassalage and loyalty. In Anglo-Saxon England there were bonds, too, that bound the warrior to his lord. This was another of William's cunning plans. It must have been clear to Harold, by now at least, that he was being stitched up. But what was he to do? If he backed off and refused the honour of a Norman knighthood, a poisoned chalice if ever there was one, what were his chances of ever persuading William to release his brother and nephew? What were his own chances of ever returning to England alive?

It is time to pause and look back at what may have been missed since that distant appearance of Mont-Saint-Michel. The Breton war is over. It has proceeded in the tapestry's threads with its own internal logic; but there is much that merits a second look. From the beginning it is attended by strange and redolent border imagery. Beneath the shallows at Mont-Saint-Michel there were two fishes swimming in opposite directions but joined at the mouth by a cord. This is clearly an image of the astrological sign of Pisces, an indication, perhaps, of the time of year – 19 February to 20 March – when the crossing into Brittany was made (but whether the year in question is 1064 or 1065 is not known). There follows a school of wriggling eels and then, beneath the passage from Mont-Saint-Michel to Dol, yet more astrological signs; in fact, a strange series of joined-up constellations that have been identified by various authors as Serpens, Perseus (or Orion or Boötes), Ursa Major (or Canis Major), Aquila, Lupus and Centaurus [scene 18].[19] The meaning of this has never been deciphered. The campaign itself is distinctly odd. Our only other source of information comes from the work of William of Poitiers.[20] In his account, Conan was besieging Dol, not holed up in it. He immediately retreated when he heard that William was advancing to Dol, fled quickly and was never subdued by the Normans. Poitiers mentions no sliding down a rope, and no circular movement by William's men, southwards from Dol to Rennes, then northwards from Rennes to Dinan; indeed he mentions no action at Rennes or Dinan at all. The reason why the tapestry's tale should differ so much is obscure. We are left to wonder how much of the truth has been embroidered and whether there is rather more to this strange vision of Duke William's Breton campaign than at first meets the eye?

Now William's men have returned to Normandy and they have made their way to Bayeux. HIC WILLELM VENIT BAGIAS (Here William came to Bayeux). The town of Bayeux is represented by an elaborate castle standing on a tall mound. This, no doubt, is the castle of William's older half-brother Odo, the bishop of Bayeux, but its exact location in the modern town can only be guessed at. Strangely, Bayeux Cathedral, which was then being built under Odo's direction, is nowhere to be seen. Nor is Odo himself, although he will later become an important figure as the story progresses. We have moved outside, or beyond, Bayeux on to a patch of open ground. If Harold's purpose was to convey a message from King Edward that William should expect to be the next king, the tapestry has *still* not illustrated him doing so. Instead, it is William who takes the initiative. Once more we are reminded of the story told by Eadmer rather than the Norman sources.

According to Eadmer, Duke William at last took Harold aside and told him what was on his mind. William said that when King Edward was an exile in Normandy, and both of them were much younger, he had once 'promised him and pledged his faith that if he should ever be king of England he would make over to William the right to succeed him as his heir'. William looked at Harold and, in the words reported by Eadmer, made the following astonishing proposal:

If you, for your part, undertake that you will support me in this project; that you will make a stronghold at Dover for my use, which should include a well of water; that you will, at a future time agreed between us, send your sister to me so that I can give her in marriage to one of my nobles; and that you will take my daughter to be your wife; if you undertake to do all these things, then you can have your nephew straight away and your brother will be delivered to you safe and sound when I come to England to be king. And if I am ever, with your support, established there as king, I promise that you shall have everything you ask of me, provided that it can reasonably be granted.[21]

Eadmer tells us that this elaborate proposal was the first indication Harold had that William seriously intended to be king of England. There was danger in this, whichever way Harold turned. It was bad enough being vaguely bound by the grant of Norman arms. Now he was being asked to give his support, in the clearest possible terms, to the Norman claim to the English throne, a pretension which hitherto he had discounted in his own mind – and which he knew would have no support in the country. But what was he to do? To refuse would be to throw himself, and his men, at the mercy of Duke William. Eadmer tells us that Harold could see no way of avoiding that fate without at least feigning to agree what William asked. He would keep up (we may imagine him thinking) this silly pretence of friendship between the two of them and then make his excuses later. An agreement extracted under such circumstances could hardly be considered binding and, besides, Harold could argue that in reality the decision was the king's. He had no authority to overrule the king's latest wish, which, almost certainly, was that young Edgar should succeed. What was William going to do about it? Invade England?

But William wanted more than a mere agreement: he was

about to raise the stakes even higher. He and his advisers were busy weaving an intricate web around Harold, a web of obligation, both secular and religious, from which the Englishman would find it impossible ever to disentangle himself. At this very spot, visible to all upon the open ground, William has had gathered together the bones of some of the holiest saints in Normandy [scene 23; plate 5]. They have been placed in two great reliquary chests. One of the chests is surmounted by a precious crystal known as the Bull's Eye.[22] The design of the other brings to mind the holiest chest of all, the portable Ark of the Convenant in which the Ten Commandments were once placed by Moses.[23] What possible objection can Harold have to taking the next step? He must swear an oath upon the bones of these holy saints. He must swear before God what he has already agreed before William. What he has already agreed by the law of man will become the law of God.

William's throne has been carried to the place so that he can witness the event. Now the duke is sitting there, smug and haughty. He is holding his ceremonial sword in one hand and with the other he is pointing at Harold. His whole posture smacks of command rather than gratitude. Harold is standing with his arms outstretched, fingers touching the two holy boxes placed on either side of him. His brow is furrowed; his eyes, narrowed to the width of a stitch, are fixed upon the first reliquary chest in fear. This is turning into a dreadful moment. The very atmosphere seems to have been pulled taut. William is pointing to Harold, commanding that he swear the oath. Like all men of his day Harold must surely believe, with all the conviction of his heart, that those who break a sacred oath will have to answer before God. On the awful Day of Judgement, or quite possibly sooner, the guilty will be mocked by monsters; they will be poked and prodded by an army of hideous devils; their lying tongues will be wrenched from their throats; or their eyes will be taken out by divine writ, which will sear like a blazing arrow from the angry heavens; and then they will be thrown for all eternity into the flames of Hell. Harold hears William commanding him to make the oath. Surely he has no other choice. How else will he and his nephew, let alone the rest of his men, ever return to their waiting homes and long-forsaken loved ones? Once he is back in England, he can probably do what he likes. Harold's fingers are touching the two holy boxes. He will take his chance; the words are uttered. UBI HAROLD SACRAMENTUM FECIT WILLELMO DUCI (Where Harold swore a sacred oath to William). This was how Harold of Wessex gambled the kingdom of England for his freedom.

The oath is made and Harold and his men are immediately shown aboard their embroidered ship as it departs towards England [scene 23]. A pair of Englishmen provide the link between the two scenes. They are looking back at Harold's oath and at the same moment they are moving impatiently towards the ship; one of them has his foot already in the water. This link, temporal and narrative, is another clue. In the written Norman accounts, Harold's oath is described in detail and it is supposed to have been given 'clearly and of his own free will'.[24] The oath is a key part of the Norman claim, but it takes place much earlier, before the Breton war (though the accounts differ as to the precise location). By reversing the order and placing Harold's oath after the Breton war and immediately before he departs for home, the tapestry's artist has accentuated the impression of duress. With pictures rather than words, he is telling us that Harold was a helpless prisoner and that he was permitted to return only because he swore the oath demanded of him.

At last Harold's ship threads a homeward course through the lapping linen waves. There are eight men to be seen on board, unnamed men, hopeful men, busy men, testing the wind, pulling up the sail, tending the rudder, longing for home. One of them must be Hakon, Harold's nephew, for even William of Poitiers confirms that Hakon was released by Duke William and allowed to return home with his uncle after more than ten years as a hostage in Normandy. Perhaps Hakon is the smallest figure; he can be seen barely above the line of shields that are laid out along the side of the boat; now he is looking up wistfully at the billowing curve of worsted rail that has caught the homeward breeze. Harold's brother Wulfnoth is not on board; he did not fare so well. It is known that he remained a prisoner of the Normans. Even after King William's death in 1087, when his son William Rufus became king, it was still considered expedient to keep Harold's last surviving brother in custody. Rufus did take Wulfnoth to Winchester, where he probably treated him reasonably well; but Wulfnoth Godwinson remained a captive until he died around 1094. By then he had been a prisoner for more than forty years. Geoffrey of Cambrai, prior of Winchester Cathedral, composed a moving epitaph for him:

> Exile, prison, darkness, inclosure, chains
> Receive the boy and forsake the old man.
> Caught up in human bonds he bore them patiently
> Bound even more closely in service to God.[25]

On the southern coast, the English are eagerly looking out for Harold's ship. Four men peer from the windows of a coastal watchtower, necks craned in anticipation. A fifth is standing on a raised platform; his hand is cupped over his eyes as he looks out towards Harold's vessel looming ever nearer across the wavy sea. HIC HAROLD DUX REVERSUS EST AD ANGLICAM TERRAM (Here Earl Harold returned to English soil). Now Harold is riding a horse along the bumpy road that is taking him back to King Edward. The first thing he must do is give the king an account of all that has happened. ET VENIT AD EDWARDUM REGEM (and came to King Edward). These five, simple words tell us very little, but the picture of the new encounter between the two men speaks a thousand more [scene 24]. Harold, here, is the epitome of apology. His posture alone shows that he is utterly crestfallen and subdued. Clothed under the myriad folds of a great green cape, he is standing with his arms outstretched in Edward's direction, as if begging forgiveness from the king; his head is not so much lowered, his whole neck has been bent over and stretched forward so that it is almost horizontal to the body. 'I have done a terrible thing,' he seems to be saying. Edward, seated on his throne, is pointing at Harold and he is clearly admonishing him with his long index finger. We do not know how long Earl Harold has been away, but in the embroidered interim the king has aged notably. His face is haggard; his fingers are gnarled and spindly; and across his lap rests the long stick he now uses to help him walk. The moment when he will die is surely nearer.

If the Norman account of the purpose of Harold's mission is true, why is Harold so apologetic on his return? Why is Edward admonishing him in this manner? By promising his support to William, Harold has surely done no more than fulfil his supposed mission. He should be congratulated, not criticised. Again we are reminded of the Canterbury tale told by Eadmer. 'On being questioned by the King,' says Eadmer, 'Harold told him what had happened and what he had done.

The King exclaimed: "Did I not tell you that I knew William well and that your going there might bring untold calamity upon this kingdom?"[26]

These words could almost be an English subtitle to the tapestry's silent scene. Once more, close observation of the Bayeux Tapestry reveals that it is not the work of Norman propaganda that popular myth would have us believe, but a covert, subtle and substantial record of the English version of events, one whose true meaning has been largely lost for well-nigh a thousand years. It is nevertheless so cleverly designed that observers who expect to see a perfidious Harold have always seen what they expect to see. Many Normans would probably have seen little to quarrel with. They might have breezed up and down the length of the work, smirking here, laughing there, glowing everywhere with the haughty satisfaction of conquerors. They would have seen what they wanted to see: but the pictorial clues tell a different story. The subtle subtext lies silently within the pictures rather than the words. Drawing on a similar or identical source, it tells much the same story that Eadmer was to record more explicitly in writing forty or fifty years later. In the process the tapestry adds considerable weight to Eadmer's already plausible story. The tapestry is much earlier than Eadmer, being almost contemporary with the events themselves, but unlike William of Poitiers, who wrote his Norman biography of Duke William at around the same time, the tapestry's artist had no motive to dissemble the facts, if he could get away with recording them, and he had no reason to spread propaganda. What we see in these threads is, therefore, very likely true.

Thus it appears that by the early 1060s King Edward no longer supported Duke William's claim. Harold, however, had been foolish enough to travel to Normandy on his own business and had fallen into a trap. He had been caught in a tragic dilemma from which he could only extricate himself by swearing a sacred oath to support the Norman claim. It is unlikely, even then, that Earl Harold had any intention of fulfilling that undertaking. He had escaped from Count Guy into the hands of Duke William and he had escaped from Duke William only by placing himself in the hands and at the mercy of his God. His journey back to Edward is accompanied by yet another border image of the ancient fable of the fox and the crow. Can there be any doubt that William is the greedy fox and that Harold is the naive and foolish crow? King Edward is frail and old; his time will soon be over and the moment when his successor must be chosen will surely arrive before the cornfields are golden again. The Bayeux Tapestry is appearing less and less as a triumphal monument. It is more with the rhythm and pathos of a Greek tragedy that the story is moving, stitch by stitch, towards its deadly climax.

7

The English Decision

As late as the summer of 1065 King Edward was still well enough for Harold to invite him hunting in south Wales, but as the days grew colder, and the barren winter blew sharply across the land, the health of the old man deteriorated rapidly. His *grand projet*, his last great offering to his God, his great legacy upon which he had lavished a large fortune, was to be a new church at the abbey of Westminster, close to his riverside palace. Westminster was then situated on a little island, known as Thorney Island; it was bounded on three sides not, as now, by roads and queuing traffic, but by the slow-flowing waters of a tributary of the Thames and to the east by the Thames itself. The king's palace was situated on land where the Houses of Parliament now stand, the abbey on the site that it still occupies. From the palace you could make out the city of London, a busy agglomeration that was home to some 25,000 people. You would have seen smoke rising from its little houses, clustered around a bend of the Thames, whilst merchants' vessels with sails aloft eased their way upriver with cargoes, so the author of the *Life of King Edward* tells us, 'of every kind for sale from the whole world to the town on its banks'.[1] The ambitious church that Edward was building at Westminster, in honour of St Peter, was to be larger than any in Christendom. It was still years from completion but the ceremony of consecration was advanced to 28 December 1065 so that the old man, supported by his walking stick or carried by servants, would be able to make the short journey from the palace and attend the moment of dedication. On Christmas Eve, however, he fell gravely ill. He recovered sufficiently to attend Christmas service in the abbey, and to be present at the banquet that followed, but on Boxing Day he was again too frail to leave his bedchamber. On the day fixed for the consecration the king's condition was found to be no better and though a great concourse 'from the whole of Britain'[2] had assembled to witness a joyous occasion, the service of dedication had to proceed more solemnly in his absence. The life of the bedridden old man was edging away.

In the Bayeux Tapestry we move directly from the scene of Earl Harold's reprimand to an exterior view of the magnificent church [scene 25]. It is as if an implicit contrast is being made between Harold's well-meant foolishness and Edward's prodigious piety. At the eastern end, a workman has climbed on to the roof in order to put a weathercock in its place. Above the nave the very hand of God has descended from the heavens in a gesture of benediction. How carefully the hand of God is drawn, how skilfully the spirit of the divine has been made material. There is no room for error in the illustration of perfection. This great church is depicted as still unfinished, but it is nevertheless by far the largest building in the whole of the tapestry. It bears little relation to the Westminster Abbey known today. In the thirteenth century Edward the Confessor's elegant building was pulled down and replaced by a

Gothic structure that was similar in size but more in keeping with the times. Of course, the latter-day Westminster Abbey is itself a medieval masterpiece, itself over 700 years old. In those 700 years so much intervening history has echoed around its vaulted chambers, the royal throne, the poets' corner and the tomb of the unknown soldier are symbols of so much British heritage, that the thought that there was once an earlier church on same site, matching it in size and grandeur, is strangely disconcerting. The earlier church seems to belong to a past which is almost unreachable now. Once more the extraordinary survival of the Bayeux Tapestry is thrown into sharp relief. The great church of solid stone that Edward the Confessor built as his lasting monument has long disappeared. It is the church of threads that survives.

From the tapestry, and a contemporary description in the *Life of King Edward*, we can make out the appearance of the building.[3] The last architectural achievement of the Anglo-Saxon age was a grand imitation of French style. It looked to the future, not the past. The Romanesque style, with its characteristic round-topped arches and clean, elegant lines, had spread north from Burgundy into Normandy and after the Conquest it was to dominate the ecclesiastical landscape of Norman England. During his long exile on the continent Edward must have visited many of the great churches of northern France and it was only natural that his own great project should be an imitation of them. The closest parallel seems to have been the monumental Norman church at the abbey of Jumièges, part of whose roofless shell still survives, but Westminster church was even longer and even more impressive. Five bays of the nave are shown as completed, represented by a series of round-topped arches stitched in wools of three different colours; the bases and capitals of the columns can clearly be seen. A line of clerestory windows runs above. To the east there is a large apse; and from here an enigmatic series of steps descends into the floor, as if indicating the presence of a crypt. The church is dominated at the centre by a monumental tower, borne aloft by a great arch and surrounded by a cluster of smaller turrets. It was the central tower which most struck the imagination of the anonymous author of the *Life of King Edward*. 'It rises simply at first with a low and sturdy vault, swells with many a stair spiralling up in artistic profusion, but then with a plain wall climbs to the wooden roof which is carefully covered with lead.'

At some point during the long, sombre night of 4/5 January 1066 King Edward the Confessor breathed his last breath and died. Now we can see his coffin being borne slowly towards the church [scene 25]. HIC PORTATUR CORPUS EAD-WARDI REGIS AD ECCLESIAM S[AN]C[T]I PETRI AP[OSTO]LI (Here King Edward's corpse is borne to the church of St Peter the Apostle). The corpse is solemnly carried on an open-topped bier, over which a richly embroidered cloth has been carefully laid. The king's body, completely wrapped in a dark green binding, lies on its side, as lifeless as an empty vessel. Eight men are shouldering the poles; two other figures ring hand bells at the sides. The solemn, metallic chime of bells is accompanied by a dirge chanted out by a group of tonsured clerics at the rear of the funeral procession; two of the priests are holding open prayer books to their breasts. 'They bore his holy remains from his palace home into the house of God,' the *Life of King Edward* tells us, 'and offered up prayers and sighs and psalms all that day and the following night.'[4]

There was genuine lamenting at King Edward's passing. On the whole he seemed to have been dignified, dutiful and pious and he belonged to the most ancient lineage in England; but was he truly wise? Beneath that pious exterior, behind that lily-white beard and wistful gaze, was Edward the Confessor as much of an enigma to his contemporaries as he appears to us? He has been seen as the archetypical weak and ineffectual king, forever under the domination of powerful nobles; and yet now and then he acted with decision, if not always with effect. In truth, it was probably his position, more than his character, that was inherently weak. Viewed in this way, Edward's acceptance of the power of the Godwins after 1052 can be seen as positive and pragmatic. Certainly, after the dust of war had settled, and the Normans dominated the land, many people were to look back upon the days of King Edward with fondness and nostalgia. Compared to the Danish maelstrom that came before, and the Norman disaster that ensued, it seemed that Edward's reign had brought England over twenty years of relative peace and prosperity. But there was a terrible price to pay. As far as may now be judged (though there is no hint of this in the tapestry) the king seems to have been using his childlessness as a diplomatic tool. In the course of his life, Edward dangled the prospect of the succession in front of far too many people – the King of Denmark, the Duke of Normandy, Edward the Exile and his son Edgar, and at the last moment Harold himself. This, of course, kept various would-be warriors friendly while he lived, but it was storing up immeasurable problems for the future. Duke William, for one, had indicated that he was deadly serious. It mattered not that many years had passed since Edward foolishly raised his hopes, nor that the King of England had since changed his mind. To make matters worse, William had outfoxed Harold into giving him that unlikely promise of support.

We have seen Edward's corpse being borne in all solemnity

from the palace to the church of Westminster, but what were his final wishes? For reasons that will become apparent, the tapestry now turns the clock back to the king's last moments, just a few hours earlier. In the upper part of a split scene, we find ourselves transported into Edward's bedchamber somewhere within the turreted palace of Westminster [scene 26; plate 6]. The billowing curtain, which would normally enclose the bed, has been pulled open and tied back so that we can observe the proceedings within. Edward is still living though he is barely alive. Here he is on his deathbed, a wearisome, weakening old man, waiting for death. Death comes to kings as it does to all men. The dying king is surrounded by four attentive, though unnamed, followers. One of them supports his back with a cushion so that he can sit up and speak. A veiled and sombre woman – the second of only three women depicted in the tapestry – is seated at the foot of the bed. The third figure is a tonsured cleric who is seen leaning over in order to catch the king's words. The cleric's unshaven face is dotted with stubble, for he has been attending at the royal bedside for many hours. The fourth witness, seated or kneeling at the front, is a noble follower; his fingers are touching the king's fingers. It is to this fourth figure that Edward is evidently addressing himself in particular. HIC EADWARDUS REX IN LECTO ALLO-QUIT[UR] FIDELES (Here King Edward in his bed addresses his faithful followers). In the lower part of the scene time has moved on, and we are at the point when all life has left the old man – ET HIC DEFUNCTUS EST (and here he has died). His corpse is tightly wrapped in green cloth. Only his linen-grey face is exposed to view; and this has been angled towards the viewer. For the first time, the gaze of one of the tapestry's figures meets the onlooker in the eye, but this is the chilling, lifeless gaze of death.

None of the four followers, gathered like chess pieces closely around their king, is given a name in the tapestry. Nor are the king's last words, faintly uttered from his own thin lips, recorded in the brief inscription. The words tell us little; the picture reveals the truth. A contemporary written account of Edward's last hours survives, and elucidates what we see in the tapestry. It is to be found in the *Life of King Edward*, the work commissioned by Queen Edith shortly after the old king died, though it was not completed until after Duke William's victory at Hastings. The author was a Flemish monk; he was clearly on good terms with the queen, and no friend of the Normans, although his name is not known. It can be deduced that some years earlier he had come to England from the monastery of Saint-Bertin at St-Omer, not far from Boulogne. By chance the *Life* survives in an early, fragile, mutilated copy dating from around 1100, neatly copied out in a Canterbury style of writing. The deathbed scene conjured up in the *Life of King Edward* is so similar to what we see in the tapestry that it is highly probable that the artist held one of the first copies in his own hands and used it as his source. It can hardly be irrelevant that, at this key moment, the artist of the tapestry was using another source from southern England, one which, moreover, was closely connected to Harold's family. According to the *Life*, the following witnesses were present at the king's deathbed and heard his last wishes: '. . . the queen, who was sitting on the floor warming his feet in her lap, her full brother Earl Harold, and Rodbert, the steward of the royal palace . . . also Archbishop Stigand and a few more whom the blessed king when roused from his sleep had ordered to be summoned'.[5]

The four persons named in the *Life of King Edward* can be matched without difficulty to the four who appear in the tapestry. These, then, are not merely representative manikins. They are not merely woollen figurines, illustrative of a death-bed scene in some generic way. They are the real people who were there at that decisive moment, the real witnesses of the king's last will and testament during the night of 4/5 January 1066. The veiled lady at the foot of the bed, by Edward's feet, must be Queen Edith. The unshaven cleric is Archbishop Stigand of Canterbury. The man at the king's back is Robert fitzWimarch, the French-born royal steward, and the one towards the front, touching fingers with the king in such a redolent, complicit gesture, must be Earl Harold himself. The finger-touching gesture is identical to the one seen when Edward met Harold at the beginning of the tapestry. Harold is thus identifiable, here at the king's deathbed, as one of the FIDELES (the faithful) who are now being addressed by their dying king.

For days he had been drifting in and out of consciousness. Like a pale winter sun appearing now and again behind sombre clouds, old Edward would awaken briefly, mumble something unintelligible and then fall once more under the shadow of a long deep sleep. At one point, however, he started and then he spoke up (the author of the *Life* tells us) in a clear and healthy voice. He told the assembled group about a dream that he had just had. Edward, in his delirium, had dreamt that two long-dead monks, whom he had known in Normandy, had come to him bearing a terrible message from God. They told him that the holders of the highest offices in England – all 'the earls, bishops and abbots and all those in holy orders' – were not what they seemed to be. They were not the servants of God; they were in league with the devil. Within a year and a day of Edward's death, the monks told him, God would punish the whole of England by delivering it into 'the hands of the enemy' and that 'devils shall come through all this land with fire and sword and the havoc of war'. Only when a green tree was cut in half at the middle of its trunk and the upper part transported three furlongs away, and the two parts joined themselves together without the slightest human intervention, and the conjoined tree then sprouted a profusion of leaves and bore fresh fruit, only then would the sins of the people be forgiven and England find respite from its suffering.[6]

The story of this strange dream owes much, of course, to the fact that the author of the *Life* was writing after the Battle of Hastings. With the benefit of hindsight he knew the subsequent course of events. The dream-story, and its implicit likening of the Normans to 'devils' sent by God, is revealing nonetheless. It shows how the Norman Conquest appeared to the English, as they tried to comprehend the totality of their defeat. It also shows how the Conquest sometimes appeared to continentals from beyond the borders of Normandy, men like the anonymous Flemish author of the *Life of King Edward*. In this view, Duke William did not have a lawful claim to the English throne. He was an unwanted pretender, but after he had won the sheer fact of his victory was undeniable. God, the author of all things, must surely have caused that victory. He cannot have done so because William was right, but rather in order to punish the English. It followed that prior to 1066 the English must have been sinful – and sinfulness is never particularly hard to find once you start looking for it in earnest. In the world-view of the time this seemed to be the lesson to be learnt from the Bible. When David sinned, the author of the *Life* notes, God's vengeance fell from the heavens upon the whole people of Israel.[7] Was this not (the people asked themselves) what had really happened to England in 1066?

The little company gathered around Edward's bed 'were sore afraid' and 'stupefied and silent from the effect of terror' when they heard him speak of this dire prophecy. The author of the *Life* now points his finger explicitly at Archbishop Stigand, whose embroidered counterpart is seen leaning over the king's bed, with his eyes fixed intently on the king. 'He ought to have been the first to be afraid ... [but] with folly in his heart he whispered in the ear of [Earl Harold] that the King was broken with age and disease and knew not what he said.' Stigand was a great survivor. He was a man with a dubious past and an even more dubious present.[8] A cleric of enormous wealth, he had risen to prominence in the days of King Canute and in the course of a long life he contrived to remain in high office under six very different kings. He had been made Archbishop of Canterbury in 1052 when his Norman predecessor, Robert of Jumièges, fled the country in haste as the Godwins returned in force. Stigand's appointment in such circumstances was regarded by Rome as null and void and although in 1058 he did obtain recognition by Pope Benedict X, Benedict was deposed a year later and was spoken of as an 'anti-pope'. Stigand's position was also dubious in that he remained the Bishop of Winchester although such pluralism was frowned upon. As a consequence he had been excommunicated by five popes and the sentence of anathema still clung to him like a nasty cold. Yet he used his wily skills and long experience to remain in office. In the aftermath of the Norman Conquest, and especially after Stigand's replacement by Lanfranc in 1070 and his death in 1072, it was easy to find a scapegoat in Archbishop Stigand and to portray him as symbolic of all that was wrong with the English Church. With a man like that occupying the ancient see of Canterbury, it was hardly surprising in this religious-minded age that it appeared

God's sleeping anger had been roused. To contemporaries it seemed that God had punished the whole nation for the sins of its leaders.

As King Edward lay dying, the question whether Earl Harold might yet adhere to the sacred oath he had given to Duke William was still hanging on a knife-edge. The *Life of King Edward* makes no reference to the oath, nor to Duke William's claim at all, but it does describe Edward's dying bequest.[9] This must be the very moment, the very gesture, that we can see in the Bayeux Tapestry [scene 26; plate 6]. 'And stretching forth his hand to [Harold], he said: "I commend [Queen Edith] and all the kingdom to your protection."' These words, reported by the author of the *Life of King Edward* and illustrated in the Bayeux Tapestry, still seem to hang in the air with an eerie ambiguity. Is Edward bequeathing the kingdom to Harold? Or is he saying that Harold should act as protector and regent, perhaps for the young Edgar? If anything like these words were truly spoken, the king's voice fell silent and he faltered and died on that very bed before he could make himself clearer. The living were left to decipher what he meant. The general view seems to have been that Harold, at the last moment, had been nominated as king. The E version of the *Anglo-Saxon Chronicle*, written at St Augustine's Abbey in Canterbury, also states in the clearest possible terms that Edward bequeathed the kingdom to Harold ('And Earl Harold succeeded to the kingdom of England just as the king granted it to him . . .'). Even William of Poitiers, the arch-propagandist of the Normans, admits that Edward on his deathbed nominated Harold.[10] This, no doubt, was an inconvenience for the Normans; but the testimony of witnesses such as Queen Edith and Robert fitzWimarch could hardly be impugned. Poitiers deals with the point by arguing that, whatever had happened at Edward's deathbed, William already had the better claim: Harold had quite simply disqualified himself by swearing to be William's man. In any event it seems that under Norman law Edward's earlier choice of William (as a *post obitum* gift) would have been regarded as final and irrevocable. In England the custom was different. Since time immemorial ('ever since St Augustine came to these parts') a gift made by an Englishman at the point of death (*verba novissima*) was regarded as valid and binding.[11] Whereas to modern eyes it might seem that a dying person's mental faculties would be at their most questionable, to the Anglo-Saxons a person's thoughts were then at their most lucid and close to God. If this is the true nature of the legal dispute between Harold and William, it has no obvious solution, for it is a dispute between the laws of Normandy and the laws of England. In the absence of an agreed system of supranational law to determine which nation's law should apply, the dispute between two such proud and determined warriors as William and Harold could only be resolved by war.

It remained for the king's nominee to be elected by the Witan, the council of the great in the land, who were already in attendance in large number at Westminster. Accordingly, in the next scene, we see two nobles offering the crown to Harold, one of whom points back at the previous image of King Edward's dying bequest [scene 27]. HIC DEDERUNT HAROLDO CORONA[M] REGIS (Here they gave Harold the king's crown). This, evidently, is the reason why the tapestry depicts Edward's funeral and death in reverse chronological order. The inscription alone tells us very little, but a visual link is clearly being made between the king's last words and the offer of the crown to Harold. If events had been portrayed in their natural sequence, the men offering the crown would have been pointing at Edward's funeral, and not his dying wishes. By pointing to the dying king, the thrust of what they are saying to Harold becomes immediately clear. 'Here is the crown,' the English nobles are telling him. 'It was Edward's last wish that you should have it and we urge you to accept.'

Once again, the story is not being told 'from the Norman point of view'. The tapestry makes not the slightest reference to Duke William's claim to the throne, which was founded upon his earlier designation by Edward, but it does show Harold's own nomination as entirely lawful under English custom. There is no sense in which Harold is a usurper, a man who, in the words of William of Poitiers, 'seized' the crown with the connivance of a few and who was 'the enemy of the good and the just'. Yet although Harold has been duly nominated by the last king he still seems reluctant to accept the highest office. He does not thrust out his arm and seize the crown of threads; he keeps his hand firmly upon his hip. This is a hesitant, pensive man; he is wondering what to do next. Without doubt, the young Edgar Ætheling had a superior blood claim to the throne, but Edgar was barely a teenager and it must have appeared to those who mattered in the Anglo-Saxon state that Earl Harold, an experienced warrior, was truly the man for the moment. Archbishop Stigand, it seems, was one of them; and it may have been his worldly-wise voice that won the doubters over. At the forefront of Harold's mind there was bound to be the memory of the oath he had sworn to William. By now he must have been convinced (by Stigand, perhaps) that the oath was involuntary and invalid – not only in the eyes of man but in those of God as well.

No one, in truth, wanted Duke William as king. Even King

Edward had long since changed his mind. In any event the Normans were hardly the sort of people whom you would expect to invade England. Who did this William think he was? Harold, we may imagine, was still smarting at how foolish he had been in Normandy, at the way he had been cornered into swearing an oath. This was his chance to show the Norman duke just how much he was scared. He would brazen the matter out; and he would do so in the most robust manner possible. Harold would be King of England. He would accept the crown himself, just as it seemed the old king had wished, and the blood of the Godwins would now occupy the highest, most glorious office in the land.

So we see King Harold seated in majesty [scene 28]. He sits on his throne, wearing his crown, proudly holding the royal orb and sceptre for everyone to see. HIC RESIDET HAROLD REX ANGLORUM (Here sits upon the throne Harold, king of the English). In the post-Conquest period, the full implications of the tendentious Norman case against 'the usurper' Harold were gradually worked out. If Harold had no right to accept the throne, he had never been king at all. The Normans therefore airbrushed the reign of Harold II out of constitutional history. Quite simply, in legal terms, it had never happened and all those who had supported him were guilty of treason and liable to confiscation and banishment. William of Poitiers, writing in the 1070s, is generally careful never to refer to Harold as 'King Harold', though he drops his guard once or twice. By the time of the Domesday Book, in 1086, Harold is always referred to as earl, never as king. By contrast, the tapestry's Harold is a truly regal figure. He is without doubt HAROLD REX, every inch the King of the English, as he stares at us without commentary in that full frontal pose, inviting our judgement upon his actions, sitting there on a royal throne which was scarcely cold from the departure of its previous occupant.

Harold was crowned the very day of Edward's funeral. Westminster must have been exceptionally busy over that Christmas period, with much backroom politicking and earnest whispering in stony halls. A great assembly of earls, bishops and abbots was already *in situ*. They had come to attend King Edward's Christmas court and to witness the consecration of the new church; they had stayed for Edward's funeral; now they took part in the election of Harold, or at least they would have been present at his coronation. It is not known for certain where the coronation took place. It is often said that William the Conqueror 'inaugurated' the famous practice of English monarchs being crowned at Westminster Abbey. This is what the abbey's own tourist material states. It would, however, be very surprising if, during the course of that short winter's day, the whole party was made to decamp from Westminster to St Paul's in London. Harold, moreover, lacked the authority of the ancient bloodline of the Wessex kings. His was to be a brave new dynasty. He would have wished, so far as he could, to associate his kingship with that of his predecessor, and what better way to do that than to be crowned in the very church that Edward had built and where he now lay buried? It is therefore much more likely that Harold, not William, was the first English monarch to be crowned at Westminster Abbey.[12]

The tapestry does not show us the ceremony of coronation that ushered in the brave new age, or rather reign, but standing next to the newly crowned king is none other than STIGANT ARCHIEP[ISCOPU]S (Archbishop Stigand). Like the enthroned Harold, Stigand confronts us in the face, inviting our judgement upon his open pose. William of Poitiers, raising every argument he could think of in order to justify the

Norman Conquest, alleges that Harold's coronation was actually carried out by Stigand. It was therefore 'an impious consecration' by a man 'who had been deprived of his priestly office by the just zeal and anathema of the pope'. A later English source, however, maintains that the rite was carried out by Ealdred, the Archbishop of York.[13] This is much more likely. Harold would have been as conscious as anyone of Stigand's dubious position. When Harold's own church of Waltham Holy Cross was consecrated in 1060 he used the services of Cynesige, the then Archbishop of York. It can also be shown that the only occasions when Stigand was chosen by the English to consecrate any bishop occurred during the period when he was briefly recognised by Pope Benedict X.[14]

All that may be so, but the tapestry is still widely interpreted as following the Norman propaganda line – that it was Stigand who anointed Harold and placed the crown on his head. As Archbishop Stigand is named and depicted adjacent to the newly crowned king, and Ealdred of York is nowhere in sight, the work is certainly open to interpretation in the Norman manner. This, however, is only a superficial reading. Any image of the coronation itself has been studiously avoided. Rather, what the tapestry is suggesting is that Stigand, by his very occupation of the see of Canterbury at this time, has sullied the proceedings. He – and corrupt priests like him – was about to draw the wrath of God upon the whole country. The *Life of King Edward*, which the artist certainly knew and used, is evidence of this perspective on events. The Flemish author's criticism of Stigand is scarcely veiled. Stigand was one of those who 'dishonour the Christian religion', one of those who were 'irreparably attracted to the devil by riches and worldly glory'. According to the author of the *Life*, God's anger is sometimes roused to such a terrible extent that there is, quite simply, no hope of mercy in this life. 'Under these scourges of the chastising God, many thousands of people are thrown down and the kingdom is ravaged by fire and plunder; and this in times past has been shown to come from the sins of the priests.'[15] Thus it seemed that Stigand's sins were so great that a whole people was about to suffer for them.

One moment the people are cheering the new king, the next their heads are tilted upwards at the night sky over Westminster, fingers pointing to the heavens in wonderment and awe [scene 29]. A strange celestial body, a glowing ball of fire with a long hairy tail, has appeared above the dark world. ISTI MIRANT STELLA[M] (These men wonder at the star). In the words of the *Anglo-Saxon Chronicle* (C and D), 'throughout all England, a sign, such as men never saw before, was seen in the heavens. Some men declared that it was the star *comet*, which some men call the "haired" star; and it appeared first on the eve of the Greater Litany, 24 April, and shone thus all week.' What they saw, in fact, was a comet and it was the same comet that was observed in 1682 by the astronomer Edmond Halley, and later named after him. Halley's Comet appears in a regular 76-year cycle, and it so happened that 1066 was one of the years when it was visible. It was last seen in 1986, but in 1066 it would have seemed much brighter to the eye, for on that occasion it passed between the sun and the earth rather than on the other side of the sun. The regular laws governing Halley's Comet were, of course, unknown in this pre-scientific age, and it is no surprise that people looked upon this strange fiery phenomenon in the night as a divinely ordained portent. It first appeared dimly above England in February, attained maximum brightness in April and was still visible well into May. It was observed elsewhere as well; chroniclers all over Europe reported its appearance and wondered what it might mean.[16] In retrospect this became clear to the Normans. In words rhetorically addressed to Harold after his death, William of Poitiers notes coldly: 'The comet, terror of kings, which burned soon after your elevation, foretold your doom.'[17]

The hand of God has descended benevolently and blessed King Edward's church at Westminster. Now he has fired a warning shot across the heavens. This is the other side of God. This is God in the image of a truculent medieval monarch. His anger, already stirred by Stigand's presumptuous hold on the see of Canterbury, has now been truly roused by Harold's breach of oath. It would have been better for Harold to have chosen exile, imprisonment, slavery or even death in Normandy than to have made a sacred oath that he had no intention of fulfilling, for it now appeared, in retrospect, that in the eyes of God an oath made upon such holy old bones could never be broken, even if it had been made under duress. What else could explain the victory of the Normans in 1066? Harold had been crowned King of England in accordance with all the laws and customs of the land; he may have sat there enthroned, majestically, with all his regalia; but this was as nothing if he did not have the approval of his God.

Perhaps the underlying meaning of the Bayeux Tapestry, this mysterious and many-layered work of genius, is at last becoming clearer. It is not a monument of Norman triumph or celebration. Nor is it a work of Norman propaganda or justification. Rather, at the deepest level, it is beginning to appear as a work of *explanation*, seen from the tragic English perspective. The artist, working under the domination of the Normans, has succeeded brilliantly in deceiving generation after generation that he is telling the story from the Norman point of view. At another level, however, the Bayeux Tapestry is nothing less than the lost chronicle of the English. It is shot through with what seems to be a true account of what happened – of Harold's journey, the involuntary nature of his oath and Edward's attitude to William – all of which directly contradicts the Norman version of events. In the final analysis, however, it reflects the belief that Duke William was to win at Hastings because Harold, Stigand and the people of England had sinned and because God ordained that the English should be punished. On this account the Normans could be regarded as merely the instruments, and not the champions, of God's will.

Harold, like everyone else, must have seen that celestial fireball passing so wonderfully across the crisp night sky. Now we see HAROLD again on his throne, only this time he is far from the self-assured, majestic figure who was seated there a moment earlier [scene 30]. He is a changed man, a worried man. His whole demeanour seems unsteady; the crown itself seems about to topple from his head; and he points at it as if to ask: 'How much longer will I be king?' A retainer is secretly explaining something. Perhaps it is the meaning of the comet; perhaps he is conveying some intelligence, recently received, about Duke William's reaction to the turn of events. William, it seems, has not taken the matter quite as philosophically as might have been hoped. Rumour has it that he has ordered the preparation of an enormous invasion force. A ghostly fleet of ships appears in the lower border as if by way of premonition.

This is worrying news. Harold needs to know exactly what William is doing and to that end he has dispatched spies on board a ship bound for Normandy. The ship of spies catches a breath of wind in the curve of its linen sail and, tossed high upon the threaded waves, it steals in secret across a swelling sea [scene 31]. HIC NAVIS ANGLICA VENIT IN TERRAM WILLELMI DUCIS (Here an English ship came to Duke William's land). Landfall is made and now a barelegged Englishman, his tunic hitched up and tucked into his belt, wades sleekly through the shallows and on to an empty Norman beach, bearing a heavy anchor in both hands. Cunningly, he has shaved the back of his neck in order to pass himself off as a Norman. The tapestry leaves the spy's fate unrecorded, but we learn from William of Poitiers that around about the spring of 1066 an English spy was, for all his guile, captured in Normandy and swiftly taken before Duke William. William dispatched him back to Harold with the following instructions: 'Take this message from me to Harold: he will have nothing to fear from me and can live the rest of his life secure if, within the space of one year, he has not seen me in the place where he thinks his feet are safest.'[18] It was a chilling riposte.

8

Invasion

Duke William's bravado was all good and well, but not everyone in Normandy was as confident about the prospect of invading England. According to William of Poitiers, many of his barons expressed reluctance, and even outright opposition, to the duke's audacious plan. They pointed out that England's resources, both military and financial, were significantly superior to Normandy's. A great army would not only have to be formed and equipped, it would also have to be transported across a hazardous sea. It was surely impossible to build all the necessary ships, let alone do anything else, within the timescale that William required; and with so many men absent from the duchy Normandy itself might be exposed to invasion. In the face of all these arguments, and anything else that the timid-hearted could bring themselves to say, the Duke of Normandy remained utterly resolute. He knew what he wanted and to that end he was as firm as granite. Was he not King Edward's blood kinsman? Had not Edward long ago told him that he would be his heir? Had he not seen with his own eyes Earl Harold utter a sacred oath that he would support his claim? There was no doubt whatever in William's mind that England should be his. It was he, William, who should be now seated upon that throne, but Harold had impudently seized it and (so it probably seemed) he was now sitting there, laughing at him.

William of Poitiers has the duke win over the Norman doubters by his powers of oratory at a great meeting, which may have taken place at the town of Lillebonne. If the lack of ships worried his barons, they should not worry, he said, because there would soon be enough. If it was the lack of soldiers, they should remember that wars are more often won by courage than by the number of fighting men. Harold was attempting to retain what he had wrongfully seized; the Normans would fight to acquire what was rightfully theirs. 'This fundamental confidence of our side, dispelling all danger, will give us a splendid triumph, great glory and a famous name.'[1] During the spring and summer of 1066 there is evidence that the duke was travelling widely around Normandy, meeting with his chief men, no doubt rallying their morale and overseeing the preparations. Every aspect of the invasion, down to the finest logistical detail, must have been painstakingly planned. The army was probably to number about 10,000 men (though some have suggested a much larger force); there were horses, equipment, transport and supplies to prepare. William was a ruthless man, but it speaks much of his personal authority and powers of man-management that he was able to organise such a great army in so short a time and to hold it together for such a risky enterprise.

He was also one step ahead of Harold in the propaganda war. He sent an embassy to Rome where his wily Norman ambassadors persuaded Pope Alexander II to give his blessing to the invasion.[2] Since Harold's case went unrepresented, it may be presumed that this result was achieved by dint of the usual one-sided arguments. The Pope's sponsorship of a war, symbolised by the grant of a papal banner, was a very recent innovation and it was notably astute of William to seek it, for this emblem of the approval of the highest authority in Western Christendom at once legitimated the expedition as a sanctified quest to oust a faithless usurper and an excommunicated archbishop. In the end William had no difficulty raising his army. The bulk of it came from within Normandy but others, sometimes his former enemies, from Brittany, north-eastern France, Flanders and even Aquitaine joined his cause as well. They were lured by the spirit of adventure, the papal blessing and the promise of English land and gold. Many would die, but if the Norman side won the survivors would become rich. The most prominent of the non-Normans who pledged his support (for the time being at least) was an old rival, Count Eustace II of Boulogne, though it is only later that we see him in the tapestry.

The tapestry distils all the decision-making into a single decisive meeting within a turreted Norman palace [scene 32]. Nowhere does it mention Pope Alexander's blessing and amongst all the flags depicted in the work (of which there are many) the papal banner has never been identified with certainty. It may, in fact, not be illustrated at all. The pivotal meeting takes place between an adviser (or informant), Duke William and a tonsured cleric. This is the meeting at which the momentous decision to invade England is taken. The inscription above is unusually spread across the upper border: HIC WILLELM DUX IUSSET NAVES EDIFICARE (Here Duke William ordered ships to be built). These words, like all other sources, make it seem as if the duke was decisive in the matter, but once again the embroidered picture tells a different story. The first man stands in front of the seated William. Perhaps he is counselling caution, referring to the difficulties that William of Poitiers has all the doubters allude to. Or perhaps he is a spy bringing news of Harold's accession. Duke William sits in the middle; he is pointing to the standing man but his head is twisted towards the tonsured cleric at his side. This is a William who is uncertain and wishes to hear the cleric's views. Like William, the cleric is seated on an important throne but he is noticeably depicted higher than the rest. It is the cleric who points to the shipbuilding that follows. Evidently, on this account, it is the cleric's advice that wins over a surprisingly hesitant duke and now, as if obeying the cleric's own words, a workman with an axe is at once hurrying out of the room in order to get down to work on the formidable task of building all the required ships.

Who is this cleric, so prominent and influential in the counsels of Duke William? He can be none other than William's half-brother Bishop Odo of Bayeux. This enormously ambitious man was as much a secular as a religious figure, and he was already growing rich thanks to William's fraternal patronage. Odo was certainly one of the duke's key advisers, but no other source gives him such a prominent role in persuading his brother to take up arms and invade England. This is another clue about the tapestry's origin. It is the first hint that the tapestry's artist is making a special point of flattering Bishop Odo of Bayeux. He is flattering him, even above the duke himself.

Shipbuilding begins in earnest [scene 33]. In the Norman forests men swing great axes to fell tall, embroidered trees; and then the wood is turned into planks and the surface rendered as plain and smooth as a stretch of white cloth. In the foreground two bearded old shipwrights are now shaping the ships out of wood with little axes; others are performing the same task in the near distance. A contemporary document, the *Ship List of William the Conqueror*, tells us that Odo contributed 100 ships to the invasion force, which is no mean contribution considering that the total fleet numbered in the high hundreds.[3] As all this activity was going on, Harold's own difficulties were becoming worse. Entirely neglected by the tapestry is the fact that in October 1065 there had been a rebellion in Northumbria against Harold's brother, Earl Tostig. It is said that the local people resented Tostig's harsh rule and wanted Morcar of Mercia in his place. The insurgents went on a rampage, killing and looting on a murderous journey into the English midlands. King Edward attempted to restore peace at a great council held at Britford, near Salisbury. Tostig, ill tempered and suspicious, now thought that Earl Harold had instigated the whole uprising and openly accused him before the whole assembly. Harold, in turn, indignantly repudiated the charge on oath. If Duke William and his brother Bishop Odo were at one about their plans, relations between the two English brothers had reached an all-time low; and they were about to become even worse.

By Christmas 1065 the dying king had resigned himself to the fact that Tostig was unpopular and that a royal army could not be raised in sufficient numbers to defeat the rebels. He gave in; the rebels had won. There can be little doubt that Harold had some hand in this pragmatic but unfortunate decision. Tostig was not only deprived of his earldom. Such was the ferocity of the insurgents that he and his wife Judith were forced to flee to Flanders. Not long afterwards Tostig must have received the news that Edward had died and that his brother Harold had ascended the throne in triumph. Maddened by fury, he was determined to revenge himself against Harold, whatever it took. He journeyed hither and thither in an attempt to find an ally in this unwavering and unnecessary vendetta. It is said by Orderic Vitalis, writing in the twelfth century, that Tostig visited Duke William of Normandy, but he was apparently rebuffed. From there it is said that he went to Norway in order to meet with King Harald Hardrada, a bloodthirsty warrior who could easily be persuaded that now was the moment to take up his own tenuous claim to the English throne.[4] That may be so. More contemporary sources describe Tostig raiding around the English coast throughout the spring of 1066, before sailing up to Scotland to stay at the court of King Malcolm.[5] The outcome was the same. He forged an alliance with the fearsome Viking magnate and by September the Norwegian Harald was poised to unleash his own invasion of England. This was the last thing that Harold needed, and Tostig knew it.

The tapestry proceeds swiftly with its own internal logic. It ignores the Norwegian dimension and omits Harold's troubles with Tostig, though in truth these all played a part, and perhaps the telling part, in his downfall. Instead we are shown the meticulous Norman preparations. There is a swarm of activity by the seashore as everything is loaded on to ships [scene 34]. The newly made vessels are dragged down to the sea. Some of the men are heaving ships to the beach with long ropes; they are struggling against the dead weight, leaning backwards as they progress step by step into the rippling water. HIC TRAHUNT[UR] NAVES AD MARE (Here the ships are hauled down to the sea). Others are carrying suits of chain-mail armour. Each suit of armour has a pole threaded through its arms; the pole is shouldered at each end by a man; borne upright in this manner, it is almost as if an invisible knight were already clothed within and ready to conquer

England. Swords, lances, helmets, axes and provisions are all carried on board. Another two men, bent forward and visibly struggling, can be seen hauling a four-wheeled cart on which an enormous barrel of wine had been loaded, together with helmets and spears. ISTI PORTANT ARMAS AD NAVES ET HIC TRAHUNT CARRUM CUM VINO ET ARMAS (These men carry arms to the ships and here they drag a cart with wine and arms). Apparently William thought it wise to take some French wine with him, rather than risk drinking any English beverage. With this on board, William himself now rides to the shore.

What an awesome spectacle he must have seen, hundreds of ships lying in wait along the narrow coast, thousands of men and horses lined up along the littoral ready to embark on their mission, a mission that William had conceived in his own ruthless mind and ordained with his own commanding words. The first part of his vision had become a reality; it remained to cross the sea and conquer Harold. If the Bayeux Tapestry were the only evidence that survived, the crossing of the Channel by the Normans would appear to be a seamless and uncomplicated affair. It is known, however, that it was a two-stage process. The fleet assembled initially at the Norman port of Dives in August 1066, where it stayed for about a month. It then moved northwards along the French coast as far as the estuary of the River Somme at St-Valéry, in Ponthieu, apparently driven by westerly gales. Here they waited a further two weeks for the contrary winds to abate. Throughout a tense, uncertain September, the Duke's qualities of leadership were tested as he held his army together. He is said by William of Poitiers to have maintained good discipline and a high morale. When some of his soldiers fell in the water and drowned during the journey from Dives to St-Valéry, William, not wishing to cause alarm, ordered the mishap to be kept secret.

All summer King Harold maintained his watch. A large defensive force was placed at strategic points along the southern coast and the English fleet of longships was stationed on the Isle of Wight, ready to intercept the Normans at sea. Spies may have informed the king that the Normans were busy assembling at Dives, for Dives lies directly opposite where he placed his own navy. Harold is also known to have confiscated the estate of Steyning in Sussex from the Norman abbey of Fécamp, fearing, perhaps, that it might be a centre of intelligence for the enemy.[6] His forces stood ready and waiting; eyes scoured the horizon on a constant watch for any sign of William's armada, but as the long days of summer grew shorter the anticipated invasion did not materialise. By 8 September there was still no sign of the Normans, and with provisions running dangerously low, and the season of autumnal storms now arriving, the king dropped his guard and decided to disband his coastal forces. It seemed that the danger of invasion, in that tense year of 1066, had at last subsided. Winston Churchill, who found himself in a not dissimilar situation in 1940, later commented dryly: 'in true English style [they came] to the conclusion that the danger was past because it had not yet arrived'.[7]

It arrived all right, but in another place. Harold had been so preoccupied by the Norman threat that events in the north took him by surprise. King Harald Hardrada had slipped across the North Sea with a formidable army numbering over 7,000 Norsemen. He picked up allies in Orkney, joined Tostig and his Flemish mercenaries, either in Scotland or at the mouth of the River Tyne, and then proceeded darkly down the English coast. As soon as Harold learnt of the danger, he hastily assembled his army of professional housecarls and raised more men from the shires. He sped north from London, hoping to reach York by the old Roman road before the invaders could take the city. He learnt *en route* that on 20 September Hardrada's army had annihilated an English force at Fulford and had probably already passed through York. This was certainly bad news, but Harold pressed on, undaunted, and the speed of his advance took the Norwegians by surprise.

At Stamford Bridge, on 25 September 1066, Harold launched a decisive attack on an unprepared Norse army. The fighting was 'very hard' and continued 'long in the day', so the *Anglo-Saxon Chronicle* (C) tells us, but it was the English who were victorious. King Harald Hardrada was killed, as were Tostig and several thousand Norsemen. In the end the rout was so great that it took only twenty-four ships to carry home the survivors of an army that had arrived on 300. Hardrada's own son and heir, Olaf, was amongst those who made the sombre journey home; Harold allowed him to return to Norway after he had sworn an oath never to invade England again. The Battle of Stamford Bridge, no less than Hastings, was one of the decisive encounters of the Middle Ages. Three centuries earlier the age of Viking terror had begun when bands of marauding Norsemen struck fear around the coasts of western Europe. Now it was effectively over. Never again was England to be seriously imperilled by invasion from Scandinavia. This, of course, could not have been known to King Harold, but he had undoubtedly won a great battle. It was his finest hour, and on the morrow of victory he could sit back and congratulate himself on the first nine months of his reign. He thought he had seen off the danger from Normandy. He had decisively defended his country against Norwegian aggression, and in the process he had defeated and killed King Harald Hardrada, the most famous and formidable of warriors. His tempestuous brother also lay dead and would trouble him no more. 1066, it seemed, was going to be a good year for Harold Godwinson.

At this point the thread of the tapestry's tale can once more be picked up. Barely three days after Harold's victory at Stamford Bridge, the wind in the Channel changed. Duke William's mighty force took their chance and left the shores of Ponthieu on the night of 28/29 September 1066. The tapestry tells us nothing of events in the north, nor of Harold's preparations, but now the great Norman fleet takes up the whole of the canvas as it crosses a moderate sea of undulating threads [scene 35]. Some of the ships are packed with men and horses; others predominantly horses; others only men. HIC WILLELM DUX IN MAGNO NAVIGO MARE TRANSIVIT ET VENIT AD PEVENSAE (Here Duke William crossed the sea in a great ship and came to Pevensey). William's ship is the largest in the fleet. Illustrated as a typical Viking-style ship, it bears a cruciform banner (or possibly a lantern) at the top of the mast. At the prow there is a carved lion's head; at the stern a sculptured child holds a horn to his lips and points towards England, to which steady progress is being made. The duke's ship, unnamed in the Tapestry, is called the *Mora* in the document known as the *Ship List of William the Conqueror*, and it had apparently been given to him by his wife Matilda. Torches attached to the masts, like so many stars, are said to have kept the fleet of 700 ships in contact with each other during the night. We are told by William of Poitiers that at one point the duke's ship, no doubt the fastest, became separated from the rest. He ordered the anchor to be dropped and hid his anxiety by taking a hearty breakfast and drinking spiced wine, cheerfully behaving 'as if he were in his hall at home' until the flickering lights of the rest of the fleet gradually reappeared.[8]

It has been calculated that at an average speed of three or four knots the whole flotilla would have taken at least twelve hours to cross the Channel.[9] They probably left the estuary of the Somme at nightfall, on an ebbing tide, an hour or so after the sun had set at 17.26 p.m. A quarter moon was then in the skies. The moon may have lit the first part of the journey, but would have disappeared from view three or four hours later. It would have been imprudent to arrive in darkness and with the sun not rising until six o'clock on the morning of 29 September 1066 it is possible, as we are told by the *Carmen de Hastingae Proelio*, that William's fleet had already dropped anchor for a while off the coast of France for a final review or tactical delay. The tapestry's illustration of the crossing is, however, entirely seamless. Under a grey-linen sky the vast armada now arrives in sight of the Sussex coast. What terror it must have struck in the hearts of anyone who saw it approach, first a few spangled dots on the dim horizon, then more and more until the dots numbered in their hundreds, gradually taking on the shape of warships, a terrifying prospect drawing ever nearer, the metal of swords and shields glinting, here and there, in the angled light of morning. The army within was intent on the mission that the English had long feared, and they were arriving only three weeks after Harold had commanded his own coastal force to disband.

The invaders disembarked without opposition from hundreds of ships on to the sloping beach at Pevensey. The tapestry's artist was impressed by the novelty of so many horses travelling by sea, for he shows us the horses, rather than men, leaving ship. One horse has a hind leg still on the boat as he clambers into the shallow water. There must have been hundreds, and perhaps thousands, of such horses being led off the ships that day. Masts are pulled down and the ships are left beached upon the shore. A foraging party now penetrates inland, riding in the direction of Hastings with orders to purloin provisions for the Norman army. Livestock is quickly found. A cow has been seized and slaughtered and now it lies on the linen ground, the first English casualty. Two Normans proceed to fell a sheep with an axe; another carries a pig on his shoulders; and a fourth is holding what appears to be a coil of rope. Behind them we see a line of empty English homes; it is their land that is being pillaged. The pillaging of provisions, though unfortunate, would have been seen as inevitable by viewers of the tapestry. It was what armies did. There is, however, a curious feature about this whole operation. The mounted Norman knight overseeing it is designated by name. HIC EST WADARD (Here is Wadard) [scene 37; plate 8]. This mysterious man is evidently not a person of rank or title, and his job is hardly the most important on the expedition. He is the third of the four obscure characters given a name by the artist.

Food has been seized by the invaders and taken back to the Norman camp. The task of cooking is illustrated in extraordinary detail [scene 38]. At the front, two men are busy boiling meat in a great cauldron, which has been hung by poles over a flickering red fire of tongue-like woollen flames. In the background a rack of spitted fowl is ready to be eaten. An army baker removes hot bread from a field oven, using a pair of tongs, and then places it carefully on a tray. The cooked birds, still on their spits, are served to the eager diners, one of whom blows a horn to announce the start of the meal. A party of knights eats at an improvised field table, a wooden structure on which kite-shaped shields have been laid as a makeshift surface, but the more important of the diners have gathered around their own semicircular table. William's half-brother Bishop Odo of Bayeux dominates the table; once more Odo takes centre stage [scene 39; plate 7]. HIC EPIS-COPUS CIBU[M] ET POTU[M] BENEDICIT (Here the bishop blesses the food and drink). This meal is not referred to in any other source, but there can be no doubt that the bishop in question is Odo; one of the diners points to the words ODO EP[ISCOPU]S (Bishop Odo) in the inscription which follows, whilst looking back at the bishop in mid-benediction.

This scene of feasting, observed in these threads, still holds many beguiling secrets. Odo's tonsured head rises above all the others in a carefully constructed composition. There is bread and fish and other food arranged about the table, which the diners eat with hands and knives (forks were not used in the eleventh century). Duke William is unnamed, but he may be the figure upstaged by Odo, seated on Odo's right and looking up at him. Another figure, an enigmatic, older man with a long, straggling beard, sits to the left of the 'duke' and, with his back turned, he rather rudely stretches across him in order to take a piece of bread from the table. At the same time he sips from a cup of wine. A further figure has engaged the older man in the eye and points to a loaf of round flatbread lying in front. It is as if reference is discreetly being made to the bread and wine of the Eucharist; but if so, it is an allusion that is completely ignored by Odo and the duke. At the other end of the table a man is about to eat a fish eye; mysteriously, he points to the vacant eye-socket in the fish. A servant at the front, with his knees bent, offers a bowl of water so that the party can clean their greasy hands and he also has a towel laid over his arm. There are parallels in the iconography of this scene with early medieval manuscript representations of the Last Supper, where the servant figure would be Judas and the man at the centre Jesus. It seems that at one level Bishop Odo is being flattered, not only by upstaging the duke, but more presumptuously by taking on the role of Jesus at this carefully embroidered repast. More discreetly, however, the reference to the bread and wine of the Christian Eucharist passes unnoticed and is ignored by him.

After the meal, Bishop Odo, Duke William and the Duke's other half-brother, Count Robert of Mortain, hold a meeting to take stock of the initial landing and the preparations for the fight with Harold [scene 40]. All three are shown seated on a cushioned bench and are named in the inscription, as if in a family portrait on the eve of the great adventure: ODO EP[ISCOPU]S, WILLELM, ROTBERT. William, as would be expected, is taking counsel from amongst his leading feudal vassals, but the highlighting of his kinsmen Odo and Count Robert, and no others, is noteworthy and it is Bishop Odo who once more takes the limelight. He appears on this occasion to be advising caution and William is evidently listening to him. A commander, presumably on Odo's advice, now orders a fortification to be built at the port of Hastings. Workmen duly take up their tools; but a disagreement arises between two of them and they are now hitting each other about the head with shovels [scene 41]. Whatever disorder occurred, it must have been quickly quelled for the workmen are now busy throwing up an earthen mound on which a makeshift timber castle is raised. The work passes without further incident, except that a stone falls off someone's spade and hits another on the head; perhaps this was the cause of the dispute shown earlier, or a continuation of it. The prefabricated wood necessary to build the castle would have been already prepared in Normandy and transported across the Channel. What is quite possibly the mound of earth that these querulous workmen built may still be seen, at the top of Hastings cliff, where pottery fragments have been found dating from the time of the Norman Conquest.[10]

William is next illustrated receiving some unspecified news of Harold [scene 42]. King Harold himself received the dire news of William's landing whilst still in the north, though it is possible that he had already commenced his journey south and met a breathless messenger *en route*. If Harold's heart sank, as it must have, he soon steeled himself to face the new challenge with formidable, almost inhuman energy. He reached London in four or five days, with little more than the core of his men, and stayed there a week in order to wait for reinforcements. He then marched swiftly into Sussex to confront the invaders with an army that could match them. If we are to believe Orderic Vitalis, a comparatively late source, Harold met his mother Gytha in London and she begged him to wait and at least take some rest after all that he had been through. His brother Earl Gyrth even offered to lead the English against William himself, but when Gytha clung to Harold in an attempt to prevent her son leaving, the king indignantly kicked her away. Harold was to fight two major battles, 250 miles apart, within the space of nineteen days.

What may have incensed Harold was that his ancestral homeland in the south was being cruelly ravaged by the invaders; and this is exactly what the tapestry now shows [scene 43]. The invaders are setting a large house on fire, from which a woman and child flee in panic. HIC DOMUS INCENDITUR (Here a house is burned). William of Poitiers himself notes that Harold 'was hastening his march all the more because he had heard that the lands near the Norman camp were being laid to waste'. The woman and child shown in the tapestry are usually regarded as representative figures, and it is tempting to see them as standing generally for the innocent victims of war. It is just as possible, however, that they are meant to stand for actual people. There are only two other women depicted in the work – the named but mysterious Ælfgyva and the unnamed but identifiable Queen Edith – and it would certainly be consistent for the third woman, who also wears aristocratic clothes, to be a real and identifiable person. If so, one wonders whether she might possibly be Harold's mistress Edith Swan-Neck and the child perhaps one of the sons she had borne to Harold. He could be a boy called Ulf who at the time when the tapestry was being made had become, like Harold's brother Wulfnoth, a hostage of William the Conqueror.[11] Whether this is so cannot, of course, be proven; it would have to be established that they were either in the vicinity at the time or else that the tapestry is alluding to an earlier flight before the Normans arrived. At some point after 1063 Harold had also entered into a strategic marriage with Ealdgyth, the sister of Earls Edwin and Morcar and the widow of King Gruffydd of Wales.

William's scorched earth policy was probably premeditated. He would have calculated that reports of men, women and children suffering on Harold's own land, people whom Harold knew and was duty bound to protect, would incense his enemy and it was to William's advantage that Harold should be provoked into a decisive early encounter. The path of the Norman rampage may still be traced in the Domesday Book of 1086, where it is noted that a succession of lands to the north and south of present-day Battle – at Crowhurst, Whatlington, Netherfield and Broomham – had been devastated and laid waste. Yet although this devastation may have played a part in Harold's decision, he had a tactical reason, too, to advance swiftly and pin William down by the coast, where the isolated invaders would eventually run out of supplies. By the evening of 13 October Harold's army had assembled only a few miles from the point at Hastings where William's forces were encamped.

It is the tense morning of Saturday, 14 October 1066 [scene 44]. William has put on his armour. He stands proudly in his full-length chain mail; he wears a helmet with tassels at the rear; his sword has been placed in his belt and his lance has been planted in the ground; a little banner tied to the top flutters in the wind. His prized warhorse is now led to him by a squire, a virile stallion which (if we are to believe later twelfth-century evidence) had been given to him by King Alfonso of Spain and brought back to Normandy by Walter Giffard, the lord of Longueville.[12] William's troops, like him, are already in armour, and they are now setting out from Hastings and advancing towards the place where it is believed that Harold's army lies assembled. In the border above there are two erotic images of a man and woman, neither wearing a stitch, and with arms outstretched they are about to embrace; the naked man's moustache reveals him to be English. In the first image he is carrying his fighting axe with his tunic draped in his arms; in the second, having discarded them, he is ready for amorous action with his genitals exposed. Have the English been indulging in the delights of the flesh on the eve of battle? Duke William has sent scouts to ride ahead, and from the top of a hill they peer down to ascertain Harold's position. One of them is now returning with fresh intelligence [scene 46; plate 9]. HIC WILLELM DUX INTERROGAT VITAL SI VIDISSET EXERCITU[M] HAROLDI (Here Duke William asks Vital whether he has seen Harold's army). The reason why this second comparatively unimportant knight is named is again obscure and Vital's identity and significance will have to be carefully unravelled.

Harold has sent out a scout of his own. His lookout has ventured on foot but he is fully armed and dressed in mail. From behind a thicket of gnarled trees, he peers through lush foliage; and with his hand raised over his eyes he can see that some of William's men are already dangerously close, just on the other side of the wood [scene 47]. The lookout returns hastily across rough terrain in order to report back to King Harold. No doubt the king would have wanted more time to prepare. Reinforcements were on the way and his ships were planning to move round the coast to cut off any Norman escape by sea. His elite bodyguard of housecarls had suffered many casualties at Stamford Bridge and they, like him, must have been utterly exhausted by the hard battle in the north and the long journey south – not to mention any other, on the whole rather unlikely, activities in the night. All in all the decisive battle looked like it was going to come rather too quickly for King Harold of England. He would have preferred a little more time.

William of Poitiers describes the two sides exchanging provocative messages (he even says that the duke offered to fight Harold in a single combat) but if Harold thought that this kind of posturing could delay matters for another day or two, he was wrong. This time it was his enemy who was advancing upon him before he was entirely ready. Clearly Duke William wished to engage the English in a decisive encounter without risking any further delay. Nevertheless, Harold, a native of Sussex, had the advantage of local knowledge and he assembled his army in a strong defensive position at the top of a ridge. The Normans and their allies would have to attack uphill from marshy ground a few hundred metres below. Now was the time for waiting, waiting nervously for the battle to begin.

9

The Battle of Hastings

Down on the Norman side, the embroidered duke is strutting proudly on his horse [scene 48]. Holding up his club, like a baton, he makes a last-minute rousing speech to his men.[1] He exhorts them to prepare manfully and wisely for the battle against the English army: HIC WILLELM DUX ALLOQUI-TUR SUIS MILITIBUS UT PREPARENT SE VIRILITER ET SAPIENTER AD PRELIUM CONTRA ANGLORUM EXERCITU[M]. It is known that he placed his Normans in a central position, with allies from Brittany arranged on one flank and the French and Flemings on the other. The lines are now drawn and, according to William of Poitiers, the moment the battle began was signalled by a harsh bray of trumpets.

In the embroidery, a squadron of mounted knights, the elite of the invaders, starts to make its move; each knight is seated upon a stout warhorse; each is protected by chain-mail armour and a conical helmet; each grips a lance in one hand and a wing-like shield in the other; each glares through his narrow eyes at the enemy ahead. The horses quicken pace. The knights are tilted forward in the saddle as they move steadily ahead of a body of archers who, just now, have launched a volley of arrows against the English position. Spurs have been kicked and muscles tensed, and now the knights are charging forward at full speed, hoof is thundering upon hoof in a magnificent, breathless attack across the wide open ground, up towards the distant wall of coloured shields behind which the English have made their stand. Some of the knights are holding their lances ready to be thrust or thrown; others tuck them under-arm, to be used as a sharp battering weapon. Up on the ridge the English have ducked and caught the lethal rain of arrows on their wooden shields. Now they stand again, and the linen air is scored with spears, and some men lie already dead, as the first horseman arrives and thrusts his couched and bannered lance into the arrow-pierced shield of a standing Englishman [scene 49]. The Englishman stands firm. He is defending his land. He is rooted tree-like to the spot, at least for the embroidered moment, and he even retaliates with his own spear. Battle is truly joined.

The English repel the attack. They are clustered on foot in close, disciplined formation behind their tall, kite-shaped shields. Harold's elite troops, his housecarls, are wearing the same armour as the invaders; but their special weapon is the two-handed battleaxe, 'murderous axes' William of Poitiers calls them, which 'easily penetrated shields and other protections'.[2] In the midst of the phalanx, a lone English archer, without armour, does his best to repel the invaders. Harold's army seems to have had fewer archers than the Normans and his men fought on foot, without cavalry. Another attack is launched by the invading cavalry, apparently from the other flank [scene 50]. The charging knights must be losing momentum as they reach the top of the ridge. Their spears pour down on the English, but the English still stubbornly stand their ground. A moustachioed housecarl prepares to swing his great axe into a horse's neck but the rider plunges his lance into his attacker's chest before he is able to do so. 'The loud shouting, here Norman, here foreign, was drowned,' William of Poitiers writes, 'by the clash of weapons and the groans of the dying.'[3] The tapestry illustrates the slaughter in all its terrible confusion. The lower border becomes a mass grave for the mute and mutilated bodies of the dead, bodies whose nationality, so important in life, is now appropriately indiscernible. One has died of arrow wounds in his mouth and leg; some have suffered lance blows to the back, throat, chest or shoulder; another's severed head, still wearing its protective helmet, lies some distance from the body to which it was formerly attached.

At some point during the day Harold's brothers, Earl Gyrth and Earl Leofwine, both perished while fighting loyally by his side. The death of both in close-quarter combat is remembered in the embroidery [scene 51]. HIC CECIDERUNT LEWINE ET GYRÐ FRATRES HAROLDI REGIS (Here died Leofwine and Gyrth, King Harold's brothers). Leofwine is stuck in the back by the lance of a mounted knight before he has a chance to swing his great axe at the attacker. Gyrth, holding a round shield, is felled by another laniferous lance plunged into his mouth. Many more men and horses are struck down in agony and tumble over and die and their bodies, broken swords and severed heads lie strewn across the lower border.

There are innumerable casualties. HIC CECIDERUNT SIMUL ANGLI ET FRANCI IN PRELIO (Here English and French fell together in the battle). In the midst of it all, a moustachioed English housecarl strikes his axe deep into a horse's head, the horse recoils in agony, but from behind another knight uses such venom with his sword that not only does he kill the Englishman but knocks the head off an axe of another surprised fighter as well. Many horses are now falling. They twist and turn and are upended on to the ground, as the riders lose their grip and tumble off. One knight struggles to throw his lance as his horse collapses underneath him. Duke William himself is said in the written sources to have lost two or three horses during the battle and he had to remount on others. On the top of an isolated hillock, a group of lesser Englishmen, with shields and spears, but without chain mail protection, continue a manful defence. They are suffering heavy losses [scene 52].

The carnage at Hastings began at the third hour after dawn. It continued for the whole day, neither side gaining a decisive advantage until late in the afternoon. The account in the tapestry is, of course, an abbreviated one. The artist presumably got his information at second hand; he reorganised some of the events for artistic, dramatic or iconographical effect; and he ignores, for example, the role played by Duke William's lesser-born foot soldiers, who probably made the first assault. The extent to which some of the details of arms and armour derive from conventional artistic templates rather than the real battle is debated. Nevertheless it is undeniable that the artist captures the essence of the contest in a flowing series of brilliant and memorable pictures. Most sources agree that there were times when the English came very close to winning. At one point, a breakout by some of Harold's troops, probably undisciplined, pursued the retreating Bretons and inflicted heavy casualties before William was able to stem the tide with own Norman cavalry.

Earlier in the day there had been another moment of panic; the ducal army almost took to flight when a rumour spread that the duke himself had been killed. The tapestry now highlights this incident and makes it the turning point of the whole encounter [scenes 53–55]. First Bishop Odo of Bayeux, named and depicted once more, rides unexpectedly into the thick of the fighting, waving his baton and shouting words of encouragement to the younger knights [plate 10]. HIC ODO EP[ISCOPU]S BACULU[M] TENENS CONFOR-TAT PUEROS (Here Bishop Odo, holding a baton, cheers on the young men). The rumour is flying around that the duke is dead, so William raises his nosepiece to show his face and reveal that he is still alive. HIC EST DUX WILEL[MUS] (Here is Duke William). At his side is Count Eustace II of Boulogne, his name displayed prominently in the upper border – EUSTATIUS [plate 11]. Eustace is carrying the greatest banner in the whole of the tapestry; it flutters high in the upper border, as he swings round on his horse and points to the indomitable duke. Battle recommences swiftly under the words HIC FRANCI PUGNANT ET CECIDERUNT QUI ERANT CUM HAROLDO (Here the French do battle and those who were with Harold fell). The momentum is now regained and the final stage of the embroidered contest draws near.

In quick succession three combatants for the Norman side are named by the artist – Bishop Odo, Duke William and Count Eustace – and these are the only three who are named. The duke, of course, could hardly be ignored, but the choice of his only identified battle companions is much more surprising. The tapestry's flattery of Odo has been noted and often discussed by many historians. The image of Odo in battle is as noteworthy as his other appearances. According to William of Poitiers, Odo was present at Hastings but only for the purpose of helping by prayer, a feat of war that was presumably accomplished at a safe distance from the action.[4] The tapestry is alone amongst contemporary sources in placing him in the thick of fighting and giving him such a remarkable starring role. Consistent, however, with his status as a bishop, Odo is not wearing chain mail but rather a padded tunic and he encourages the troops with a mace, not a sword. Less commented upon, but even more remarkable, is the named appearance of Count Eustace II of Boulogne. A thousand books and postcard images persist in calling the pointing Eustace a 'Norman', but he was, of course, not a Norman at all but rather a Frenchman whose lands straddled the border between northern France and Flanders. Count Eustace II of Boulogne, a noted descendant of the Emperor Charlemagne, was the most high-ranking and prestigious of William's foreign allies and he was Duke William's equal as a grand feudatory of the king of France. He had previously been hostile to the duke and he had only recently joined forces with him, perceiving that the risk of leading his Frenchmen in the fight against King Harold was worth taking. What is more, some time in the autumn of 1067 Count Eustace attacked Odo's castle at Dover and embarked on a mysterious, though ineffectual, rebellion against his one-time Norman allies. He may even have been attempting to advance his own rival claim to the English throne. As a result of this abortive invasion, Eustace was disgraced, and lost his share of the spoils, although he was able to contrive a remarkable reconciliation with the Normans during the early 1070s.[5]

Contrary to popular belief, very few of William the Conqueror's companions at Hastings can be identified with certainty. William of Poitiers names a small roster of men. He singles out for special praise Robert of Beaumont, and names several others whom he viewed as Normans such as William fitzOsbern, Walter Giffard, Hugh of Montfort and William of Warenne.[6] None is named in the tapestry. Poitiers also confirms the presence of Count Eustace; but he was writing after Eustace was in disgrace and perhaps because of that describes him as a rank coward. According to William of Poitiers, Eustace's most notable contribution at the battle was to advise the duke to retreat, before receiving a blow between the shoulders and being carried away half-dead by his men, with blood streaming profusely from his nose and mouth. This, then, was the Norman view of Count Eustace II of Boulogne, after his disgrace, and it is quite clearly different from what we see in the Bayeux Tapestry. What is going on? Why, out of a ducal army of thousands, is the artist choosing to highlight the 'rebel' Eustace, of all people, and to ignore so many high-ranking Normans? The date when the Bayeux Tapestry was made is not certain, but whether it was made before or after Eustace's reconciliation with Duke William in the early 1070s, the appearance of such a rival and enemy at the pivotal moment in the embroidery is striking. It deserves much greater attention than it has ordinarily received.

The Bayeux Tapestry's treatment of Count Eustace is more akin to the *Carmen de Hastingae Proelio* (*The Song of the Battle of Hastings*) than it is to any Norman source. The *Carmen* is the very earliest surviving account of the battle. Its author, Bishop Guy of Amiens, was a close kinsman of Count Guy of Ponthieu and Count Eustace II of Boulogne. In the decade after the Battle of Hastings there was a very lively polemic between the Normans and their less numerous French allies as to who had really made the most telling contribution to the victory. The non-Norman French got in first with the *Carmen*. In the *Carmen*'s account of Hastings, the Normans are hardly mentioned at all; indeed the only Norman mentioned by name is the duke himself. Instead, the stress is placed on the contribution of the non-Norman Frenchmen (*Galli* or

Franci) and, like the tapestry, their leader Count Eustace II of Boulogne. William of Poitiers seems to have written his pro-Norman account shortly after the *Carmen*. Without doing so in express terms, he set about correcting what he perceived to be an unsavoury downgrading of his fellow Normans by the Bishop of Amiens and especially the latter's heroic portrayal of Count Eustace.[7] With more than a hint of exaggeration, he concluded that 'Duke William with the forces of Normandy subjugated all the cities of the English in a single day ... without much outside help.'[8] Since the *Carmen* was only re-discovered in 1826, and William of Poitiers' work was known, directly or indirectly, to later medieval writers, it is the Norman account that has dominated subsequent historiography and popular myth. In the process it is the Norman account that persists in colouring interpretations of the Bayeux Tapestry and obscuring some of its extraordinary meanings.

The momentum of battle is regained in the tapestry under the specific words HIC FRANCI PUGNANT (Here the French do battle) [scenes 55–56]. For the second time the tapestry calls the invaders 'French' (*Franci*). Nowhere, in fact, does it call them 'Normans' (*Normanni*). 'French' was an ambiguous term. It could mean the people from Francia generally, the French-speakers, and in that sense, common enough in England, it included the Normans as well as people from Paris, Picardy, Boulogne, Maine, Aquitaine and many other regions. In the more restricted sense, which is used both by William of Poitiers and in the *Carmen de Hastingae Proelio*, the *Franci* are quite distinct from the Normans; but the term undoubtedly includes men from north-eastern France who were the followers of Count Eustace II of Boulogne.[9] We are so used to thinking of the Battle of Hastings in purely binary terms, as a conflict between Anglo-Saxon and Norman, that the rivalries between the disparate elements of Duke William's army are easily overlooked. It is, however, improbable that the artist of the tapestry, an obviously well-informed person, was so naive as to be unaware of the lively polemic that was going on between the French and the Normans in the aftermath of the battle. Once more, he is playing a dangerous double game. Does he mean FRANCI in the inclusive or exclusive sense? He is, in fact, purporting to illustrate the Normans at all in these famous battle scenes?

It is the picture, not the words, that shows where his sympathies lie, for the word FRANCI is pictorially linked, inextricably, to the preceding image of Count II Eustace of Boulognes [scene 55]. A great lion in the upper border marks out the letters F and N with its paws whilst Eustace's enormous banner shares the same, uniquely elongated compartment in the border and even touches the lion's chest. What is more, the knight who takes up the charge carries a lance which underlines the very word FRANCI and at the same time he is pointing back at Count Eustace with his index finger. To make the connection even more explicit, the far end of the lance is touched by Eustace's left hand; it even seems to grow out of his skin. There can surely be no doubt, at this deeper level, that it is the French under Count Eustace, and not the Normans, who are indicated by the word FRANCI. Extraordinary as it may seem, all those charging knights in the Bayeux Tapestry, so often described as 'Normans', are at the deeper level nothing of the sort. This is a whole new layer of meaning, a layer of meaning which has lain hidden and unsuspected for almost a thousand years. The implications are profound. The tapestry began by undermining the Norman claim by subtly recording the English viewpoint and now it has discreetly highlighted the controversial Count Eustace II of Boulogne and his northern Frenchmen over and above the Normans. So much for telling the story 'strictly from the Norman point of view'.

Roused by the trio of Odo, William and Eustace, the bloody fighting resumes in earnest and the battle is now entering its final bitter stage. Up to now no clear advantage had been gained by either side, and a great many lay dead or maimed. If William could not deliver a killer blow before dusk the situation would probably be dire. Harold's reinforcements would soon arrive, perhaps the next day, perhaps in the days that followed, and the battered ducal army would be no match for fresh troops eager to defend their country and to repel the invaders.

The embroidered knights press on with another attack deep into the redoubtable English position. A French knight seems to be intent on pursuing one housecarl in particular, for he ignores the nearest enemy and thrusts his sword straight at the face of the one standing behind [scene 55]. Another French knight has been knocked out of the saddle but he still manages to ride on the neck of his horse and strikes down a goatee-bearded Englishman with a single blow of his sword. Presumably these two incidents really happened. Next, in a very enigmatic picture, a knight with spurs on his heels is standing on the ground; he is the only knight not on horseback in all the battle scenes. Grabbing the hair of an unarmed Englishman, he is about to decapitate him in a formal-style execution [scene 56]. His victim's decapitated body lies beneath, in the lower border, together with the sword that did the job. As he performs this gruesome task, the knight has another sword in his belt. The handle of his belted sword protrudes from his groin as if it were a penis, whilst its tip seems about to obscenely penetrate a stallion behind. The meaning of this scene remains obscure.

The lower border is now full of archers, shooting skyward in a desperate attempt to inflict further damage on the English position. Harold is standing amidst his men by the dragon banner of Wessex. He is still holding fast; but the end is near. Under the inscription HIC HAROLD REX INTERFECTUS EST (Here King Harold was killed) the King of the English appears to have been suddenly hit in or around the eye by an arrow [scene 57; plate 12]. He must be in agony now, as he tries to extract the shaft from his face, but then a mounted knight arrives at the scene and swinging down his heavy sword he strikes Harold on the thigh. The king collapses. A great English battleaxe, presumably representing Harold's military power, splits in two under his falling weight. The sprightly Harold Godwinson, whose tragic story has been animated so poignantly and memorably in the Bayeux Tapestry, now lies dead upon the very ground that he was attempting to defend.

The tapestry's image of Harold stuck by an arrow in the eye is one the most famous and enduring in English history; but it is not universally accepted as the correct reading. It has sometimes been argued that Harold is not, in fact, the famous figure wrenching an arrow from his face under the word HAROLD but rather that he is only the second figure, the one struck on the thigh beneath INTERFECTUS EST (was killed).[10] This has never been entirely persuasive.[11] It rests upon some doubtful generalisations about the conventions followed by the artist and ignores the obvious implication that the arrow-in-the-eye figure who stands under (and even breaks up) the letters HARO/L/D must be the eponymous casualty. He even looks up at the letter O in his name. Moreover, the tapestry is not alone in telling the arrow-in-the-eye story, or something like it. The arrow story may have been circulating in some Norman accounts even before 1080[12] and in the first third of

The following is a reproduction of the Bayeux Tapestry in its entirety.

1

2

King Edward

Where Harold, Duke of the English,

3

4

and his soldiers ride to Bosham

The church

Here Harold sailed across the sea

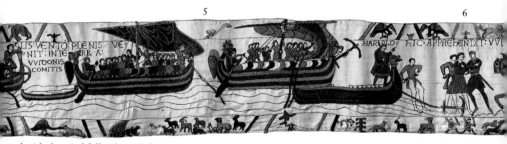

5

6

and with the wind full in his sails he came to the land of Count Guy

Harold

Here Guy seizes Harold

7

and led him to Beaurain and he held him there

Where Harold

and Guy confer

Where Duke William's
messengers came to Guy

Turold

Duke William's
messengers

Here Duke William comes to
his palace with Harold

And here they crossed the river
Couesnon. Here Duke Harold
pulled them out of the sand

And they came to
Dol and Conan fled

Rennes

Here William came
to Bayeux

Where Harold swore a sacred
oath to Duke William

Here Duke Harold retuned to English soil

12 13 14

Here a messenger came
to Duke William

Here Guy brought Harold to William,
Duke of the Normans

17 18

Where a cleric
and Ælfgyva

Here Duke William and his army
came to Mont-Saint-Michel

21 22

Here Duke William's soldiers fight
against the men of Dinan

And Conan surrendered
the keys

Here William gave
arms to Harold

24 25

And came to King Edward

Here King Edward's corpse is
borne to the church of Saint Peter
the Apostle

Here King Edward in his bed
addresses his faithful followers
And here he has died

Here they gave Harold
the king's crown

Here sits upon the
throne Harold, King
of the English

Archbishop
Stigand

Here Duke William ordered
ships to be built

Here the ships are
hauled down to the sea

Here Duke William crossed the sea in
a great ship and came to Pevensey

And here soldiers have hurried
to Hastings to seize food

Here is Wadard

Here meat is cooked and here
the servants have served it

These men   Harold   Here an English ship came to
wonder at   Duke William's land
the star

These men carry arms to the ships
and here they drag a cart with
wine and arms

Here the horses leave
the ships

Here they held a feast   Here the Bishop blesses   Bishop Odo,   This man has ordered a fortification
                          the food and drink   William, Robert   to be thrown up at Hastings

42   43   44

Here news of Harold
is brought to William

Here a house is burned

Here the soldiers set out from Hastings and
advanced to do battle against King Harold

47

This man gives King Harold
news of Duke William's army

49

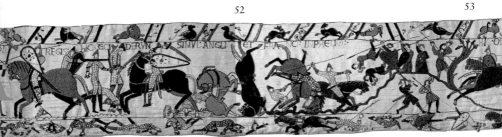

52   53

Here English and French
fell together in the battle

Here Bishop Odo,
holding a baton, cheers
on the young men

45

46

Here William Duke William asks Vital
whether he has seen Harold's army

48

Here Duke William exhorts his soldiers to prepare themselves
manfully and wisely for the battle against the English army

50

51

Here died Leofwine and Gyrth,
King Harold's brothers

54   55

Here is   Eustace
Duke William

56 57

Here the French do battle and
those who were with Harold fell

Here King Harold was killed

58 59

And the English have turned to flight

the twelfth century two Anglo-Norman writers recorded a version of Harold's death that seems very close to the tapestry. The first, William of Malmesbury (c. 1125), wrote that Harold's 'brain' was 'pierced by an arrow' before 'one of the knights hacked his thigh with a sword as he lay on the ground'.[13] The second, Henry of Huntingdon (c. 1130), was the earliest known English writer explicitly to mention Harold's eye: 'the whole shower sent by the archers fell around King Harold and he himself sank to the ground, struck in the eye', whereupon 'a host of knights broke through and killed the wounded king'.[14] Whether these writers were basing their accounts on an interpretation of the Bayeux Tapestry or were recording a similar but independent tradition, the view that the Tapestry is following the arrow story is rendered more probable. Moreover, in his poetic re-rendering of the work as a luxurious wall hanging around Countess Adela's bedchamber, written between 1099 and 1102, Baudri of Bourgeuil writes that Harold was hit by an arrow, albeit without specifying the point of impact: 'a shaft pierces Harold with deadly doom'.[15] This was evidently Baudri's interpretation of the tapestry and as a contemporary observer it may be assumed that he was familiar with the artistic conventions of his day.

A more serious challenge to the traditional view proceeds upon the fact that this section of the tapestry was much restored in the nineteenth century.[16] Did the restorers faithfully follow the evidence of original stitch holes or did they do a bit of embroidering of their own? In the earliest known drawing of this scene, rendered by Antoine Benoît in 1729, the figure standing under the word HAROLD is apparently not wrenching an arrow from his face but appears possibly to be holding up his own English spear which he is about to throw. Certainly the weapon has no arrow flights on it, whereas arrows in the tapestry are invariably depicted with flights. It is, therefore, suggested that the arrow-in-the-eye, complete with little flights, was a nineteenth-century 'restoration' by persons who thought that they could 'improve' upon the original. The force of this argument is undermined by the fact that the eighteenth-century artists were not infallible; nor can Baudri's evidence – that the embroidered Harold is pierced by a shaft – easily be dismissed; and if Benoît's drawing shows no flights on the 'arrow', equally it shows no point on the 'spear'. If the nature, path and length of the weapon in Harold's hand really were drastically altered in the nineteenth century, evidence of the original stitch holes should presumably still be discernible through a close forensic examination of the fabric itself. The generally accepted view is that Harold is shown twice, first hit by an arrow and then struck down by a sword. It may be that the arrow-in-the-eye interpretation of the embroidery will one day have to be jettisoned, but until forensic evidence proves otherwise beyond doubt, the current view will probably continue to prevail.

This is not to say that the Tapestry, or any other source, is necessarily giving a true account of Harold's death. Battles are confused; stories differ. The most that can be said is that there is nothing inherently implausible about the notion that an arrow hit him around the eye and that he was then struck down by advancing knights. An arrow-wound in the face, leaving him bloodied and maimed, would have allowed the interpretation that the shaft had struck him specifically in the eye, whether or not this was actually the point of impact. It has been argued by an American historian, David Bernstein, that blinding would have had symbolic value in contemporary thought: the perjurer had received an arrow in his eye, his eye had been put out as God's punishment.[17] Such a story would have quickly spread and the tapestry's artist may be following it on account of its resonant symbolic overtones. This may be so; but the tapestry does not actually show the arrow in Harold's eye, rather it enters his head at some undisclosed point on the other side of his helmet. Strictly speaking, the belief that it has hit him specifically in the eye is merely a matter of surmise on the part of the observer. Had the artist wished to show the arrow entering Harold's eye, he could no doubt have done so more explicitly.

Are we being teased again with double meaning? Is the artist hinting at another version of Harold's death? The story of the arrow was not the only early story. In the *Carmen de Hastingae Proelio*, the very earliest account of the battle, the description of Harold's death is quite distinct from any Norman or Anglo-Norman source and it makes no mention of any arrow. Instead Harold is killed by four aristocrats, or rather the poem singles out the four aristocrats who led a mêlée that descended upon Harold all at once: 'Others indeed were there,' the poet admits, 'but [these four] were better than the rest.'[18] The *Carmen* is quite clear about the identity of one of the four: it is none other than Count Eustace II of Boulogne, who apparently arrives first at the scene. As to the other three, the passage is unfortunately ambiguous but they are probably Duke William himself, Hugh of Ponthieu (Count Guy's younger brother) and Robert Gilfard (another French baron). Of these four persons only one, the duke, is Norman; the rest are French in the narrow non-Norman sense.[19] Curiously William of Poitiers is silent on the manner of Harold's death, although in other respects he set about correcting the French bias of the *Carmen*. Was this because the thrust of the *Carmen*'s story was uncomfortably close to the truth, that the French, and specifically Count Eustace, had played the greater part in the killing of

Harold? It seems at first sight that the tapestry leaves us guessing as to the identity of the knight who is portrayed as cutting Harold to the ground. However, we shall return to this enigma in chapter 15. There are reasons to believe that the name of this person, shown as he inflicts the mortal blow at the very climax of the battle, is not unknown at all but has been ingeniously encoded in the tapestry: it is, once again, Count Eustace II of Boulogne.

The death of King Harold is the decisive moment. The morale of the English, an already exhausted and depleted force, has been cruelly sapped by the loss of their leader. The fighting seems to continue for a short while, but it is not long before any further resistance becomes futile. The last straggling remnant of Harold's worsted army is now pursued off the field of battle. Duke William has won, his enemy is dead and he can look forward to wearing the crown that he covets. Even as battle is still raging, looters have arrived in the lower border, hoping to retrieve anything of value from the littered dead. One man bundles more swords into his arms than he can possibly hope to carry. Two more quarrel over a shield, pulling it greedily between them as if it were a Christmas cracker. Others are slipping chain-mail suits off the sprawled white corpses of the dead, nonchalantly removing armour from fallen warriors as if they were doing no more than help the wearer undress. One of the looted corpses may even be Harold's, for William of Poitiers notes in his own account that Harold's body was 'despoiled of all signs of status'.[20]

Eadmer summed up the Battle of Hastings and all the death, turmoil and suffering it caused in a way that made sense to his fellow countrymen: 'although fickle fortune veered from one side to the other, so great was the slaughter that the victory they gained is truly and without doubt to be ascribed to the miraculous intervention of God who by punishing the evil crime of Harold's perjury in this way showed that He is not God that countenances iniquity'.[21] This, too, is the most basic underlying meaning of the Bayeux Tapestry, and as such it would not have displeased the Normans. We have seen, however, how the story is told in an enormously subtle way, one that secretly undermines the Norman claim to the throne and records the English version of the succession, long before Eadmer was able to put that version in writing. Ultimately the tapestry seems to add its own twist by covertly turning the French under Count Eustace II of Boulogne into the true champions of divine will.

When evening fell on 14 October 1066 a large part of England's warring classes lay lifeless with their king on the field of Hastings. The body and face of Harold are said by William of Poitiers to have been so horribly mutilated that no one could be sure which corpse was his. Thus, according to one later story, his mistress, Edith Swan-Neck, was brought on to the scene of carnage and, picking her way over the corpses, was able to identify her lover – not by his face but by marks on his body known only to her.[22] William of Poitiers tells us that Duke William took charge of the corpse. Harold's mother, Gytha, then approached him and pleaded to have custody of her beloved son so that she could give him a fitting burial. She even offered Harold's weight in gold in return for his body. William refused. In his view, Harold was a faithless perjurer; he had opposed God's will and his army had fought for an unjust cause. Had not the result proved William right? William of Poitiers tells us that the duke ordered that the mass dead of the English should be left where they fell, unburied and unremembered, and that Harold's body should be taken away and placed unceremoniously under a simple cairn of stones at the seaside. There, the Normans joked, he could continue to guard the coast that he had sought in vain to defend. It has recently been suggested that the bones of an eleventh-century warrior discovered in Bosham church in 1954, adjacent to the supposed remains of Canute's little daughter, may be those of King Harold.[23] The evidence of written sources, however, indicates that Harold's body was shortly afterwards moved to his foundation of Waltham Abbey.[24] An important tomb once marked his grave there but it was destroyed at the time of the dissolution of the monasteries under Henry VIII. Today only a simple plaque on the ground within the ruined Waltham Abbey bears witness to the final resting place of Harold Godwinson, King of England.

There are a few final images in the embroidery, but they have been poorly restored and may not reflect the original. The yarn ends abruptly in the immediate aftermath of battle. In the upper part of a split scene, several prisoners, most linked by a rope, are filing past [scene 59]. Two of them, interestingly enough, seem to have arrows in the eye. In the lower part riders with whips are chasing a man who appears to be hiding in a bush. Originally, no doubt, there were some further scenes – the tapestry probably continued for several more yards – but even in the drawings of 1729 it ends where it ends now. The extremities of the work were no doubt especially vulnerable to damage. The ending must have been destroyed at some point before 1729, but rather than lamenting the loss, we should remind ourselves how amazing it is that so much has survived.

Modern embroiderers have produced reconstructions of the missing last section.[25] This, of course, is largely guesswork as far as the details are concerned, but the gist of the lost scenes may probably be deduced from the poem of Baudri of Bourgeuil.[26] Baudri probably saw the original tapestry before

1102. His poetic description of the one he imagined in Countess Adela's bedchamber may be taken as a broad, personal account of the original work. After the death of Harold, Baudri tells us that the Normans attack the remaining English 'more savagely than a tiger' and that the English fall 'more meekly than a sheep'. When night falls the English take flight and hide wherever they can; some occupy caves while others 'find shelter in bushes'. Thus far it is possible that Baudri is describing what survives of the existing work. The following day, so Baudri tells us, William's army resumed the business of war. Baudri writes that the houses of the English resounded with wailing: 'No woman, youth or elder is spared the tears.' It thus appears that there was a second scene of civilians caught up in the conflict. A city, no doubt London, is surrounded. The men of the city are leaderless and disorganised and without proper arms. 'What shall they do?' asks Baudri. 'The frightened people imagine their walls torn down, their houses burned, themselves murdered.' In a pathetic effort at defence 'an unwarlike legion' of 'girls, old men and boys' gird up the city walls with whatever they can find. At this point, however, William offers peace. The city gratefully accepts the offer and the tapestry, as described by Baudri, ends with William's triumphant acclamation as king.

This abbreviated version of events between October and December 1066 is much as would be expected if the Bayeux Tapestry had continued until Duke William's coronation. It is known that he stayed for about a week at Hastings before moving slowly into Kent and taking Romney, Dover and then Canterbury. By late November he had advanced to Southwark and was ready to cross the bridge over the Thames at the site where London Bridge now stands. He judged, however, that the people of London still needed softening up and instead he led his army on a rapid rampage through Surrey, northern Hampshire and Berkshire. Once again his forces ravaged the countryside and the trail of devastation can still be traced in the Domesday Book written twenty years later. The English will to resist was sapped by this crude display of military might. The first major submissions, including that of Archbishop Stigand, took place at Wallingford, where William crossed the Thames. Queen Edith submitted to a Norman delegation at Winchester. Although she was Harold's sister she was able to retain for herself an honoured position as Edward's widow.

For a brief moment it seemed as if the city of London would hold out. The remaining English leaders rallied around the boy Edgar and in London they elected him as king. But the hopeless reality of their plight soon dawned on them and Edgar, Earls Edwin and Morcar, Archbishop Ealdred and the chief men of London all submitted to William at Berkhamsted, Hertfordshire, by late November or early December 1066. William eventually came to terms with Edgar Ætheling, who went on to lead an eventful life and was still living in the English countryside as late as the early 1120s.[27] On Christmas Day 1066 Duke William of Normandy was crowned king of England at a tense service in Westminster Abbey, less than twelve months after Edward had been buried and Harold crowned within the same great walls. He was the third of England's kings in that tumultuous year of 1066. Of his two battle companions highlighted by the embroidery, Odo of Bayeux became Earl of Kent and was granted enormous landholdings in many English counties as his reward. Count Eustace had arrived back in Boulogne by Easter 1067.[28] By the autumn of that year, and perhaps already at Easter, he was not a happy man.

10

English Art and Embroidery

We have seen that the Bayeux Tapestry is a many-layered masterpiece, how cleverly it seems to be shot through with the English viewpoint and how its account of the Battle of Hastings subtly and unexpectedly puts the emphasis on the controversial Count Eustace II of Boulogne and his Frenchmen rather than the Normans. Is there any further evidence of this? What can be known of the true origin and meaning of this extraordinary work?

When Bernard de Montfaucon found the Bayeux Tapestry in the late 1720s he reported that 'the common opinion in Bayeux is that Queen Matilda, wife of William the Conqueror, had the tapestry made'. 'This opinion,' he wrote, 'passes for a tradition in the region. It seems highly probable.'[1] In this way one of the most enduring myths about the Bayeux Tapestry was propagated. To eighteenth-century observers, the most obvious thing about the tapestry was that it told the story of Duke William's famous conquest of England. How natural it must have been to assume that Queen Matilda and her ladies-in-waiting spent their idle hours, with needle in hand, embroidering the Conqueror's famous triumph over Harold while the man himself was busy reducing the English to final and complete submission. Despite the lack of evidence this story was for a long time accepted as true. In the nineteenth century a debate did occur between those who attributed '*la tapisserie de la Reine Mathilde*' (Queen Matilda's Tapestry) to William's wife and those who thought, for various reasons, that it must be a later work and that it was, therefore, to be ascribed to another Matilda, the Empress Matilda who was the Conqueror's granddaughter. No one, however, seemed to doubt that it was the work of some Queen Matilda or other. The only problem was choosing the right one.

Study of the Bayeux Tapestry has always been hampered by the fact that there is not a single reference to it in any surviving contemporary document. Step by step, however, close examination of the tapestry itself and ingenious detective work have enabled these early assumptions to be discarded. Early observers assumed that this heroic frieze, which at first glance seemed to be a straightforward celebration of the Norman triumph, must itself be of Norman origin. Several distinct clues quite apart from its subversive content have overturned this belief.[2]

The Bayeux Tapestry is an embroidered wall hanging, and herein lies the first clue which suggests an English origin. From surviving texts it is known that Anglo-Saxon women, in particular, were renowned for their skill at embroidery. No tradition comparable in either quality or quantity seems to have existed on the other side of the Channel. The Normans excelled at building, the English at the smaller arts. Pious Anglo-Saxon nuns and wealthy noblewomen alike occupied their hands making exquisite vestments and decorative wall hangings.[3] The skill, in particular, of Harold's sister Edith, the Confessor's queen, is attested by contemporary sources. In *The Life of King Edward* there is fulsome praise for Edith's needlework. The anonymous author tells us that Queen Edith was 'another Minerva' in this art and according to William of Malmesbury she herself embroidered the costly robes which King Edward wore on festive occasions.[4] It cannot be without interest that Edith appears unnamed, almost inconspicuously, at Edward's deathbed in the Bayeux Tapestry. It could even be that her hands, not Matilda's, were among those that stitched this famous work – making it the tragic record of a brother's death rather than the triumphant account of a husband's victory.

Edith aside, there were certainly many female embroiderers in England. Even William of Poitiers, no friend of the English, noted that 'the women are very skilled at needlework and weaving gold thread'.[5] Similar remarks were made by another foreigner, an expatriate Fleming named Goscelin, who became English by adoption (and who may possibly be the author of *The Life of King Edward*).[6] Written sources attest to Anglo-Saxon embroideries being frequently embellished with gold thread and fine jewels, although the Bayeux Tapestry, being so vast, has no such rare adornment, a fact that may have helped its survival intact through so many centuries. In addition to fine garments, wall hangings which commemorated Anglo-Saxon heroism on the field of battle were certainly not unknown. The lost work presented to the church at Ely by Ælfflaed in memory of her late husband's heroic death at the Battle of Maldon in 991 is evidence of this.[7]

Although the conquerors generally despised the language and culture of the Anglo-Saxons, scoffing at English saints with their uncouth names like Egwin and Aldhelm, and pulling down unstylish English churches, they seem to have made an exception in the case of English embroidery. This was what the natives were good at. Some items the Normans purloined for sending home, some they commissioned anew. The Domesday survey of 1086, the great landholding record in England commissioned by William towards the end of his reign, intriguingly mentions some English needleworkers who were still esteemed for their art and in possession of land. One, Æflgyd, held land at Oakley in Buckinghamshire 'which Godric the sheriff granted her . . . on condition of her teaching his daughter gold embroidery work'. Another, Leofgyd, held a moderate estate at Knook in Wiltshire, because 'she made and makes the gold fringe of the king and queen'.[8] There is further evidence for Queen Matilda's taste for English embroidery. When she died in 1083, her will reveals that she bequeathed two exquisite items of English embroidery to her favoured church of Holy Trinity in Caen. The will specifically mentions that one of these items, a chasuble, was as yet in the course of being embroidered and it names the embroiderer as 'Aderet's wife' at Winchester.[9] This is not to say that there was no embroidery in Normandy or France; but the evidence for the quantity and quality of English work is much more abundant. The accumulated evidence thus strongly suggests that the Bayeux Tapestry was not made by triumphant stitchers. It was made by Englishwomen and they would have had sadness in their eyes, as their needles picked like crows over the corpses of their mutilated menfolk.

The next, and most vital, clue came from a close examination of the artwork of the tapestry. It is important to distinguish the designer of the work from the embroiderers who carried out the task of stitching. There is no similar surviving embroidery and historians of art have thus been obliged to draw parallels with manuscript illumination and drawings. In

the 1950s the art historian Francis Wormald turned his attention to the Bayeux Tapestry.[10] He found that he was able to
identify a number of stylistic affinities, narrative analogies and
visual quotations which strongly suggested, as many now suspected, that the tapestry's master artist was working within
the Anglo-Saxon world, and not in Normandy at all. In particular, the designer seems to have drawn inspiration from a
number of illuminated manuscripts which were produced at,
or possessed by, the monasteries at one specific place – Canterbury. There were two monasteries at Canterbury: Christ
Church Abbey and St Augustine's Abbey. The closest connections have been found to be with St Augustine's Abbey, the
oldest and most prestigious abbey in England, founded by
St Augustine himself in the sixth century as part of his mission
to convert the pagan Anglo-Saxons.

Since the 1950s, Wormald's pioneering observations have
been built on by other art historians.[11] Once again, those who
have assumed that nothing new awaits to be discovered about
the Bayeux Tapestry have been proved to be very wrong; much
of the most exciting and intriguing art historical work was
done in the 1990s, and it is entirely possible that more remains
to be discovered. The artist of the tapestry seems to have made
much use of the *Old English Illustrated Hexateuch* (a copy of
the first six books of the Bible produced at St Augustine's
Abbey in the mid-eleventh century). He also drew from a
collection of texts known as the *Canterbury Miscellany* and
a sixth-century work known as *The St Augustine's Gospels*.
In the eleventh century *The St Augustine's Gospels* were kept
on the high altar of the abbey church at St Augustine's Abbey.
The *Gospels* are said to have been brought to Canterbury in
597 by St Augustine; they are still used in the ceremony for
the enthronement of archbishops of Canterbury. So impressive

is the range of parallels that, in the words of one recent historian, 'the art historical evidence for the design and manufacture of the Tapestry at St Augustine's Abbey, Canterbury is now so extensive and formidable that it should be taken as an established fact'.[12]

These parallels are drawn with artwork produced at male monasteries and the master artist of the tapestry was probably (as has often been assumed) a man, although it is also likely that the embroiderers were women. The tapestry's unity of style suggests that there was a single master designer, though he may have worked with one or more assistant. The designer could have been a monk at St Augustine's or a layman with a close connection with the abbey. Not all those who lived and worked in monastic communities had taken the vows of monks or were fully accepted as monks. The artist may have transferred his parchment designs on to the linen surface with a charcoal marker, although no trace of the outline has been found. Embroiderers would have then set to work with needle and thread. How long it took can only be guessed. The fact that it took two years for the Leek embroiderers to complete their nineteenth-century facsimile is of little help, for it is not known how many embroiderers were employed to stitch the original. Intriguingly there was a small nunnery in Canterbury on part of the estate owned by St Augustine's Abbey, though no positive evidence has been found indicating that this is where the tapestry was made. The linen could, of course, have been taken anywhere for this purpose. The surviving tapestry has been found to consist of eight joined-together sections; it is thus conceivable that a number of different workshops were engaged on the task.

In sum, it now seems well established that the artist of the Bayeux Tapestry was someone with a very close connection with St Augustine's Abbey in Canterbury and that the tapestry was made by English embroiderers, probably at or near Canterbury. This is entirely consistent with our analysis of the tapestry's story. Covertly the work tells the same story about Harold as the one later told, around forty or fifty years afterwards, by Eadmer, a monk of the other great Canterbury monastery, Christ Church. It does not seem unreasonable to conclude that this was a story known to and preserved by the monks of Canterbury.

11

A Connection with Bishop Odo of Bayeux

It is commonly assumed that a single wealthy patron would have commissioned the Bayeux Tapestry. Misgivings about Queen Matilda's supposed involvement – whether as patron, designer or embroiderer – began to be voiced in the early nineteenth century. Some, for instance, found that the occasional lewdness in the borders was not to their taste and accordingly they doubted that either of the esteemed Matildas could possibly have been responsible for such crude indelicacies. Taking up this point, a French antiquarian, Honoré François Delauney, speculated in 1824 that the tapestry might have been given to Bayeux Cathedral by a cleric of perhaps less than perfect morals.[1] Bishop Odo of Bayeux, William's half-brother, is depicted four times in the embroidery and he fitted in nicely with this somewhat anachronistic conjecture. Odo was known to have had a mistress and a son; he was present at Hastings; and his position of power gave him the requisite authority to commission such a vast work on the great events that had just taken place.

Delauney's observations prompted others to examine more

closely Bishop Odo's appearances in the work. It was noted that the tapestry gives him much greater significance than any of the written sources. In those sources Odo is merely one of two distinguished prelates accompanying the expedition, neither of whom is described as playing any significant role during the battle itself. In the tapestry Odo is not only the sole Norman ecclesiastic identified, he also appears (and indeed virtually steals the scene) at some of the most important moments: he is present at William's council at which the decision is taken to construct an invasion fleet; he says grace at the banquet after the landing at Pevensey [plate 7]; he dominates the subsequent council of war; and he rallies the young knights at a critical juncture at the Battle of Hastings [plate 10]. A further scene in which Bishop Odo had an interest is Harold's oath scene, which seems to be sited by the tapestry at or near Odo's cathedral city of Bayeux. The main written sources place it either at Bonneville (William of Poitiers) or Rouen (Orderic Vitalis).[2]

Another clue then emerged. There are only four obscure characters identified by name in the whole tapestry: Turold, Ælfgyva, Wadard and Vital. The last two are minor Norman knights depicted as taking part in the invasion. Their names are more unusual than the others, particularly Wadard's. In 1838 an English antiquarian named Bolton Corney wondered whether the Domesday Book might assist us in understanding who they were and why they are named in the Bayeux Tapestry.[3] It was found that Wadard and Vital had at least one thing in common: both were knights who owed allegiance to Bishop Odo and in the great share-out of the spoils of victory they were granted lands in Kent under the protection and patronage of Odo. Wadard also held lands from Odo in several other counties. In Lincolnshire he is nine times called '*homo episcopi baiocensis*' (the Bishop of Bayeux's man).

Even some of the very first observers concluded that the style and presentation of the story meant that the tapestry was much more likely to be broadly contemporary with the events depicted than to be of subsequent date. In particular, the inclusion of these obscure characters suggests that the tapestry was made at a time close enough to 1066 for observers to remember these people and why they were being portrayed.[4] Historians also noted that the styles of dress and armour are not inconsistent with an eleventh-century date. Today no one doubts that the work was made quite soon after 1066.

These clues, together with the tapestry's historical association with Bayeux (although this cannot be proved earlier than 1476), seemed to link it firmly with Bishop Odo. By the middle of the nineteenth century the Matilda theory was beginning to be eclipsed. The hypothesis that Bishop Odo was the patron also seems to dovetail neatly with the Canterbury connection. After the victory at Hastings, William made Odo Earl of Kent. Canterbury was the principal town in Kent; it was also its artistic centre; and both Wadard and Vital held land in Kent from Bishop Odo. A general consensus has therefore emerged that the Bayeux Tapestry was 'probably' made to the orders of Bishop Odo of Bayeux, at a workshop in or near Canterbury, perhaps with a view to adorning his new cathedral at Bayeux, which was consecrated with great pomp in 1077, and at any rate before Odo dramatically lost favour and was imprisoned by his half-brother King William in 1082. In popular books, or where space precludes the usual caveats, the 'probably' and the 'perhaps' have been hardened into statements of fact.

Presented in this way these conclusions can, indeed, seem entirely reasonable. But there are many problems. In precisely those respects where one would expect the tapestry to be most emphatic, to proclaim loudly and expressly Duke William's case, it is silent, shifty or ambiguous and ultimately downright subversive. The closer one looks the more the Norman case evaporates before our eyes. We see the true reason for Harold's journey to the continent; we see that in the early 1060s King Edward the Confessor did not support Duke William's claim; and at the Battle of Hastings it is the French under Count Eustace II of Boulogne who take the starring role – the same Eustace who, for obscure reasons, attacked Odo's castle at Dover in 1067 and was promptly disgraced. None of this could conceivably be described as a 'Norman point of view'. Bishop Odo of Bayeux was the Conqueror's own half-brother. He was one of the architects of the Norman invasion. His castle was attacked by Eustace in 1067. Can it really be that the Bayeux Tapestry was produced under his directive eye? There may, moreover, be yet another, even more astonishing, anti-Norman undercurrent running through the work – a subversive parallel with the Babylonian Conquest of the Jews in the sixth century BC.

12

The Bayeux Tapestry and the Babylonian Conquest of the Jews

In the biblical account, a puppet ruler of Judah, Zedekiah by name, had been installed by Nebuchadnezzar, the king of powerful Babylon.[1] Nebuchadnezzar took the precaution of requiring Zedekiah to swear an oath in his favour but in the ninth year of his reign Zedekiah rebelled. It was not long before he was captured by the Babylonians and was charged with having broken an oath of fealty. Like Harold, terrible punishment was now wrought upon him and his country. His sons were killed before his eyes and Zedekiah himself was blinded and taken in chains to Babylon. The Jewish kingdom of Judah was reduced to the status of a colony. Its royal officials, warriors and intellectuals were killed or exiled. The Temple and the houses in Jerusalem were burnt down and a large amount of treasure was carried off as booty. So began the long, sorry Babylonian Captivity of the Jews.

The Bible was the most widely read and studied book in the Middle Ages. People looked to its stories in order to make sense of the present. They regarded history as a complex working out of the will of God and chroniclers frequently interwove into their accounts allusions and references to biblical events, which they took to be illustrative or explanatory of the events of their own day. The Jewish disaster of the Babylonian Conquest must have seemed very much like a precursor of the Norman Conquest of England. It seemed clear from the Bible that God's anger had been roused by Zedekiah's breach of oath and that the Babylonians had been the instruments of God's anger in punishing the Israelites for their sins. Thus, having described Zedekiah's breach of oath, the prophet Ezekiel reported: '"As I live," says the Lord, "surely my oath which he despised and my covenant which he broke, I will requite upon his head . . . And all the pick of his troops shall fall by the sword, and the survivors shall be scattered to every wind; and you shall know that I, the Lord, have spoken." '[2] Harold, too, had broken a holy oath and the country had been conquered and plundered by foreigners. It could well have seemed that God had punished England, just as God had punished even the 'chosen people' by inflicting upon them the scourge of the Babylonians.[3]

In a book published in 1986, the American historian David Bernstein examined the subversive symbolism of the Bayeux Tapestry more closely than had ever been done before.[4] He identified some intriguing clues suggesting that the artist of the tapestry was drawing just such a parallel. Thus a pair of winged lions in the upper border seems to be associated with the appearances of Duke William. Two of these lions, in particular, appear above William in the famous oath scene [plate 5]. Is it possible that the winged lion has a particular meaning in this context? In the Old Testament Book of Daniel the eponymous author is said to have a dream of four great beasts, the first of which 'was like a lion and had eagle's wings'.[5] Commentators from the first century AD onwards interpreted the four beasts as standing for a succession of four worldly empires: and the winged lion, or lioness, was universally taken as representing the Babylonian empire. Thus a French illuminated copy of Jerome's *Commentary on Daniel*, produced in the eleventh century, depicts the mythical beasts with labels identifying them and adjacent to the winged lioness are the words: *leena alas aquile habens regnum babilonium* – 'a lioness having the wings of an eagle is the Babylonian kingdom'.[6] Could it be that Duke William was being deliberately associated with the pagan Nebuchadnezzar?

Bernstein further suggested that the artist's choice in depicting Harold as struck in the eye by an arrow may be another pictorial echo of the blinding of King Zedekiah. It will also be recalled that, shortly before the slaying of Harold, there is a very curious illustration of the death of an Englishman, who bears neither arms nor armour [scene 56]. In the midst of battle, a French knight grabs this man by the hair, revealing the Englishman's naked outstretched neck; the French knight's sword is poised to decapitate the helpless victim. Here we find an image that bears marked similarities with early medieval illustrations of the death of Zedekiah's sons; in Spanish Bibles of the ninth and tenth centuries, the two sons are likewise shown as decapitated by an executioner who triumphantly grasps the victim's head by the hair. This imagery was possibly based upon a lost but common stock of illustrative material about the Babylonian Conquest with which the tapestry's artist was familiar.[7]

The most intriguing, though ultimately unprovable, of the parallels identified by Bernstein concerns Duke William's mysterious Breton campaign. Nebuchadnezzar had led campaigns against two of Zedekiah's predecessors, the similarly named father and son, Jehoiakim and Jehoiachim. The latter was known by the nickname Coniah, a name which is uncannily similar to Conan.[8] Moreover, according to early rabbinical legends, although not, it should be stressed, the Old Testament itself, the father, Jehoiakim, escaped from Jersusalem by 'gliding down from the city walls . . . by a chain'. When his son 'Coniah' was subsequently attacked by Nebuchadnezzar the young man climbed on to the roof of the Temple in order to hand over its keys. The illustrations of Conan escaping down a rope from Dol and handing over the keys to Dinan are uncannily reminiscent of these old rabbinical stories. Such stories were certainly known in Jewish circles by the eleventh century. Although no evidence has yet been found that they were known in Christian circles, the parallel with the Bayeux Tapestry is again certainly suggestive.[9]

Norman writers liked to portray Duke William as a latter-day Julius Caesar, and indeed as a military leader even more successful than Caesar himself. 'Caesar,' wrote William of Poitiers, 'twice crossed over to this same Britain (for the ancient name of England is Britain) with a thousand ships, but he did not perform deeds as great the first time, nor did he dare to advance far from the coast or to stay long on the coast.' 'The Britons often gave battle to Caesar,' William of Poitiers continued, 'whereas William crushed the English so thoroughly that afterwards they could not muster the courage to fight him again.'[10] If William the Conqueror could be compared by the Normans to Caesar, a parallel with the Babylonian Conquest of the Jews is nowhere to be found in surviving Norman texts. Such a parallel carried with it a completely different political and psychological resonance. Caesar was a mighty warrior who had invaded a backward people. As understood in the Old Testament, however, the kingdom of Babylon was no more than a great pagan power, used as an instrument of God's wrath, so that his 'chosen people' might be punished for their error and sins. After years of subjugation, the Babylonian kingdom was eventually destroyed and the Jews were able to return to Jerusalem in 539 BC. Such a parallel therefore carried with it not only the solace that the Norman Conquest of England was part of a wider divine plan, but also the hope of eventual liberation.

The Bayeux Tapestry seems to be shot through with a subversive undercurrent rather than any sense of Norman triumph. If Bernstein is right, there is yet another layer to this extraordinary undercurrent. This is hardly inconsistent with the growing body of evidence that the tapestry is not a Norman work at all but was made by English people in conquered England.

There is a twist, however, to all this evidence of the tapestry's 'Englishness'. For a long time it was thought that the inscriptions revealed the work's Anglo-Saxon origin as forcibly as its imagery. For example, the use of the abbreviation '7' for 'and' is said to have been, in the eleventh century, a distinctively Anglo-Saxon usage and the name of Harold's brother Gyrth is also spelt in the Anglo-Saxon style with a barred D (Ð) instead of a TH. It had long been pointed out that there were one or two Latin words in the tapestry whose usage seemed to be more French than English but this was normally brushed aside. In the late 1990s, however, Professor Ian Short, a specialist in medieval French at the University of London, carried out a fresh analysis of the tapestry's written text.[11] Short pointed out that, time after time, the Latin words used in the tapestry were ones that would have been most naturally employed by a native speaker of French rather than English. Thus 'sand' is rendered ARENA in the tapestry, which corresponds to the Old French word *'areine'*, rather than the synonyms that might have been used in the context, '*grava*' or '*sabulum vivum*'; horse is CABALLUS, corresponding to the Old French '*chevaus*' rather than '*equus*'; talk is PARABOLARE, corresponding to '*parler*' rather than '*loqui*'. Short's conclusion is as unequivocal as it is surprising: 'The embroidery was conceived by a gifted artist . . . whose first language was French.'

The words and the pictures are so closely intertwined, relating to each other in many subtle ways, that it is natural to assume that the same man was responsible for both. It is, however, possible that the person who devised the inscriptions (a Frenchman) was different from the artist (an Englishman). Alternatively perhaps there was a single writer-artist who was a French émigré, long resident in Canterbury, since before the Conquest, and heavily influenced by the manuscript library at St Augustine's Abbey. In either case, it seems that a Frenchman was intricately involved in the actual making of the Bayeux Tapestry.

At this point it is even more important than ever to avoid the endemic assumption that 'French' means 'Norman'. It is entirely possible that the Frenchman concerned was not Norman but from some other part of France. Indeed the tapestry's favouring of Count Eustace II of Boulogne and his French army over and above the Normans suggests that our mysterious Frenchman might well have been a native of Boulogne or the surrounding lands in Picardy or Flanders which looked to Count Eustace as their leader. A non-Norman Frenchman would not have been predisposed to favour the Normans and he could easily have been sympathetic towards the English viewpoint, especially if he had long been resident at Canterbury.

We have, then, a work that was probably made by English embroiderers at Canterbury, either to the designs of a long-standing French émigré or to those of an English artist who was working closely with a French colleague. Although at one level the tapestry flatters Bishop Odo of Bayeux, it is also shot through with a succession of subversive viewpoints, all inimical to Norman interests. Despite the widespread modern view that Odo was the patron, there must be a growing sense of doubt that this was ever the case, for a work produced under the directive eye of the Conqueror's half-brother would surely have been a much more straightforward piece of Norman propaganda. The Tapestry also favours, in covert and subtle ways, Count Eustace II of Boulogne. These two men, Odo and Eustace, are the only two companions of the Conqueror who are named by the artist in his very personal depiction of the Battle of Hastings – two men who came into conflict in 1067 when Eustace launched an unsuccessful attack on Dover Castle. This is surely an important clue. The next stage in our quest is to examine the contrasting lives and overlapping careers of Bishop Odo of Bayeux and Count Eustace of Boulogne.

13

The Tanner's Grandsons

The Bayeux Tapestry gives us only a snapshot of the colourful life of Bishop Odo of Bayeux.[1] It is a mere cross-section of a long career, lived out by a flawed man, on a grand scale, a career that encompassed everything from the heights of power to the loneliness and disgrace of imprisonment. The key to this turbulent life was the patronage of Duke William of Normandy and the key to that patronage was the fact that Odo and William shared the same mother, a lowborn woman called Herleva. Herleva was the daughter of Fulbert, a tanner (some say undertaker) of Falaise. At the age of about seventeen she became the lover of Robert of Hiésmois, brother of the then reigning Duke of Normandy. William was the illegitimate son of this union; Odo and his brother Robert were the offspring of Herleva's subsequent marriage to Herluin of Conteville.

The story of Herleva's beauty and of her first meeting with Robert of Hiésmois is a captivating tale that has long passed into legend.[2] According to the most well-known version, Robert first set eyes on Herleva when he returned to his castle at the end of a day's hunting. He happened to look down from within his keep and caught sight of the beautiful young Herleva, her lily-white legs exposed to the sun as she washed linen in a nearby stream. At length Robert persuaded Fulbert to allow his daughter to pay him a secret visit at his castle but she, in turn, insisted on arriving in broad daylight and on a fine horse, which she rode proudly, for all to see, through the main gates of the building. Inside the castle, the poets of the twelfth century continued the tale with relish. Within the privacy of the comital bedchamber the lowly maiden was at once more erotic and yet strangely more demure. Herleva, so it was said, ripped open her underskirt, tearing it from top to bottom, so that her torn and unworthy clothes lay open and her pure white skin was revealed in the flickering candlelight. She had done this, so the story goes, so that her lowly garment would need to be lifted up towards Robert's face or mouth. We are then told by the poet Wace that the two of them remained awake for some time ('for I do not wish to say anything more,' he explained, 'about the way a man disports himself with his beloved'). In the fullness of time Herleva fell asleep; but as she lay beside Robert, sleeping, her body suddenly began to shudder uncontrollably before once again resuming a state of peaceful slumber. On awakening at dawn, Herleva explained that she had had a strange dream. She had dreamt that her womb had suddenly begun to grow – it had grown out of her body, she said, like an enormous tree, becoming bigger and bigger until it was eventually so vast that the whole of Normandy and the whole of England lay under its incredible shade.[3] Such, according to the old stories, were the portentous circumstances in which William the Bastard, the future Duke of Normandy and King of England, was conceived one night by his parents.

This story is, of course, almost entirely legendary. There is

no contemporary account of the meeting of Robert and Herleva; and during William's lifetime the subject of his illegiti-
macy remained strictly taboo. It was the poets of the twelfth
century who invented these tales, giving them an aura of
romance and mystical, divine approval, in order to please a
courtly Plantagenet audience who were then the inheritors of
William's achievements. The essential facts remain: in the late
1020s Robert formed a non-marital liaison with Herleva, the
daughter of Fulbert, a tanner or undertaker of Falaise, and
that William was the child of this union. Robert seems to have
treated Herleva well, but presumably wishing at some stage
to make a more advantageous match he found her a suitable
husband, Herluin of Conteville, a minor lord with some land
on the south bank of the estuary of the River Seine. The
bastard William was to remain distinctly touchy on the subject
of his birth. It was a matter which could be broached with
him only circumspectly, indeed if at all. Many years later,
when as Duke of Normandy he was besieging the town of
Alençon, a number of the townsmen thought it would be a
good idea to string out animal hides in order to taunt him
about the low birth of his mother. Once in control of the
place, he had the culprits rounded up.[4] He then had their limbs
cut off and their eyes put out. It is not recorded that the jest
was ever repeated.

Not long after William was born, Duke Richard III of
Normandy died and Robert of Hiésmois inherited the duchy.
It was rumoured that Richard had been poisoned by Robert.
At this distance in time a charge of fratricide can neither be
sustained nor rebutted, although Robert certainly had the
motive, and presumably the opportunity, to do away with his
brother. His own rule of Normandy was short and unsettled.
It came to an abrupt end in July 1035 when he died in Nicea,

in modern-day Turkey, on the journey home from a pilgrimage to Jerusalem. Thus it was that one of the most turbulent territories in Europe fell to the rule of his only son, an illegitimate boy of some seven or eight years.

There followed a decade of grim disorder, from which the child duke was lucky to escape with his life, let alone with his position intact. William's two half-brothers, Robert, afterwards count of Mortain, and Odo, the future bishop of Bayeux, were born to Herleva and Herluin in the 1030s and also grew up during this period of civil unrest. In theory they could expect to gain substantially from a connection with the duke. In practice the little boy's position was desperately insecure. Rival magnates vied for control; for long periods any authority at all was widely lacking. William's own life seems to have been sorely threatened several times. Four of his guardians were murdered in turn and one of them, Osbern the Seneschal, was stabbed to death in the very room where William slept. Such was the danger that Walter, Herleva's brother, had to smuggle the young duke out of his castle at night in order to conceal him for his own safety in poor men's houses. This was a harsh and unsettled upbringing. William's ruthless determination – without which the conquest of England can hardly be imagined – was born out of the brutalising experiences of his youth. The turning point did not come until 1047. In that year, the twentieth of his life, Duke William won a crucial victory over the rebels at the Battle of Val-ès-Dunes, near Caen. This had not been achieved without the welcome support of King Henry I of France who had ridden out of Paris at the head of his own army in order to come to his young vassal's aid. Nevertheless the victory at Val-ès-Dunes marks the true starting point of Duke William's effective rule over Normandy.

Odo's life and whereabouts during this dark period remain unknown. It is only in about 1049 that we hear of him, at which point it is recorded that William, who was now able to exert his authority more firmly in western Normandy, appointed him as the Bishop of Bayeux. Odo was certainly young for such an important promotion. There is conflicting evidence as to his precise year of birth, but it is quite possible that he was only thirteen years old and at any rate he would have been well below the canonical age of thirty. Despite William's sensitivity on the subject of his bastardy, he remained on close terms with his mother and the preferment of Odo was the first of many favours that he would grant his half-brothers. This is not surprising. Nepotism was a widely accepted practice, and in a dangerous and untrustworthy world reliance on ties of blood cannot be said to be entirely without purpose. William governed Normandy, and afterwards conquered England, with a closely knit network of loyal nobles, often related to the ducal family. Odo's brother Robert was made Count of Mortain around 1055 and so began his own long and rather colourless career of loyal service to William. Odo was made of different stuff: he was too self-important to be a sycophant and his ambitions knew few bounds. Before 1066, however, the evidence of his activities is sparse. The office of bishop that Odo had acquired was as much political as religious. It also promised considerable rewards, something which no doubt stimulated his appetite for further wealth and luxury. He appears as a witness to some of William's charters, attended ecclesiastical councils and would have overseen the establishment of the cathedral school at Bayeux, which later became something of a training ground for Norman bishops and administrators in conquered England. The cathedral itself, so intimately connected with the later history of the Bayeux Tapestry, was at this time steadily being rebuilt on the foundations of an older Carolingian edifice. The construction of the new building, which had already commenced under Bishop Odo's predecessor, continued under his youthful direction.

In about 1051 William married Matilda, the daughter of Count Baldwin of Flanders. Politically, it was a good match and it was achieved despite the initial opposition of the Pope on grounds of consanguinity. William's continued attachment to his lowborn mother is illustrated by the fact that prior to the wedding Matilda, a lady of the noblest blood, was placed in the care of Herleva. Not long afterwards the newly-weds founded two abbeys in Caen and the two abbatial churches still stand there today, proud monuments to their founders, gazing across at each other from opposite sides of the town. So far as is known, William remained faithful to his wife and together they had nine children. They must have made an odd couple, though. William was a large man, increasingly given to corpulence as he grew older, whereas Matilda was unusually small. The lady to whom the Bayeux Tapestry was so often attributed was (on the evidence of the bones discovered in her grave at her church at the Abbaye aux Dames in Caen) only about 4 feet 3 inches tall.[5]

Despite this astute marriage, the early 1050s were a time of considerable danger for William. There was nothing certain about his hold on the duchy, still less was his rise to pre-eminence in northern France inevitable. To the leaders of neighbouring territories his growing power was an increasing threat and they readily joined attempts to depose him. In 1053 Duke William's uncle, William of Arques, plotted to usurp the duchy for himself and to this end assembled a coalition of neighbouring rulers hostile to William. To make matters worse, King Henry dramatically reversed his earlier policy and in alliance with Count Geoffrey of Anjou launched an invasion of the duchy as well. The duke swiftly besieged and defeated William of Arques; amongst the latter's supporters, Count Enguerrand of Ponthieu, brother of the tapestry's Guy, was killed in action. King Henry retreated for the moment but he and Count Geoffrey were soon back, in the early part of 1054, and this time they had a much larger force that contained warriors from many regions of France. William split his own army into two parts. The first blocked Henry's advance towards Rouen; the second launched a surprise attack against the French at Mortemer, where they had been enjoying the spoils of plunder. So great was the rout at Mortemer that upon hearing the news the French king hastily retreated to Paris. The victory was significant, not least in the way it pacified Normandy's easterly borders. In particular Count Guy of Ponthieu was captured and imprisoned at Bayeux, an experience he would remember. By the time Guy was released two years later Ponthieu had been reduced to the status of a client state.

King Henry's last invasion of Normandy was defeated by Duke William at Varaville in 1057. The political circumstances of northern France now became remarkably favourable to Normandy. In 1060 William's principal enemies on the continent, King Henry of France and Count Geoffrey of Anjou, both died in quick succession. The new French king, Philip I, was a minor whose regent was Count Baldwin of Flanders, William's compliant father-in-law. A peace treaty with the king of France was shortly agreed; Anjou succumbed to a decade of weak rule and disputed succession. In 1063 William's position was further enhanced by his conquest of Maine, a smaller territory lying to the south of Normandy. William's pretence for invading Maine, following the death of the reigning count, appears to have been extremely slender. His main rival, Count Walter of Maine, soon surrendered and both Walter and his wife Biota died shortly afterwards in mysterious circumstances in William's custody. Walter was Edward the Confessor's last surviving nephew and might have been considered a contender for the English throne in 1066. William's show of force into Brittany in 1064 or 1065, depicted on the Bayeux Tapestry, was sufficiently effective to complete 'the curtain of friendly or acquiescent powers around the Norman duchy's borders'.[6] The way had been cleared for what was to come. By strong rule, astute generalship and good fortune, William had transformed beyond all recognition the precarious position in which he began his reign thirty years earlier.

William must never have abandoned the hope that he might one day succeed to the English throne. Edward's tantalising words of encouragement, apparently first heard when William was a boy, before Edward's return to England, and later, it seems, confirmed in 1051, had not been forgotten. It mattered not a jot that Edward had since changed his mind. When Earl Harold of Wessex unexpectedly fell into his lap, William seized the opportunity and exploited his luck superbly. Now, with the invasion of England, Bishop Odo of Bayeux comes out of the shadows and moves into the centre stage of history. It was a major turning point in his career, just as it was, in different ways, for Count Eustace II of Boulogne.

14

The Scion of Charlemagne

The maternal ancestry of Count Eustace II of Boulogne could hardly be more different to the lowly origins of the mother of William, Odo and Robert, for in Eustace's veins ran some of the noblest blood in Christendom.[1] His mother, Matilda of Louvain, was a granddaughter of Charles of Lorraine, the last lineal male descendant of the Emperor Charlemagne (747–814). A contemporary genealogy traces Eustace's maternal ancestry even further, beyond the Carolingians to the earlier Merovingian kings of France, whose dynasty began in the fifth century AD, and through them to mythical beginnings with Priam of Troy. Count Eustace's father, too, could trace his ancestry to Charlemagne, through the ninth-century union of Judith, the emperor's great-granddaughter, with Count Baldwin I of Flanders.[2] How Eustace must have looked down upon Duke William of Normandy, the grandson of an artisan, and a bastard descended in the male line only from a tenth-century pagan, Rollo. Above all, in the eleventh century, it was the blood of Charlemagne that was prized most. Eustace's dual Carolingian bloodline was the richest of any of his eleventh-century contemporaries and it gave him a lustre that was widely recognised. Even William of Poitiers begrudgingly notes near the end of his work that Eustace was 'illustrious in many ways and a distinguished count'. The *Carmen* refers to him as 'the scion of a noble dynasty', while Orderic Vitalis calls him 'a man of the very highest birth, sprung from the stock of Charlemagne, most renowned king of the Franks'.[3]

Throughout the Middle Ages the name of Charlemagne was held in awe and mystique. As King of the Franks from 768 to 814, Charlemagne had conquered Lombardy, subdued Saxony, annexed Bavaria, campaigned in Spain and Hungary, and he held the war banner of Christianity aloft against the pagans on many fronts. Allying himself with the papacy, he created a papal state in central Italy and in 800 was crowned by Pope Leo III as the Emperor of the West. At the height of his power Charlemagne ruled over a veritable superstate comprising practically all the lands of Western Christendom, with the exception only of the Asturias in Spain, southern Italy and the British Isles. After his death, however, this agglomeration quickly splintered into rival and warring territories. It is not surprising that, in retrospect, people looked upon the age of Charlemagne as a golden era, a time when Christendom was led by the true prototype of the Christian king and warrior. Stories of Charlemagne were told and retold in castles and halls and along the pilgrim routes; his achievements were celebrated, magnified and mythologised. Two and a half centuries after Charlemagne's death some of these stories took shape in the *Chanson de Roland* (the *Song of Roland*), the first great work of French literature. The origin and authorship of this poem remain mysterious but the story it tells, of the death of Charlemagne's nephew Roland fighting against the

Muslims in the Pyrenees and of Charlemagne's subsequent revenge, was undoubtedly circulating in the France of the second half of the eleventh century. Charlemagne, as he appears in the *Chanson de Roland*, is a impossibly old figure in a flowing white beard, an indomitable and ceaseless warrior, a wise ruler with the aura of an Old Testament prophet, a man singularly favoured by God and palpably in touch with the divine. To have the blood of Charlemagne running through your veins was prestige indeed.

Prestige, however, was not enough; Charlemagne's dynasty had long ceased to reign over France. In the ninth century a series of weak and divided kings resulted in the kingship passing out of the Carolingian lineage. The heirs of Charlemagne regained the title sporadically from 893 but their reign finally came to an end in 987 with the death of the childless King Louis V. Hugh Capet, the duke of the Franks, supported by Archbishop Adalbero of Rheims, persuaded the magnates of France that the kingship was elective rather than hereditary and that Louis' uncle Charles of Lorraine was unfit to rule. Hugh was thus elected king. The subsequent attempts of Charles of Lorraine to wrest the crown from Hugh Capet came to naught. He was captured and imprisoned in 991 and died shortly afterwards. Although the Carolingian lineage continued to flourish in the noble families of Lorraine, Vermandois, Blois, Flanders and Boulogne, never again was it to assume the royal title of France.

As Count of Boulogne and neighbouring Thérouanne, Eustace was a vassal of the Capetian kings of his day. From 1054 he was also the Count of Lens, which he held from the Count of Flanders, himself a vassal of the French king. Such ties were limited in effect. Within his own territories Eustace, like William of Normandy, was virtually a sovereign prince, with power of life and death over his subjects and the ability to build castles, mint money and pursue his own independent policies. Though small by comparison to Normandy or Flanders, Boulogne was a prosperous county. Its geographical position, as the gateway between England and the continent, had long been a source of wealth. We have a description of Wissant, the chief port of Eustace's county, in 1068, from which we learn that it could be a bustling place, full of noisy merchants and pilgrims waiting for their ships to leave.[4] The commerce of Boulogne was certainly active enough for the county to mint its own coins. Boulogne also attracted pilgrims. In the seventh century, in the days of King Dagobert, the Virgin Mary was believed to have arrived miraculously on an unmanned boat at the harbour of Boulogne and she made an apparition to the inhabitants while they were at prayer in their little hilltop chapel. The story made Boulogne one of the most important centres of pilgrimage in France throughout the Middle Ages. But it was still a small county, surrounded by powerful neighbours. Eustace had to strive hard to maintain his independence, in particular from Norman interests to the south and Flanders to the north. He had everything to fear from a powerful Normandy and much of his early policy was inimical to the interests of the Norman duke. Equally, although his links with Flanders were strong, his relations with the Count of Flanders were not always cordial. Eustace was always his own man and of necessity he was a schemer. He needed to construct deft alliances and to shift with the times in order to steer his lands through the turmoil of the age. It also seems quite likely that he harboured a secret hope that one day the House of Boulogne would occupy a throne worthy of its bloodline. Eventually it would.

There are no surviving chronicles written from the perspective of Boulogne, and Count Eustace, for the most part, is a shadowy figure. Despite the obvious respect that chroniclers held for his noble ancestry, Eustace generally appears only briefly in the chronicles of other lands, only fleetingly in stories whose central concern is someone else. It is only recently that historians have begun to put the spotlight more closely on Boulogne, to unpick the evidence and rediscover something of the importance that he once had in the contemporary world of northern France and Flanders.[5] It was probably in about 1036 that Eustace's father, Count Eustace I of Boulogne, arranged that he should marry Godgifu, the sister of the two English princes, Edward and Alfred, who were then living in exile in Normandy as England lay under Danish rule. The first consequence of this English alliance was to entangle Boulogne in the cruel tragedy of Alfred's murder. Alfred had been lured back to England during the period of confusion that followed the death of King Canute.[6] Refusing aid from Flanders, he came instead with a bodyguard of knights from Boulogne. Once in England, however, the party was deceived and disarmed by Earl Godwin, who then delivered them all into the hands Harold Harefoot, Canute's illegitimate son; in this period of confusion Harefoot was attempting to impose his own rule over England and, suspicious and disreputable by nature, he perceived them as a threat. The Boulonnais knights were shackled and many were promptly slaughtered in cold blood; others were sold into slavery. Alfred was cruelly tortured and he subsequently died of his wounds in the care of the monks of Ely. This episode, one of the darkest in English history, cannot fail to have made a deep impression on the young Eustace, who was perhaps then around twenty years of age. Alfred was the brother of his new wife and he must have known – and perhaps even grew up with – many of the knights of Boulogne who were so cruelly murdered. Though Godwin later insisted that he had played no active part in the murders, and that he was only obeying Harefoot's orders, many thought otherwise. The tragic events of 1036 must have left Count Eustace, like Edward the Confessor, nursing an abiding grudge against Earl Godwin – a grudge that could easily be transferred against Godwin's son, the future King Harold.

This was hardly an auspicious start to Eustace's alliance with England's exiled royal family, but the gamble soon paid off. In 1042 Edward became King of England. By then the surviving sons of Canute – the bastard Harold Harefoot and the legitimate Harthacanute – had both died young, after reigning only for short periods, and the way was open for Edward's peaceable succession. Eustace was now the brother-in-law of the reigning English monarch. By 1047 he had also inherited the county of Boulogne from his father, Eustace I. How different the fate of England might have been if Count Eustace and Godgifu had produced children, who, as nephews of Edward the Confessor, might have stood to inherit the crown in 1066. It seems, however, that their union was entirely without issue and, as best as may be judged from the evidence, Godgifu died before 1049.[7] By her previous marriage to Drogo, Count of the Vexin, she left two children who became Eustace's stepsons, Ralf, whom King Edward made Earl of Hereford, and Walter, Count of Maine. Eustace next married Ida of Lorraine, who, like himself, was a descendant of Charlemagne; she was to provide him with three sons. As with Duke William's marriage with Matilda, there was papal opposition on the grounds that Eustace and Ida were too closely related, and Eustace was excommunicated in 1049. It was an obstacle that must have been shortly overcome and the new marriage added to Eustace's prestige as well as increasing his network of alliances.

In 1051 Count Eustace visited England.[8] The purpose of this visit seems to have been a secret even to his contemporaries and it remains mysterious to this day. The *Anglo-Saxon Chronicle* (E) tells us merely that the Count of Boulogne spoke with King Edward 'about what he wanted, and then turned homeward'. Eustace would have been concerned at the prospect of Duke William's marriage with Matilda of Flanders, for it was an alliance of the two great powers on either side of his county and as such a potential threat to his interests. Uppermost in his mind may have been the need to reiterate his ties with Edward. Whatever the true purpose of the visit, its result is clear. Eustace unwittingly became the catalyst for some of the most dramatic events in Edward's reign and once more he came into conflict with the Godwin family. According to the E version of the *Anglo-Saxon Chronicle*, which may be the best informed, Count Eustace was returning from his meeting with the king and was on his way through Kent to the port of Dover. Perhaps with the events of 1036 fresh in mind, he and his men took the precaution of putting on their chain mail some way before they had reached the town. Once there they highhandedly set about seeking the best private lodgings they could find. One of Eustace's men demanded quarters at the house of a certain townsman, and this Englishman, valuing his privacy above providing hospitality at the point of a sword, refused to let the man cross his threshold. In the ensuing scuffle the householder was wounded. He promptly retaliated and on the spot killed his Boulonnais assailant. Eustace was enraged. He and his men mounted their horses and riding straight to the house in question they swiftly dispatched the townsman on his own hearth. More

Englishmen then joined in the riot. Twenty or so were killed on each side, many were wounded by the sword, others by horses' hoofs, before Eustace was able to escape from Dover with his men and hurried back to King Edward. Naturally enough he gave the king his own version of events. The king, believing that the men of Dover were entirely at fault, ordered Earl Godwin to harry the town as punishment. It was Godwin's refusal to harry his own people that led, unexpectedly, to the dramatic showdown between Godwin and Edward. Ultimately, civil war was only prevented by Godwin's flight to Flanders. It seems to have been during the brief period of freedom from Godwin's influence that King Edward felt able to confirm to Duke William of Normandy his then intention that William should succeed him. The following year the Godwins returned in force and Edward, unable to resist, was obliged to reinstate them.

The outcome of these events was hardly in Eustace's interests. He was no friend of the Godwins and he was no friend of Duke William. At the same time a feud had also developed between his stepson Ralf, the Earl of Hereford, and Swein, the most violent and irresponsible of Godwin's sons, whose lands were in the same region. The response of Eustace and his allies to the growing threat posed by Duke William was to support the rebellion of William's uncle, William of Arques. When this came to naught in 1053, Eustace provided the Count of Arques and his wife with exile in Boulogne and thereafter it appears that the Normans made a retaliatory raid into Eustace's county.[9] In 1056 we find Eustace at the court of Count Baldwin of Flanders at the same time as Earl Harold was also visiting. Eustace, too, was a witness to the charter dated 13 November 1056 along with his cousin Count Guy of Ponthieu and Earl Harold. History unfortunately does not record whether Eustace and Harold spoke on this occasion or what they thought of each other. Their relations on this occasion were probably cold but correct.

In the year 1066, when Harold had succeeded to the English throne and an angry Duke William was laying his plans to invade, Eustace made the fateful decision to throw in his lot with the Normans. It was certainly not any sense of loyalty to William that moved him to take this course. Nor can he have been impressed by William's invasion of Maine three years earlier and the subsequent deaths of Eustace's stepson Count Walter of Maine and Countess Biota in Norman custody. Eustace must have weighed matters in the balance and concluded that his best chance of advancement was, for the time being, to reverse his policy of hostility towards Normandy and ally himself with Duke William's plans. Rich rewards were no doubt promised should the invasion succeed. It has even been suggested that Duke William proposed, if victorious, to share the whole kingdom of England with Count Eustace II of Boulogne, but there is really nothing to support this claim.[10] Perhaps what tipped the balance in his mind was the chance to gain revenge on the Godwins.

William's father-in-law Baldwin, the Count of Flanders and regent of France, had maintained close ties with the Godwin family as well as with Duke William of Normandy, and he chose to remain neutral and aloof from the conflict. Many individual Flemish knights, however, seem to have joined Count Eustace's army; Baldwin's neutrality did not extend to preventing them doing so. It is known that during the tense summer of 1066, as preparations were made for the invasion, Eustace travelled into Normandy and met Duke William at Bayeux.[11] Here, no doubt, they discussed terms and laid down the tactics. For the first time, so far as recorded history is concerned, Eustace met with Bishop Odo as well. The precise contribution of Boulogne and its allies to the invasion force is impossible to determine (the *Ship List* deals only with Norman contributions). William of Poitiers mentions at one point that Eustace had fifty knights in his following[12] but the implication of the *Carmen* – as well as the hidden import of the Bayeux Tapestry – is that the French contribution to the whole was significant. Notwithstanding Eustace's pledge of support, Duke William remained suspicious. It was accepted only upon condition that Eustace hand over his young son (who may have been the first born, Eustace III) as a hostage.[13] This hostage was possibly handed over at the meeting at Bayeux and held in the custody of Bishop Odo. Such, on the eve of the invasion of England, was the level of mistrust between Duke William of Normandy and Count Eustace II of Boulogne.

15

Count Eustace and the Death of King Harold

Eustace in the Bayeux Tapestry is a striking figure, swinging around on his horse and pointing out the duke, and above him in the upper border the inscription spells out his name in prominent letters, or at least it used to, and herein lies a very curious anomaly [plate 11]. At some point before the rediscovery of the tapestry in the eighteenth century a semicircular tear in the border obliterated most of Eustace's name. The tear is large; it seems deliberately centred around the name and may well have been an act of deliberate censorship.

Whether deliberate or not, it left observers in ignorance who the pointing figure was. The first person in modern times to identify the figure as Eustace was the English artist Charles Stothard. Stothard spent many hours poring over the Bayeux Tapestry during the years 1816 to 1818. When he first examined this scene, all that could be made out were the letters VS, evidently at the end of the name. The torn and ragged edges around the inscription had been doubled under and sewn down. Stothard carefully unpicked the stitching and was able to discover three more letters. The first letter, at the beginning,

191

was an E; the other two, TI, came just before the letters at the end, VS. Stothard then noted that the letters of the name appeared to alternate between green and buff colours (this is not now the case, presumably as a result of subsequent restoration). From this, and the size of the space in the middle, Stothard deduced that there were four letters missing, giving him E—TIVS. 'V' in Latin is equivalent to either a 'u' or a 'v' in our own script. 'I therefore conjecture,' he wrote, 'that the letters as they now stand may be read *Eustatius*, and that the person bearing the standard beneath is intended for Eustace, earl of Boulogne, who I believe was a principal commander in the army of William.'[1]

The very few doubts that have since been voiced about this identification appear to be misplaced.[2] That the figure is Eustace is confirmed by a remarkable further detail, apparently missed by Stothard. Eustace's nickname in Old French was Eustace 'als gernons', a sobriquet which meant 'Eustace the Moustachioed' or 'Eustace the Whiskered': for he was apparently well known for his flowing moustachios.[3] At the time of the Battle of Hastings it was the fashion for the Normans and other northern Frenchmen to wear their hair closely cropped at the back and their faces clean-shaven. It was the English, not the French, who typically wore moustaches. Count Eustace stood out as a grand and exceptional figure, a Frenchman with a magnificent set of whiskers; and there on the tapestry we can clearly see them, a full moustache and whiskers, drooping in an elegant blond curve from beside his ears to under his nose. There is, moreover, no doubt that Eustace's facial hair is an authentic part of the embroidery, for the wool has every appearance of being original, rather than subsequent repair work. The whiskers also appear in the earliest unpublished drawing by Antoine Benoît around 1730.[4] Interestingly, after the Norman Conquest the French nickname 'als gernons' became more widely used in England and over the course of subsequent centuries it evolved into the English first name Algernon – a name whose aristocratic resonance provides another faint echo of the seismic social impact of the Norman Conquest.

In the Norman account of William of Poitiers Eustace is a coward who advises Duke William to retreat before suffering a blow in the back and being carried off the battlefield 'more dead than alive'. In the slightly earlier account of the battle, the *Carmen de Hastingae Proelio*, written by Eustace's kinsman Bishop Guy of Amiens, the story is very different. In the thick of battle, Eustace, the 'scion of a noble dynasty', is singled out for special praise for rescuing the duke, who had been unhorsed during an intense bout of fighting. Eustace valiantly gives up his own warhorse for William's use. One of Eustace's knights then gives Eustace his horse and together Eustace and William remount and return to fight 'where the weapons gleamed the most'. 'By their two swords,' the *Carmen* continues, 'they clear the battlefield of English troops. A good number desert, hesitate and are destroyed. Just as a wood, when the axe is applied, is chopped to pieces, so the English forest was reduced to nothing.'[5] The *Carmen* makes no mention of Eustace receiving any injury; indeed in its account Eustace continues fighting to the end.

In putting the emphasis on Eustace the tapestry is following the tenor (though not the detail) of the *Carmen*'s story. We have seen how the word FRANCI in the tapestry is also a subtle indication where the artist's sympathies lie, for pictorially it appears to designate the French fighting under Count Eustace rather than the Normans. There is further intriguing evidence of this. Few things are more obscure than the origins of heraldry, the system of inherited family devices, painted on shields, that has traditionally been taken as first appearing only in the twelfth century. Clues as to the life and customs of Count Eustace II of Boulogne are few and far between, but in her groundbreaking book published in 1980, *Origins of Heraldry*, Beryl Platts ingeniously argued that heraldry has its origin in the practices of the counts of Boulogne and their kinsmen, men who shared a common inheritance from Charlemagne. According to Platts, following the Norman Conquest it was Count Eustace II of Boulogne, and not the Normans or the Angevins, who first brought heraldry to the British Isles.

The Bayeux Tapestry is usually thought to belong to a preheraldic age and the emblems on its banners and shields have generally not been considered as heraldic or even protoheraldic symbols. Eustace's own banner in the tapestry has, frustratingly, defied conclusive identification.[6] However, Platts pointed out that in the great depiction of the advancing knights at Hastings, the leading horseman – the one who bears down on the line of upright English axe men – carries a banner on his lance-tip that seems to bear the three roundels or balls (*boules*) arranged in a triangle that to this day are part of the heraldry of Boulogne [scene 49].[7] This is an extraordinary discovery, not only for the history of heraldry but for that of the Bayeux Tapestry as well. It would be hard to overemphasise the iconographic significance of this particular banner. The depiction of the charge at Hastings is one of the most vivid and exciting scenes in the whole of the work. The moment when the first charging knight reaches the first standing English housecarl and plunges his bannered lance into the Englishman's shield marks the true commencement of the historic battle. It is as if everything else has been leading up to this point and the tapestry shows Boulogne, not Normandy, leading the way. Once more the argument that the tapestry is covertly pro-Boulogne seems to find dramatic support. Platts has also identified (albeit very tentatively) other lance-tip banners borne by the invaders as being emblems of Senlis, Alost and St-Pol or Hesdin – all subsidiary or allied territories of Boulogne.

In the *Carmen*, the high point of Eustace's role at the Battle of Hastings comes with the death of Harold, for he is said to be one of the four men who delivers a mortal blow to the last Anglo-Saxon king. It is not hard to imagine that, justly or unjustly, Eustace looked upon Harold as the representative of his old adversary Godwin and sought at Hastings to gain revenge for the bloody crimes of 1036 and the humiliations of 1051. It might seem at first sight that the tapestry leaves us guessing, or is simply non-committal, as to the identity of the knight who cuts Harold to the ground [plate 12]. There is, however, an astonishing clue that has lain unnoticed for centuries. As the knight leans over, ready to strike Harold on the thigh, the top of his helmet points horizontally at the disjointed letters TUS:EST, which have been separated out of the words INTERFECTUS EST (was killed). There is no reason why these six letters should have been separated and placed on a lower line in the way that they are, for there would have been ample room for the lettering to have continued on the same line. Are we being told something else? It takes little imagination to reverse the two triplets TUS:EST so that they become EST:TUS, which gives us, in the correct order, six of the nine letters of Eustace's name, as it is spelt in Latin (EUSTATIUS). This raises the extraordinary possibility that the so-called 'Norman knight' who delivers the killer blow to Harold is not an anonymous figurine but a coded portrait of Count Eustace II of Boulogne and thus that in its secret

treatment of Harold's death the tapestry is once again following the tenor of the *Carmen de Hastingae Proelio*. An open-
mouthed bird in the upper border even points to the vacant
space with its wing, as if to draw our attention to the unnecessary gap. A hand grasping a golden sword appears almost out
of nowhere, from the back of an Englishman, pointing also
at these same letters, TUS:EST, from the other side. Can it,
therefore, be that this is a coded way of identifying Count
Eustace of Boulogne as the man who struck the killer blow
to Harold and that TUS:EST should be read EST:TUS, an
abbreviation for EUSTATIUS?

The fact that the figure in question does not have whiskers
and that he bears no obvious resemblance to the named Count
Eustace II of Boulogne is not particularly relevant. The tapestry's artist was following the conventions of his day. Realism
was not a priority; what mattered was to tell his many-layered
tale, cleverly and subtly within the artistic conventions he was
familiar with, and to draw the moral. The crown that Harold
wears when seated on his throne, for example, looks different
from the one that is handed to him just before; and Harold
sometimes loses and regains his moustache. Moreover, had
the figure who strikes Harold been shown with whiskers, the
secrecy of the message that this is Eustace would have been
destroyed. Of greater relevance is to compare this image with
what we read in the *Carmen*, for in the *Carmen* Eustace is
explicitly mentioned as one of those who killed Harold.

In the *Carmen*'s account, Duke William calls upon Eustace
to join him in an attack on Harold, whom he had spotted
fighting fiercely on top of the ridge. With them go Hugh, who
was the brother of Count Guy of Ponthieu, and Robert
Gilfard, a French baron.[8] Each of these four delivers a mortal
blow to Harold, although the poet admits that others were

there as well. In the words of the *Carmen*: 'The first of the four, piercing the king's shield and chest with his lance, drenched the ground with a gushing stream of blood. The second with his sword cut off his head below the protection of his helm. The third liquefied his entrails with his spear. And the fourth cut off his thigh and carried it some distance away.'[9] If we are to take the order in which these actions are described as reflecting the order with which the actors are first mentioned, William is the one who pierces Harold's chest with his lance; Eustace cuts off his head with a blow of his sword; Hugh pierces him in the stomach; and the fourth, Robert Gilfard, strikes him on the thigh. The figure shown on the tapestry striking Harold on the thigh might, therefore, seem to be Robert Gilfard rather than Eustace, with Eustace, Duke William and Hugh nowhere in sight.

Nevertheless, the letters TUS:EST adjacent to the figure and the pictorial clues are teasingly suggestive. The fact that the *Carmen* has Eustace strike a fatal blow of any sort makes the case for the coded message more than just arguable. It is quite possible that the artist of the tapestry, like the author of the *Carmen*, is giving us a set-piece scene, a scene that is designed to show up the contribution of one man in particular, Count Eustace, rather than portray an accurate depiction of what happened. In other respects, in highlighting Count Eustace's role at Hastings, the tapestry follows the tenor of the Boulon-nais story told in the *Carmen*, rather than the specific details (such as Eustace giving up his horse for William), and there is, in fact, no proof that the artist knew the *Carmen* or if he did that he properly understood it. The artist may be simply giving us his own impression of Eustace's involvement in the killing of Harold, of a story that was circulating at the time amongst the followers of Count Eustace II of Boulogne. If this

197

is so, the artist is merely paying lip service to the story that Harold was killed by an arrow in or near the eye; the telling blow is struck by Count Eustace with his sword.

It is even possible that the next *eight* Englishmen (including two in the lower border) are also meant to stand as symbolic representations of Harold, for they are all framed by an H shape, formed by an oddly flying lance and two swords [scene 58]. One lance pierces an Englishman's shield and then enters his chest, echoing one of the ways that Harold is said to have been killed (apparently by Duke William) in the *Carmen*. Another lance enters an Englishman's mouth, the mouth of a perjurer if we take this man as another symbolic representation of Harold. One of these figures falls over, pierced by a lance. Another, as he falls, is trampled underfoot by a horse. Two bodies lie in the lower border; one has a lance still planted in his chest and the other apparently is the one struck in the mouth. The conjecture that all of these figures are meant as symbolic representations of Harold is strengthened by the fact that the lances which attack them *are not directed by any human hand*. Close observation shows that the hand of the knight that appears at first sight to hold one or other of them is, in fact, completely empty. The three lances have already been directed on their course by the paws of two great lions (without wings) in the upper border, presumably illustrating the contemporary belief that the outcome of the battle was directed by the hand of the God.

Count Eustace II of Boulogne, who in orthodox studies of the Bayeux Tapestry has been typically brushed aside in a sentence or two, may, in fact, be the central and most important person in the work. Perhaps, for the first time in almost a thousand years, we are beginning to understand some of its deepest and most beguiling secrets. The anomaly of Eustace's appearance with Bishop Odo in the battle scenes is all the more remarkable if we remember (though it has long been overlooked) that Eustace took up arms and joined English rebels in an attack on Dover Castle in the autumn of 1067 and that when he did so he was attacking the English castle which now belonged to one man in particular: Bishop Odo of Bayeux.

16

Eustace and the Attack on Dover

The attack that Eustace launched in 1067 on Dover Castle is one of the most curious episodes of the Norman Conquest. It is described in some detail by William of Jumièges, William of Poitiers and Orderic Vitalis, and all these sources are in agreement on the essentials.[1] King William had returned to his business in Normandy in March 1067, and the country had been left under the harsh rule of his regents, Bishop Odo of Bayeux and Earl William Fitz-Osbern. Odo had been granted Dover Castle with responsibility for guarding the south-eastern coast and pacifying Kent; he held it with the assistance of Hugh of Montfort, another important Norman noble. For some obscure reason, however, Count Eustace had fallen out with William. When a group of envoys representing the men of Kent crossed in secret to Boulogne and urged him to join them in attacking Dover Castle, Eustace readily agreed. In theory the Kentish men should have considered Eustace as their enemy, given what had happened at Dover in 1051, not to mention at Hastings the year before. However, William of Poitiers tells us that they hated the Normans even more than they disliked Eustace and, he continues, 'they thought that if they were not to serve one of their own countrymen, they would rather serve a neighbour whom they knew'. Eustace's motive in all this remains mysterious.

The moment to attack was chosen well. Both Odo and Hugh of Montfort were absent from Dover, together with most of their knights, having been called away to deal with a disturbance to the north of the Thames. Dover Castle was thus sorely undermanned. The English of the 'whole district' were under arms and ready to join, says William of Poitiers, and if Eustace was able to maintain a siege of two days, more men from the surrounding areas are said to have been ready to augment the rebel forces. During the early part of the night Eustace slipped across the Straits of Dover in a small fleet of ships. He was accompanied by many knights but they took only a few horses with them, hoping to seize the undermanned castle quickly by surprise. It is not known where, or how, the rebels launched their assault, whether by force or by ruse, but they certainly found the Norman garrison much better prepared than they had expected. Several hours of intense fighting ensued; and suffering setback after setback, the morale of the attackers began to flag. Eustace must finally have become exasperated, for he ordered a withdrawal. Aware of this, the defending Norman knights, though few in number, threw open the gates and launched their own sally on horseback. The cry went up that Odo had returned at the head of a mighty army. It was not true; but in the general panic of the situation the return of the dreaded Bishop Odo was widely believed.

Eustace's troops at the rear were quickly scattered in confusion. The Norman horsemen pursued them, and amid cries of alarm and much slashing of swords, they killed many and took others captive. More lives are said to have been lost as, in their hurry and ignorance of the local paths, the Boulonnais soldiers fell over precipices and were dashed to death on the rocks below. Of those that made it down to the English shore, many crowded on to frail ships, which sank, and they were drowned under the weight of their chain mail. Eustace himself was better prepared. A fleet horse had been always at the ready for him; and knowing the way back to his ship, he made fast for it. Now with the remnant of his forces the humiliated count sailed back to Boulogne. A large part of the English contingent was also able to escape across land by using local knowledge. But Eustace's young *nepos* (a word traditionally translated as 'nephew'), apparently taking part in his first battle, was captured by Odo's knights. The chronicles do not name this youngster, evidently a close kinsman of Eustace, but they stress that he was of the highest nobility ('*nobilissimus*'). The Anglo-Boulonnais attack on Dover Castle thus ended in utter disaster for Count Eustace. That Christmas, at the king's traditional gathering of his court, William condemned Eustace to exile from England and confiscated the English lands that he had been given as his share of the spoils of victory only a year earlier. His poor *nepos*, in all likelihood, remained Odo's prisoner.

Eustace's purpose in attacking Dover remains deeply mysterious. It has been suggested that he was hoping to take Dover and the surrounding countryside so that he could control both sides of the straits of Dover, something that would have given him enormous political benefits as well as substantial economic gains. Alternatively, he may have been disappointed at his share of the spoils of conquest and, in particular, at not regaining the lands of his former English wife Godgifu.[2] Having taken Dover Castle, he may have hoped to renegotiate his share of the victory with William from a position of strength. Another possibility, though rather speculative, is that the son he had given to William as a hostage had not been released despite, perhaps, an agreement to the contrary. It is possible that Odo was given charge of the hostage prior to the invasion when Eustace and he met in the summer of 1066, and just possible that the hostage was at that very moment being held in Dover Castle.

Undoubtedly the most intriguing possibility, however, is that Count Eustace was attempting to pursue his own claim to the English throne. This idea has been proposed by many historians. Eustace stood in the same relation to the former English king, Edward the Confessor, as Harold had done in January 1066: both were brothers-in-law of King Edward. Eustace had the prized blood of Charlemagne running in his veins and beyond that contemporaries traced his maternal ancestry to the earlier Merovingian kings of France and through them on more dubious grounds to Priam of Tory. This was a bloodline that gave Count Eustace greater prestige than perhaps any of his contemporaries and yet here was a man who was not a king; he was merely the count of a relatively small region. It is not hard to imagine that he hoped one day to raise himself and his family to a position more worthy of such an illustrious lineage.

What is more, Eustace could also trace a distant line of descent from the greatest of all the insular kings, Alfred the Great, through the marriage of one of Alfred's daughters to Count Baldwin II of Flanders. This connection, albeit distant, would have certainly recommended him in the eyes of the English, assuming it was known. William the Conqueror's kinship with Edward the Confessor was entirely based upon the fact that Edward had a Norman mother; William was not in any way descended from the ancient line of Wessex kings.

The young Edgar Ætheling had been taken as a hostage by William to Normandy when he returned there in March 1067. In these circumstances, without further hope or choice, the Kentish rebels might well have turned to Eustace as the leader of a potential rebellion against the absent William. The statement by William of Poitiers that the inhabitants of Kent wished 'to serve' someone that they knew hints, perhaps, at this larger ambition.

The identity of the *nepos* is also obscure. Nor is it known when, if ever, the *nepos* was released. As used in medieval Latin, the term *nepos* is often translated as 'nephew', but it could also mean 'grandson', 'bastard' and even 'cousin' generally. Much ink has been spilt on who the *nepos* might have been; but the question remains unanswered. Whether Eustace had any nephews is disputed; he certainly had a bastard son called Geoffrey.[3] The most intriguing possibility again turns on a Boulonnais claim to the English throne. Professor Barlow has suggested that Eustace's marriage with Godgifu, Edward the Confessor's sister, may not have been childless after all. A daughter of theirs might well have had a son, a grandson of Eustace, who could have been just about fighting age in 1067. Such a grandson, another great-nephew of the Confessor, would have been a prime candidate around whom English opposition to William could have gathered. In this scenario Eustace was bringing with him, on that mysterious assault on Dover Castle, a young pretender to the English throne, a grandson who, however, was promptly captured and perhaps never heard of again.[4]

Although the identity of the *nepos* remains a mystery, what matters for our purpose is the known set of facts. In the latter part of 1067 Eustace attacked Odo's castle at Dover, suffered a humiliating defeat and a young kinsman of his, of the highest birth, was captured by Odo's men. In accordance with contemporary practice the young man was probably held by Odo for a large ransom. What became of him is not known. Realistically the Bayeux Tapestry can only have been made after Eustace's attack, in other words after Odo and Eustace came into such public conflict in the autumn of 1067. It is scarcely believable that the tapestry could have been conceived, organised, designed, approved and embroidered in the interim between William's coronation at Christmas 1066 and Eustace's attack on Dover in the latter half of 1067. With this in mind, the orthodox idea that Bishop Odo of Bayeux commissioned the Bayeux Tapestry, a work that is shot through with the English viewpoint and that makes Count Eustace into a hero at Hastings, is becoming even more unlikely.

William the Conqueror was not a man to flail about wildly at his enemies. His actions, if often crude, were cold and calculating, and if his interests required it he was quite capable of coming to terms with a former foe. So it was that in the 1070s Eustace and King William became reconciled again.[5] A motivating factor, from William's point of view, may have been his deteriorating relations with Flanders. When William's father-in-law Count Baldwin V died in 1067, Flanders was inherited by his son Baldwin VI. Baldwin VI died only three years later, and the county descended into a civil war. William and Eustace took the same side in this conflict, supporting Baldwin's young son Arnulf III and his mother Richilde against the opposing claims to the county made by Arnulf's uncle, Robert the Frisian. Robert the Frisian, however, emerged victorious in 1071 and a new alliance then emerged between Robert, as the new Count of Flanders, and Philip I of France, now an adult, and both of them were hostile to Normandy. With his resources stretched in England, and Flanders now hostile, the Norman king would have been in need of a strong ally in Boulogne in order to protect the northern border of his duchy.

Given the events of 1067, the settlement that Count Eustace renegotiated with King William in the 1070s was remarkable. Eustace was granted lands so extensive that by the time of the Domesday Book in 1086 the Count of Boulogne appears as the tenth largest landholder in England. Most of his vast estates were concentrated in Essex and Hertfordshire, but he also held lands in many other counties as well. It is noteworthy, however, that in this second settlement he took nothing in Wiltshire or Gloucestershire, and very little in Surrey, counties where his initial reward in the wake of Hastings may have been concentrated. It is not known when Eustace died, although his eldest son, Eustace III, appears to have inherited the county and the English lands before 1088. If Eustace II ever hoped to be a king, he had failed in this grander ambition, but he had overcome the disaster of 1067 and he left the comital house of Boulogne much more powerful and considerably richer than it had ever been. On the foundations he laid his sons were able to raise the blood of Boulogne to the highest ranks in Christendom.

The most famous of the sons of Eustace and Ida was Godfrey of Bouillon, the leading Crusader who, when Jerusalem fell in 1099, modestly refused the name 'King of Jerusalem' but took the title of 'Defender of the Holy Sepulchre'. Godfrey's reputation was soon mythologised and he was shortly to become one of the most celebrated figures in the whole of Christendom. When Godfrey died in 1100, his brother Baldwin of Boulogne was crowned, this time without demur, with the resonant title of King of Jerusalem. When Baldwin died in 1118, the third and eldest son, Count Eustace III of Boulogne, was also invited to be King of Jerusalem but he learnt, *en route*, that the crown had been given to his cousin Baldwin of Le Bourg and he returned to France. The daughter and heiress of Eustace III was Matilda of Boulogne. She married Stephen of Blois. When in 1135 Stephen became King of England Matilda of Boulogne became his active and capable Queen. Their son, Count Eustace IV of Boulogne, was named by Stephen as his heir. Count Eustace IV of Boulogne stood for a while on the threshold of becoming King Eustace I of England. But Eustace IV died in 1153, a year before his father, and the throne passed on Stephen's death to the rival house of Plantagenet.

In the eyes of medieval posterity Countess Ida herself seems to have eclipsed the fame of her late husband, Eustace II. After her death in 1113, miracles were reported, a cult of sainthood developed around her and she was popularly recognised as a saint. The bones of St Ida have undergone a most curious journey through the ages. First buried at Wast, in the county of Boulogne, they were taken in the seventeenth century to Paris by a nun named Catherine of Bar, who had founded the order of the Benedictine nuns of the Saint-Sacrement. In 1808, in the wake of the French Revolution, St Ida's bones were removed again and this time they were placed in the care of the Benedictine nuns of Bayeux, where they still reside, hundreds of miles from Boulogne but only a few hundred yards from where Ida's husband is portrayed in all his glory on the Bayeux Tapestry. The curious thing about all this is that it was only ten years later, with the work of Charles Stothard, that it actually became known that Eustace was depicted on the tapestry.

By the second half of the twelfth century, new legends were circulating about Countess Ida and the ancestry of Godfrey of Bouillon. In these strange stories Ida is the daughter, not of Godfrey of Lorraine, but of the fabulous and romantic Swan Knight, the scion of swans, and her destiny is to marry Count Eustace of Boulogne and raise a trio of famous Crusaders. According to these stories the Swan Knight must never be questioned about his true origin; and when one day Ida's mother, overcome by curiosity, asks him the forbidden question he suffers a violent reaction and departs at dawn for ever. Once again, in these fantastical tales a century after his death, Eustace II, son-in-law of the Swan Knight, appears only as a shadowy character with a secondary role in a story dominated by others. It is in the famous battle scene of the Bayeux Tapestry that we truly see him take centre stage.

17

The Downfall of Bishop Odo

The conquest of England was the great watershed in Odo's life.[1] As the new king's grip on the country tightened, he divided the lands of the dead and dispossessed English among his followers. Bishop Odo's share of these spoils was immense. His initial reward was the earldom of Kent, and in that county alone, as well as holding Dover Castle, he possessed at least 184 manors; he has been described as 'perhaps the greatest single figure in Kentish history'.[2] By the 1080s Odo held large estates in twenty-two counties dotted throughout England. The Domesday Book of 1086 records that Odo's total landed income was in the region of £3,000 per annum, an extraordinary amount for the times; it was at least three times more than the amount Eustace gleaned from his own English lands and that in itself was a very sizeable sum. Domesday also reveals that the yield extracted from the men and women who day-long toiled in Odo's fields and did his bidding had risen by 40 per cent from what it had been in 1066.

A striking measure of Odo's newfound wealth was provided by the *Sunday Times* in 2000 when it compiled a list of the richest non-royal Britons during the last millennium, the 'Richest of the Rich' list.³ Odo's English fortune was estimated in modern terms as £43.2 billion, putting him in fourth place overall. Such estimates are deceptively precise but they certainly reveal the broad scale of Odo's wealth. Such was the rapaciousness of the invaders of the Norman Conquest that three out of the first four places in the *Sunday Times*'s list, covering the whole of the period from 1066 to date, were held by men who accompanied William the Conqueror to England and who owed their fortunes to the spoils of invasion: William of Warenne (£57.6 billion), Odo's own brother Robert of Mortain (£46.1 billion) and Bishop Odo himself. When one takes into account the sizeable income Odo continued to receive in his capacity as Bishop of Bayeux, he must have as good a claim as anybody, so far as evidence permits, to be regarded as the richest non-monarch ever to have lived in England during the whole of the last millennium. This should have pleased the tanner's grandson, but the appetite of a greedy man is rarely sated and ultimately Odo's boundless greed and ambition were to be the cause of a sudden downfall.

Not all the land that Odo claimed was of unimpeachable title or undisputed by others. The most famous dispute of all brought him into direct conflict with the Italian-born Lanfranc, the new Archbishop of Canterbury who had been appointed by King William in 1070 from the Abbaye aux Hommes at Caen. The encroachments that Odo was accused of seem to have dated back to pre-Conquest times; they were already part of the Kentish lands of the Godwin family that Odo had 'inherited' following the victory at Hastings. Odo, however, strove hard to retain as much as he could. A dispute such as this between two of William's closest advisers, the scholarly Lanfranc and the avaricious Odo, had to be settled by due process of law. It gave rise to one of the most important legal trials of William's reign. The old shire court of Kent was convened at its traditional meeting place on Penenden Heath, where the Anglo-Saxons had met in the years before. It was presided over by another great Norman magnate, Bishop Geoffrey of Coutances, who, like Odo, was renowned for his secular lifestyle and leadership of knights. No one was deemed wiser as to the laws of England than old Æthelric, the deposed English bishop of Selsey. An invalid in his declining years, he was wheeled before the court in a cart in order to give forth his valued and learned opinions. After three days of evidence the judgment, in the main, favoured Lanfranc; Odo lost out. Lanfranc evidently had a poor view of Odo and the two remained legally and politically at odds. It was not long before their personal relations degenerated into little short of hatred and it was, perhaps, under Lanfranc's influence that William began for the first time to suspect Odo's loyalty and to disapprove of his greed.

As his wealth and power increased, the baronial, worldly-wise side of Odo's character came to the fore and on this side of the Channel he emerges as a fully-fledged secular baron, more at home in his castles and halls than in the quietude of any church. A surviving drawing of Odo's seal revealingly depicts him, on the one side, as a dutiful man of the cloth and, on the other, as a proud knight riding on his horse. When William was absent in Normandy Odo seems to have had wide powers to rule the country in his stead, together with William Fitz-Osbern. It is clear that he used his powers with considerable severity. The English would long remember their sufferings under his rule. According to the *Anglo-Saxon Chronicle* (D), when Odo was left in charge of England in 1067 the people were sorely oppressed: 'Bishop Odo and Earl

William [Fitz-Osbern] . . . built castles widely throughout this nation and oppressed the wretched people and afterwards it always grew very much worse. When God wills it, may the end be good.' In the first half of the next century, the half-English, half-Norman Orderic Vitalis also complained that Odo and Fitz-Osbern protected Normans and paid no heed to the legitimate complaints of the English: thus, said Orderic, 'when their men-at-arms were guilty of plunder and rape, they protected them by force, and wreaked their wrath all the more violently upon those who complained of the cruel wrongs they suffered. And so the English groaned aloud for their lost liberty.'[4] On another occasion, Orderic wrote that Odo was 'dreaded by Englishmen everywhere'.[5] In 1075 Odo was called upon to lead an army against the rebellious Earls Waltheof and Ralf the Staller. Five years later he led a ferocious reprisal against the turbulent north of the country following the murder of Bishop Walcher of Durham.

Wealth poured into Odo's coffers, and it was wealth from England that must have given the final impetus for the completion of Bayeux Cathedral in 1077. Certainly Odo did not forget his episcopal city. He also built a palace there for himself, constructed several houses for canons and funded the education of young clerics. The cathedral, which was served by a body of clergy of unprecedented size, was completed in grand Romanesque style. The edifice he built has, of course, been much altered since 1077; but the two monumental cliff-like towers framing the western portal and the crypt beneath the nave remain as reminders of Odo's great building. Orderic Vitalis commented that Odo did both good and evil in the fifty years that he ruled over the see of Bayeux, but the Anglo-Norman monk was evidently impressed by Odo's conventionally pious largesse, ostentatious as it was. Odo, he commented,

'enriched his church in every way with gifts of precious ornaments. There is evidence of this in the buildings he raised and
the furnishings – gold and silver vessels and precious vestments
– which he lavished on the cathedral and clergy.'[6] Another
monk who visited Odo's cathedral commented approvingly
that he had never seen the like.[7] There is, however, no mention
of the Bayeux Tapestry in any of these reports, no indication
that it was among the ornaments which Odo provided for his
cathedral, as is so often stated. All that is known is that the
tapestry was at Bayeux Cathedral 400 years later – in 1476 –
and that at that time it was the practice to hang it around the
nave on certain days.

By the early 1080s Odo was at the height of his power and
wealth. He would have done well to follow the example of
his brother, Robert of Mortain. Robert contented himself with
the role of an unimaginative servant in the shadow of William's triumph, and he benefited enormously in the process,
with almost 800 manors to his name, from the moors of Yorkshire to the meadows of Cornwall, and a string of valuable
castles to boot. One later account called Robert 'dense and
slow-witted'[8] but he was evidently shrewd enough to keep on
the right side of the king. Odo, however, was not Robert.
Greedy and energetic, arrogant and irrepressible, and with a
thoroughly misplaced sense of his own importance, he forgot
that he owed his position solely to William's grace and favour,
and his downfall, when it came, was dramatic.

The precise cause can only be gleaned from later accounts;
the matter was passed over circumspectly by contemporary
chroniclers.[9] It seems that Odo heard that a soothsayer in
Rome had predicted that the next pope would be called 'Odo'.
It did not take much to spark the flames of new ambition in
Odo's heart. Thus he set about bribing his way to succeed

the reformist and altogether more spiritually minded Pope Gregory VII, stuffing the wallets of pilgrims with letters and coins in order to smooth the way for a grand arrival at the papal see. Through agents, he acquired a splendid palace in Rome, furnishing it at great expense; and with lavish gifts and promises he secured the alliance of the leading Roman families. In England he assembled a large body of knights, and by 1082 they had moved with him to the Isle of Wight in readiness to depart. None of this seems to have had William's foreknowledge, and certainly not his approval. Gathering such a private army and removing it from the country was both a threat to the security of the land and an affront to William's authority. Odo, in any event, was meant to be one of those responsible for the government of England in William's absence. It was the final straw. The king was in Normandy when he learnt of Odo's plans. He raced back across the Channel and arrested Odo without warning on the Isle of Wight. The bishop's underlings were compelled to reveal the whereabouts of his treasure. Hidden in various secret places, wrote William of Malmesbury in about 1125, was such a quantity of gold that it 'surpassed anything that our age could imagine'. Many sacks of beaten gold were hauled out of rivers, where they had been secretly stashed away; and apparently those who already knew the whereabouts of Odo's secret hoards were able to make off with much of the treasure before the king's men arrived.

Odo protested that he was a clerk and a priest of God and that William had no right to condemn a bishop without papal authority. To this William replied, on the advice of Archbishop Lanfranc, that he was arresting not the Bishop of Bayeux but the Earl of Kent, subtly turning Odo's hitherto successful duality firmly against him. Wace, writing in the second half of the twelfth century, tells us that at times Odo had even coveted the throne of England, making discreet enquiries as to whether there was any precedent for a bishop to succeed to a kingdom.[10] Whatever the truth in this, William now conceived an utter hatred for his half-brother. The arrogant and over-mighty Odo languished as William's prisoner in the dungeon of Rouen for the next four years.

In July 1087 King William was fatally injured while fighting at Mantes. His last years had not matched the achievements that preceded them; it would have been remarkable if they had. In the period between 1068 and 1075 William ruthlessly suppressed a series of revolts in England, of which the cruel harrying of the north in 1070 was the most notorious example, and he saw off the threat of invasion from abroad. By the mid-1070s Norman rule was firmly established across the country and William increasingly turned his attention to safeguarding his continental interests. The last chapter of his life was marked by military setbacks in France and disunity within his family. His army was routed by the Bretons at Dol in 1076. His eldest son Robert Curthose rebelled against him and inflicted another defeat at Gerberoi in 1079. Odo's disloyalty in 1082, Queen Matilda's death a year later and a fresh rupture with Robert shortly afterwards must have all taken their toll. Moreover it soon became clear that there was a new danger on the horizon, for King Canute IV of Denmark and his uncle Robert the Frisian, Count of Flanders, were planning to mount a massive invasion of England. It was in this context, at Christmas 1085, that William ordered the preparation of the famous Domesday Book, a record of landholding in England that seems to have had a dual purpose: to enable the inevitably numerous disputes over possession to land to be settled and to pave the way for an increased tax, partly in order to fund a defensive war against the Danes. A combination of English administrative efficiency and Norman zeal, the Domesday Book was an incomparable achievement for its age and it remains one of the most remarkable legacies of William's reign. Though the threat remained, the invasion from Denmark never arrived. It was entirely in keeping with William's character that he should have received his last injury in the saddle, aggressively campaigning in the French Vexin in the summer of 1087. One account tells us that when his horse attempted to jump over a ditch William was pushed forward in the saddle and the pommel ripped into his stomach.

Taken to a monastery just outside Rouen, the ailing Conqueror issued his last wishes. Robert Curthose, his rebellious son, was now to be the Duke of Normandy, as he had always been promised, but the kingdom of England passed to the second son William Rufus. The third surviving son, Henry, had to be content with a gift of £5,000, but it was to be under Henry, as King Henry I, that Normandy and England were eventually to be reunited under single rule in the early twelfth century. The old king, now faced with prospect of imminent death, made a pious display of gifts to churches and ordered the merciful release of all prisoners – all, that is, except one: Odo.[11]

The darkest dungeons were to be emptied of murderers and thieves; disloyal barons and political hostages were happily to see the light of day at last; but on no account, said William, was his half-brother Odo ever to be released. To those who urged him otherwise, William was adamant. Describing the scene from the perspective of the 1130s, Orderic Vitalis put his own opinion of Odo into William's mouth. In Orderic's account the dying William now launched into a tirade of invective against Odo. Odo, he said, had long held religion in contempt, he was a cunning instigator of rebellion, he was the worst oppressor of the English, he was a destroyer of monasteries, he was frivolous, he was ambitious, he was devoted to the delights of the flesh and to deeds of great cruelty, he would never give up his vices and frivolities. 'I imprisoned not a bishop but a tyrant,' Orderic has William continue, 'and if he goes free, without doubt he will disturb the whole kingdom and bring thousands to destruction.'[12]

This, of course, is Orderic's opinion. Odo's spoliation of monastic land was probably not as great as Orderic here (and elsewhere) implies, and as evidence of Odo's sexual liaisons only one bastard is known – John of Bayeux, afterwards found 'in the court of King Henry'.[13] Nevertheless it is undeniable that William's hatred for Odo, his once trusted lieutenant, was still as extreme as it was implacable. The men gathered around William's bedside, including Robert of Mortain, continued to press him to have pity on Odo, offering to give security for the bishop's future conduct. William, a weak and dying man, finally gave way to their constant entreaties. 'Unwillingly I grant that my brother may be released from prison but I warn you that he will be the cause of death and grievous harm to many.' William died soon after, on 9 September 1087, and was buried in the enormous cathedral-like church he had had built at the Abbaye aux Hommes in Caen, one the greatest of all Romanesque churches still standing, just as Matilda was buried at her Abbaye aux Dames.

With William dead, four years in the dungeons of Rouen had left Odo neither contrite nor subdued but ready and eager to quench his thirst on the drug of power that had been so abruptly denied him. He swiftly ingratiated himself with Robert Curthose, the new Duke of Normandy, and by early 1088 they were together plotting to overthrow King William

Rufus of England and reunite Normandy and England under Robert's single authority. There would be little difficulty, Odo thought, in overcoming King William Rufus; he may well have considered him weak and effeminate. Later chroniclers, all monks, agreed that times had changed for the worse; they complained that the new king's courtiers wore their hair long and in curls, and that they minced around effeminately in wide-sleeved robes and wore shoes that curled up extravagantly at the toes like scorpions' tails.[14] It was all a far cry from the hard men in crew cuts who had invaded England in 1066. Others were persuaded to join Odo's plot, including old Bishop Geoffrey of Coutances and (with the events at Dover in 1067 now long forgotten) the young Count Eustace III of Boulogne. The plan seems to have been that Odo would secure a strong foothold in the south-east of England and Robert would invade from Normandy. One of Odo's first acts in this rebellion was to send his knights on a petulant rampage through the lands of his old adversary Archbishop Lanfranc. Odo then marched from Rochester to the castle at Pevensey, where he holed up, waiting patiently for Duke Robert's invasion.

Faced with this widening Franco-Norman revolt, King William Rufus had no choice but to appeal to his lowly English subjects for help. He made rash promises of good government and low taxation that, as ever, were rather over-optimistically accepted by the populace: 'he promised them,' the *Anglo-Saxon Chronicle* (E) advises us, 'the best law that ever was in this land; and forbade every unjust tax and gave men their woods and their coursing – but it did not last long'. By dint of these promises, Rufus was able to assemble a large Anglo-Norman force which surrounded the castle at Pevensey so that Odo could not escape. The English, so the *Anglo-Saxon*

Chronicle continued, were particularly keen 'to get Bishop Odo' whom they regarded as the brains behind the 'foolish' revolt. After six weeks the besieged bishop's provisions ran out and, with no sign of any serious attempt at invasion by Duke Robert, he was forced to surrender. He promised, perhaps already without sincerity, to hand over Rochester, and that he would then leave the shores of England and never return without the king's consent.

Odo was taken under relatively light guard to Rochester in order to arrange for the fortification there to be delivered up. Within its walls, however, were his allies Count Eustace III of Boulogne, the three sons of Earl Roger of Montgomery and perhaps as many as 500 knights. They were in no mood to surrender. Sallying out, they captured the king's men and then took them back within the castle. Odo, seizing the moment, also scurried within. Once more Rufus had to lay siege to Odo. Once more the young king proved a shrewder and more formidable enemy than the bishop had expected. During May 1088 Rufus blockaded the walls of Rochester Castle and erected two siege towers to cut off his uncle's escape. Over the next weeks provisions within ran out and conditions rapidly deteriorated. If we are to believe Orderic Vitalis, Odo and his allies were additionally inconvenienced by a plague of flies truly biblical in scale.[15] Unable to endure any longer, they finally opened negotiations to surrender.

It was the custom of the time for the victors at a siege to herald their triumph over the defeated with a fanfare of trumpets.[16] To avoid this final humiliation, Odo tried to win from the king the concession that, although he might be defeated, banished and deprived of his wealth, at least the trumpets would not be blown. Rufus refused. Not for 1,000 gold marks would he agree to his uncle's request; he wanted to enjoy the moment. So it was that Odo and his allies emerged in shame from Rochester to a loud blast of trumpets; apparently Englishmen all around jeered at 'the traitor bishop' and taunted him with cries that he deserved no better than to be strung up from a gallows. Although King William Rufus subsequently forgave many who had taken part in the revolt, including Count Eustace III of Boulogne, Odo was deprived once and for all of his vast possessions in England. He was banished for good, never to set foot on English soil again.

The great English adventure, begun in hope and trepidation in 1066 and recorded so remarkably in the stitches of the Bayeux Tapestry, was finally over for Odo. Now in his fifties, he contrived to interfere, as best he could, in the government of Normandy under the ineffectual rule of Robert Curthose. In November 1095 Odo journeyed to the centre of France, into the rounded mountains of the Auvergne, in order to attend a great council of bishops at the city of Clermont, one of the periodic gatherings of the Catholic Church. In the event it was to be a momentous occasion and its outcome defined the age to come. Over 300 clerics were present; Pope Urban II himself presided. The first nine days of the Council of Clermont proceeded uneventfully, or at least as expected, but as the council neared its end it was announced that Pope Urban was to make a momentous statement. News spread around the city. People flocked to hear what Urban had to say and they arrived in such vast numbers that the council had to be moved from within the cathedral to an open field beyond the city gates. Urban's words survive in only second-hand and mutually inconsistent versions (including one by Baudri of Bourgueil). But the gist is known. He appealed to Western Christians to aid their co-religionists in the East. The beleaguered Emperor of Byzantium had asked for help in his battles against the

Turks. Pilgrims making their way to Jerusalem were facing greater and greater difficulties. All this time the knights and armies of the West were slaying each other when it was the duty of Christians, he said, to march in aid of their brethren on a 'righteous war'. For those who died there would be absolution and remission of sins. The enthusiasm with which this revolutionary call was taken up took everyone, including Urban, by surprise. Its primary goal became, if it had not already been at the outset, the capture of Jerusalem from Muslim hands. Thus was born the terrible, tragic, bloodthirsty and ultimately fruitless movement now known as the Crusades.

Hardly in the first flush of youth, Odo was amongst those who decided to take the cross. He may have been fired by religious fervour. Duke Robert himself decided to become a Crusader and, having made his peace with King William Rufus, mortgaged the duchy of Normandy in Rufus's favour. The prospect of being left behind at the mercy of his old enemy Rufus may well have influenced Odo in his decision. We do not know the whereabouts of the Bayeux Tapestry, but if it was now in Odo's possession it is not difficult to imagine the old bishop, on eve of his departure, having the tapestry spread out and displayed for him for one last time. If so, he would have probably received fresh inspiration from what he saw; if not, he would have at least remembered what it showed. By his words, his advice, his prayers, his very presence at the battlefield, he had influenced the outcome of the fight against the English at Hastings. Might he not now also affect the outcome of the forthcoming struggles in the Holy Land?

After travelling around Normandy with the papal legate, presumably in order to preach the Crusade, Odo finally departed the duchy in September 1096. Different crusading armies took different routes. The famous brothers Godfrey of Bouillon and Baldwin of Boulogne took an overland route through central Europe. Odo of Bayeux travelled southwards through France and Italy in the company of Duke Robert of Normandy and, it seems, Count Eustace III of Boulogne. He visited Rome and afterwards met Pope Urban at Lucca. The large party moved south again and wintered in Apulia and Calabria at the southern end of Italy. All talk, no doubt, was of plans for the coming year. Northern Frenchmen would have felt at home in these parts, for these were territories which were ruled by Normans, too. Earlier in the century Norman adventurers had carved out their own principalities in Italy, a private enterprise by hardened mercenaries that had succeeded beyond their dreams. By 1059 Robert Guiscard, whose family hailed from Hauteville, not far from Bayeux, had become the powerful Duke of Apulia and Calabria. Under his command the island of Sicily had been invaded in 1061. Long in Muslim hands, Sicily had now been added to the empire of the Hautevilles.

As 1096 drew to a close, Bishop Odo, apparently still in good health, made the short sea crossing to Sicily in order to visit Count Roger the Great, Guiscard's brother, at Palermo. It was here, in January 1097, that Odo caught his last illness. Gilbert of Evreux, Odo's episcopal colleague from Normandy, remained at his bedside to the end. His final ambition dashed, Odo's last act was to leave his movable wealth, of which there was no doubt plenty, to Arnulf of Choques, a churchman of Boulonnais birth who was to end an eventful career as Patriarch of Jerusalem. A fine tomb in Palermo Cathedral was erected for Odo by Count Roger, but in the last quarter of the twelfth century it was taken down and nothing of it now remains. It is possible that Odo's bones were removed and that they now lie, together with those of other noble Normans, in a side chapel dedicated to Mary Magdalene.

Two eventful lives had ended: Eustace, the noble heir of Charlemagne, who sought to raise the fortunes of his comital house of Boulogne, and Odo, grandson of a tanner, a man who became rich and powerful thanks to his half-brother's achievements but whose greed and ambition ultimately caused a dramatic downfall. Their paths had crossed as a result of Duke William's audacious plan to seize the English throne and they came into conflict only a year later when Eustace launched his attack on Dover Castle. Why should these two men, so recently foes, be highlighted on either side of Duke William in the Bayeux Tapestry?[17] An intriguing alternative to the orthodox theory of Odo's patronage of the work has long been overlooked. Was the patron of the tapestry not Odo at all, but rather Count Eustace II of Boulogne?[18]

On the face of it, this overlooked possibility has a great deal of explanatory power. Eustace could have commissioned the tapestry as a gift to Odo, as part of the process of their reconciliation in the early 1070s and perhaps also in order to gain the release of the *nepos* who had been captured by Odo's knights. The tapestry's highlighting of Odo, in the various ways that it does, would then be a case of flattery rather than self-promotion, but at the same time the role of Eustace and his French army at Hastings, the great charge under the banner of Boulogne and Eustace's role in felling Harold, were all subtly rendered in threads. The English undercurrent consistent with the fact that in 1067 Eustace sided with English rebels. Despite earlier events, he had evidently found some common ground with the men of Kent. Moreover, as a non-Norman, Eustace could easily have been open to alternative views about the legitimacy of William's claim to the throne.

Could it, therefore, be that this forgotten and enigmatic man, Count Eustace II of Boulogne, was ultimately responsible for the most famous work of art in English history?

18

Turold the Dwarf

Turold the dwarf is perhaps the most captivating of all the figures depicted in the Bayeux Tapestry [scene 10; plate 1]. We see him in the county of Ponthieu, holding the two horses of Duke William's emissaries, who have just arrived at Count Guy's residence on their mission to demand Harold's handover to the Norman duke. There are only fifteen characters named in the whole work; all but four are easily identifiable, known from other sources for the part they played in the drama of 1066. Who is this dwarf engaged in such a menial task, and why has he been singled out so enigmatically by name?

For reasons that must lie at the very heart of the mystery, whoever designed the tapestry has taken pains to point out that the dwarf is called Turold, for the name has been carefully lowered and placed immediately above the dwarf's head. There has been some controversy in the past as to whether the person called Turold is the dwarf or the Norman emissary standing next to him.[1] But it is important to note that the word 'Turold' stands alone and does not form part of any sentence. Five other times a person is named in the tapestry by a stand-alone name. Harold (twice), William, Robert and Eustace – all are on occasions designated in this way. In each case the name has been placed above the head of the person in question. So, despite the objections of some, there can really be little doubt that the name 'Turold' refers to the dwarf. It is possible that it refers to the knight as well; we have seen how fond the artist was of teasing us with multiple meanings, and Turold was a common name.[2] What can be stated with more probability, however, is that the dwarf is called Turold, and it is the dwarf who provides us with the most compelling mystery.

Turold is a dwarf in the strictest medical sense. Some observers have questioned this, preferring to see his apparently small stature as an attempt at perspective.[3] Strangely, however, this debate has proceeded without bringing even minimal medical evidence to bear on the issue. Not only is Turold small. His head is especially large for the rest of his body; indeed his head and neck account for almost a third of his total height. In this, he is unlike any other figure in the tapestry; more normally, the proportion of head and neck to the rest of the body is a fifth or a sixth. It is, of course, unrealistic to expect an anatomically correct portrait. But the disproportionately large head is a key symptom of a type of dwarfism known as achondroplasia. Caused by a random genetic mutation, achondroplasia is the most common form of dwarfism encountered today; its incidence cannot have been any different in medieval times. Thus *'la teste ot grosse'* 'the head is large' – was how the twelfth-century poet Béroul described a dwarf named Frocin. Achondroplastic dwarfs have normal intelligence and lifespan. They also tend to be well built. Turold's normal intelligence and upper body strength are shown by his ability to control the two horses. His pointy beard shows that he is not a child. Very short limbs, strong upper body, disproportionately large head, normal intelligence, beard – all this goes a long way towards showing that the artist of the tapestry has left us with a portrait of an adult male achondroplastic dwarf.[4]

But who can this dwarf be? Our quest to answer this question is not helped by the fact that 'Turold' was a common name. Unfortunately for us, many a proud Norman parent chose to call his or her infant son 'Turold' for it was a forceful name, carrying a *frisson* of the pagan past; it was ultimately derived from the Old Norse personal name Thorvaldr, which literally meant 'the Power of Thor'. Introduced into Normandy by invading Vikings of the ninth century, it became extremely popular in the form of Turold or Thorold (and other variant spellings). Surviving documents represent only the tip of the iceberg but they attest to twenty-eight Turolds living in Normandy before 1066.[5] The name was particularly common in the east of the duchy, but it is also found as far west as the Channel Islands. The *Domesday Book* listed fourteen invaders called Turold who by 1086 had established themselves in England.[6] The popularity of the name in medieval times has left its mark in the current surnames of Thorold in England, Torode in Guernsey and Théroude (among others) in France, and in several place names in Normandy as well. On the island of Jersey it is recalled by the district still known as Trodez and by a little lane called Rue de la Fosse Tauraude. What is more, a clutch of medieval Turolds can be found in other parts of France, and elsewhere on the continent as well.

There is, of course, no reason why a dwarf should not be someone of remarkable achievement. One very intriguing theory about Turold, advanced from time to time, is that he was the genius who designed the Bayeux Tapesry.[7] Could this be the answer to the enigma of Turold? Did he cast himself in a modest cameo role within his own masterpiece, much as Alfred Hitchcock was to do in our own times? Intriguing as this theory is, it is unlikely to be the case. We must not forget that the evidence suggests that the designer of the tapestry was English, or at least connected with St Augustine's Abbey in Canterbury. Several factors show Turold to be French and to be based in France. The tapestry's Turold is shown in Ponthieu, rather than Normandy, but we should not be overly surprised to find this typically Norman name in a region which lay just over the Norman border. That Turold is French in a broad sense is further confirmed by the fact that the back of his head is shaved. At this point in the tapestry the Normans and other Frenchmen are invariably identified by their shaven napes.

Nor does the general style of eleventh-century self-portraiture lend weight to the hypothesis that Turold was the tapestry's artist. In illuminated manuscripts the artist did sometimes depict himself in small form. But typically the diminutive artist seems to be shown in a position of deference or supplication to a divine or saintly figure, drawn much larger, or to his ecclesiastical or secular superior, similarly illustrated as large.[8] This was the whole point of the artist's minimised appearance. Turold, as we have seen, is a dwarf and his diminutive appearance is not to be confused with this modest convention. Moreover, he specifically turns his back on the others depicted in the same scene. Other examples of manuscript self-portrait show the artist in the course of his work or in possession of his tools.[9] Once again, there is nothing in the tapestry which would indicate that Turold is a draughtsman or artist. On the contrary, his costume seems to suggest that his profession is specifically something else. What that profession is turns out to be the next important clue.

Turold's unusual costume comprises a pair of short, wide breeches with a pair of 'under-trousers' beneath. In 1966 Rita Lejeune pointed out that from other evidence this curious costume can be identified as that of a '*jongleur*' – in other words, an entertainer who might be a jester, acrobat, juggler, minstrel, bard or other performer.[10] The dwarf Turold, it seems, is a *jongleur*. *Jongleurs* added a sparkle and colour to medieval life that is not often evident from the dry tomes of history.[11] Most of the surviving information comes from the centuries that followed 1066, but things cannot have been so very different in Turold's day. The repertoire of a troop of *jongleurs* was as exciting as it was various. They plied their trade in marketplaces, along the pilgrim routes and in the great baronial castles. Some would juggle with apples, balls or knives. Others sang exciting tales, long heroic sagas told from memory, or showed off their skill at rhyming and repartee. There were *jongleurs* who could imitate the sound of birds; others performed tricks with dogs, horses and other animals or recounted bawdy jokes. Many were musicians who might be heard playing viols, rotes, lyres, cymbals, tambourines or bells. In fact, *jongleurs* could be seen doing practically anything that an audience eager for distraction might pay to see. Only one aspect of a *jongleur*'s performance survives in the English word 'juggler'.

At the lower end of the social scale was the *jongleur* of the ordinary people, a poor, ragamuffin busker, who was seen at markets and fairs and at stopping points along the pilgrim routes. Then there was the *jongleur* who would travel from castle to castle, knocking on great oak doors and offering his services to the lord and lady. At the announcement of an important event, such as a noble or royal marriage or the dubbing of a knight, *jongleurs* would converge from far and wide. Sometimes eager and impoverished *jongleurs* arrived in such numbers that it was necessary to turn them away.

At the very top of the profession was the *jongleur* who had become attached to the court of a wealthy patron. The resident *jongleur* would provide the entertainment at his lord's castle and would accompany him when he visited other important persons. His standard of life would have been immeasurably better than that endured by his itinerant confrères. Indeed, he might even be rewarded with a grant of land, the most important and enduring form of wealth. The names of a few of these eleventh-century stars survive. The *Domesday Book* of 1086, for example, reveals that a lady *jongleur* (or possibly the wife of a *jongleur*) called Adelina held land in Hampshire under the patronage of Roger of Montgomery, the Earl of Shrewsbury.[12] The Domesday survey also tells us William the Conqueror employed a *jongleur* called Berdic, whom he rewarded after the Conquest with three villages in Wales.[13] But of Berdic himself nothing more is known. Nor is William the Conqueror the only person depicted in the Bayeux Tapestry known to have employed a *jongleur*. His Breton adversary Conan II (1040–66), whom we see in the embroidery escaping down a rope from the town of Dol, retained a singer-harpist named, curiously enough, Norman.[14]

As for Turold, the fact that he is named and depicted in the tapestry suggests that he was one of these more important *jongleurs*, a performer who had been patronised by a member of the nobility. And his specific association with Count Guy in the embroidery suggests that he was none other than the count's own *jongleur* and household dwarf. The tapestry shows Turold only once; his feet are firmly set on the soil of Picardy; and he is depicted in the same scene as the Count of Ponthieu. There is certainly nothing that suggests that the dwarf has, just now, travelled from Normandy, as a companion to Duke William's two knights.[15]

Count Guy of Ponthieu was a rich man and he wielded significant power within his region. Closely related to the King of France and a cousin of Count Eustace II, he comes across in the sources as greedy, callous and camp; this was, after all, the man who held the marooned Harold for a large ransom.[16] The idea that he might have employed a household dwarf as his *jongleur* certainly does not jar with other reports of his character. If we are right in taking Turold to be a court dwarf, he stands in the line of a long tradition. Dwarfs have found employment in wealthy households in many periods of history, stretching back to ancient Egypt and imperial Rome, and through to Renaissance times and beyond.[17] For the medieval period with which we are concerned the evidence for court dwarfs is not abundant but it does exist. Thus in the 1060s Bishop Gunter of Bamberg is recorded as having a dwarf named Askericus.[18] In the late twelfth century Count Henry II of Champagne, the King of Jerusalem, possessed a dwarf named Scarlet, who, in a bizarre accident, perished with him as he tried to save his lord and master from falling absent-mindedly out of a window.[19] The examples can certainly be multiplied as the ages progress. The pages of medieval literature, especially from the twelfth century onwards, are full of additional evidence of the medieval fascination for dwarfs and for the existence of court dwarfs in particular. The golden-haired harpist Cnú Deireóil of Celtic myth played music that was so sweet that his listeners invariably fell asleep. The court dwarf in the German Arthurian poem *Wigalois* (c. 1200) sang songs so wonderful that they could not be erased from memory. In Chrétien de Troyes' poem *Erec et Enide* (c. 1160) we come across a more sinister dwarf who accompanies his lord and lady on their travels, brandishing a whip and barring the way to innocent strangers. There were also stories of wild dwarfs who dwelt in forests and caves, with magical powers and great hoards of gold, even a whole race of dwarfs with their own king and queen. Wild dwarfs could look up at the night sky and read the stars as if the whole of the heavens were a vast illuminated manuscript, and when the chance beckoned they would cast magic spells on the world asleep.

There is thus sufficient evidence, over an extended period, for the medieval fascination with dwarfs and we should not to be surprised if Turold is a *jongleur* attached to the noble household of Count Guy of Ponthieu. This certainly remains no more than an implication from what we see in the tapestry; no written evidence supporting it survives. But it seems an entirely reasonable hypothesis on the basis of which to continue our investigation. Let us now consider what kind of *jongleur* Turold might have been. Some churchmen held *jongleurs* in very low esteem, regarding them as typically blasphemous, vulgar and drunk. Honorius of Autun (c. 1080–c. 1117) fulminated that they were all the servants of Satan and would end up in hell. The image of a *jongleur* in hell, in the process of having his tongue torn out by devils, can be seen above the west door of the early twelfth-century church at Conques in central France. In the same vein, Orderic Vitalis, writing around the 1130s, tells the story of a *jongleur* who, having made an irreverent joke about certain holy relics, was said to have been struck dead by lightning that very night.[20]

Our Turold was surely no disreputable fellow like this. He was a high-class *jongleur*. His name has been embroidered proudly in the company of kings and nobles. There were some high-minded clerics who were prepared to tolerate the art of the *jongleur*, provided that it was put to some useful purpose.

Jongleurs could, after all, sing to the people about edifying or uplifting subjects and in a language they could understand. It did not have to be all scandalous songs or idle tricks and dirty jokes. They could sing the lives of saints and moral fables or the famous heroic tales of feudal and Christian valour known as *chansons de geste*. Above all else, it is in this last role, as performers, and sometimes authors, of *chansons de geste* that *jongleurs* are nowadays best remembered. *Chansons de geste* were the epic poems of Old French literature. They were tales of exciting and heroic deeds, usually set in or around the age of Charlemagne, sung by a *jongleur* to an audience of lords and courtiers. The great popularity of *chansons de geste* is testified by the fact that more than 100 survive, dating from the latter part of the eleventh century to the first half of the fourteenth. So is this how we should see Turold? As a performer, and perhaps author, of *chansons de geste*? Interestingly enough, *Gormont et Isembart*, the very earliest *chanson de geste* that survives, albeit in fragmentary form, is known to come from Ponthieu. The monk Hariulf, writing in the 1080s at the monastery of Saint-Riquier, just outside Count Guy's capital of Abbeville, tells us that the story of *Gormont et Isembart* was 'remembered and sung every day by the people of the land'.[21] But there is something more than this, something that is much more intriguing. The very greatest of all the *chansons de geste* is the *Chanson de Roland* (the *Song of Roland*) and it is familiar, if only by name, to every French schoolchild. It is the first great work of French literature, a monumental celebration of Charlemagne and his kin. It occupies a position in French literary history equivalent to the English *Beowulf* and it may be counted among the world's classics. Scholars have long argued over the authorship, origin and date of the *Roland*. Mystery surrounds these issues. But in the very last of the 4,002 lines of the earliest extant version of the *Chanson de Roland*, preserved in the twelfth-century Anglo-Norman manuscript kept in the Bodleian Library in Oxford, we read the following extraordinary clue:

> *Ci falt la geste que Turoldus declinet*
> Here ends the story which Turold relates[22]

At once we must remember that Turold was a very common name. Moreover, the precise meaning of line 4002 of the *Chanson de Roland*, and in particular the role of 'Turoldus', has remained frustratingly obscure; the Turold mentioned could have been the author of the poem, the performer of the poem, the author of its source material or even the twelfth-century copyist who made the only surviving copy of this version of the tale.[23] We are in a grey area; but grey as it is, the possibility is truly intriguing. It is a possibility that is even more intriguing now that we have seen that the dwarf is probably a *jongleur* and that the tapestry brings to the fore Count Eustace II of Boulogne, the man who had the richest blood of Charlemagne running through his veins and who may even have been the patron of the tapestry itself. Could it be that the dwarf in the tapestry is the forgotten genius who wrote and composed the *Chanson de Roland*? Was this his claim to fame?

The *Chanson de Roland* is a masterpiece which was written, so far as historians have deduced, by a Frenchman, from somewhere in the north of what we now call France, or possibly conquered England, during the latter part of the eleventh century. But though its author may justly be called the founding father of French literature, his identity has always remained a mystery. Apart from his possible name, Turold, nothing is known of him.

As a topic of study, the *Chanson de Roland* is matched only by the Bayeux Tapestry in terms of the vast number of scholarly books and articles that medievalists have devoted to it. Yet despite this intense interest, the theory that the two Turolds are identical persons has only very rarely been suggested, and nowadays it is not mentioned at all. As Gerard Moignet wrote in 1972, scholars have 'abandoned all hope of finding the author of the *Chanson de Roland* [in the Bayeux Tapestry]'.[24] In all this, however, the intriguing fact that the dwarf in the Bayeux Tapestry seems to be a *jongleur* has not widely been noted and it has never been truly brought to bear on the issue.

The story of the *Chanson de Roland*, which is very loosely based on fact, is set in the year 778, during the age of Charlemagne. The manner in which the poem was written or evolved has long been a subject of debate; it probably existed in a variety of earlier forms, now lost, before being reworked in the eleventh century by a single poet for new times and for a new audience. It tells of how the traitor Ganelon betrayed the rearguard of Charlemagne's army to the Muslim Saracens of Spain. As a result Roland (Charlemagne's nephew) and many others, including his companion Olivier and the warrior Archbishop Turpin, come under a devastating attack as they return to France through the Pyrenean pass of Roncevaux. Under Roland's leadership they fight long and heroically. Archbishop Turpin, Olivier and Roland all stand out for their fighting prowess but inevitably they all perish. In due course, however, Charlemagne, aided by God, exacts revenge against the Saracens, swiftly in one battle and then again on a vast scale as the forces of Islam and Christianity face each other in a further epic conflict.[25] The traitor Ganelon is finally brought to justice and executed for his crime.

In the figure of Roland medieval Europe found one of its

greatest feudal and Christian heroes. He was the epitome of valour, battling for his God and his king, and dying a heroic death. The fame of the poem quickly spread. Versions of it were to be composed in High German, Old Norse, Welsh, Dutch and Middle English. In the fourteenth century both Dante and Chaucer knew the story. In Renaissance Italy stories of Roland continued to inspire Boiardo and Ariosto. Images of Roland and his companion Olivier may be found in art and sculpture from the twelfth century onwards and Roland's horn, which, out of his sense of honour, he refuses to blow to summon help, attained iconic status.

There is, of course, much in the poem that the modern reader finds objectionable; the poet's religiosity is ignorant, racist and violent. But in truth he could not have been otherwise, given where and when he lived. The opposition he sets up between the two great companions-in-arms, the brave but reckless Roland and the wise and cautious Olivier, still succeeds in engaging the reader and in stimulating debate. The poet is also a master at milking the tension. He can dramatically hold up the action, describing the same knife-edge moment in succeeding stanzas with subtly different words. If he was a performer, it shows; he knew how to keep his audience on edge. The scene that recounts Roland's death, in particular, has been described as one of the greatest in world literature.

There are several intriguing parallels between the respective stories told by *Chanson de Roland* and the Bayeux Tapestry. Many historians have noted in passing that the artist of the tapestry may well have known the *Chanson de Roland* and that he was perhaps consciously echoing themes found in the poem.[26] Harold, for example, reminds us of the traitor Ganelon: both are brothers-in-law of their sovereign; both undertake a dangerous mission in a foreign land; both are brave and noble opponents who are brought down as a result of breaking the bonds of feudal duty; and the penalty of death is the price of their sin, for them and their kinsmen.

Most impressive, however, is the parallel that can be drawn between the fighting Archbishop Turpin and Bishop Odo of Bayeux. Alone among contemporary accounts the tapestry places Odo in the thick of the fighting. It is true that the embroidered Odo carries a mace, not a lance or sword, apparently reflecting a prohibition against those in holy orders shedding blood. The legendary Turpin is a hardened warrior who has no such inhibition. Turpin also dies in battle, a fate certainly not shared by Odo. But the image of the swashbuckling cleric, bravely taking part in the midst of a 'holy' battle, is strikingly shared between the tapestry and the *Chanson*. There is a passage in the *Chanson de Roland* that may even have been the direct inspiration for what we see in the embroidery. Surrounded by the enemy, and in the thick of battle, Roland's knights begin to panic and they call upon Roland and Olivier to protect them. Turpin, riding amongst them, steels their resolve:

> Lord barons, do not indulge in base thoughts;
> In God's name I beg you not to flee,
> So that no man of worth can sing a shameful song.
> It is far better for us to die fighting.[27]

The designer of the tapestry sought to flatter Bishop Odo in a variety of ways and it is more than possible that he was here deliberately fawning to him by implying that he was a second Archbishop Turpin [scene 54; plate 10]. At the same time, however, he carefully avoided any implication that Odo was directly involved in the slaughter. The point of comparison was carefully chosen.

If Ganelon is Harold and Odo Turpin, who in the embroidered story is the Emperor Charlemagne and who is Roland? Here the messages seem to be mixed. The leader of the invasion is Duke William and it might seem that he should naturally have the starring role and enjoy the implication of being another Charlemagne. Yet the presence of Count Eustace, the emperor's noble descendant, suggests on the contrary that he is the one who stands for the Carolingian bloodline, perhaps Charlemagne and Roland all rolled into one. On this account, William's counterpart in the poem would be a merely secondary figure, the 'Norman' vassal of Charlemagne who is anachronistically identified in the poem as Duke Richard the Old (who was in reality Duke William's great-grandfather). If these parallels with the *Chanson de Roland* are really there, as they seem to be, we have further evidence that the artist of the tapestry, although working in England and in an English genre, was actually French-speaking.[28] More than that, we can now well understand that the artist might wish to reinforce the parallels with the story of Roland by a passing depiction of the author of the poem itself, in Ponthieu and in the presence of Count Guy, where he would normally be found.

The place of origin of the *Chanson de Roland* has long been debated. On the basis that the twelfth-century Oxford manuscript was copied out in the Anglo-Norman dialect of its day, some have argued that it is a Norman work.[29] Others, however, see the original poem as emanating from somewhere else in northern France, perhaps the area around Paris known as the Ile-de-France, or in Champagne, Anjou or Lorraine.[30] Chartres, too, has been suggested.[31] That it may have been written in Ponthieu is a novel suggestion; but the possibility should not be dismissed out of hand. Count Guy of Ponthieu was a great-great-grandson in the male line of Hugh Capet, the French king who finally ended the rule of the Carolingians in 987. Hugh Capet himself, however, was an indirect kinsman of Carolingian lineage and Guy could presumably trace a descent from the emperor in several female lines. Moreover the links in the region with the age of Charlemagne were as strong as they were anywhere else. It was here that Charlemagne is said to have placed his son-in-law Angilbert (740–814) in control of the region. Angilbert was also one of the most celebrated former abbots of the monastery of Saint-Riquier, the chief monastic centre of Ponthieu.[32] The distinction in the poem between the 'French' and 'Norman' divisions of Charlemagne's army seems to mirror the very same distinction made in the *Carmen de Hastingae Proelio* when it describes Duke William's invasion force, where the 'French' are (or include) the men of Ponthieu and Boulogne. The *Chanson de Roland* thus appears to reflect sentiments of 'French' identity that are very similar to those expressed in the *Carmen*. On the other hand, the notion that the *Chanson de Roland* is a Norman work is undermined by the fact that it is always the French who are given the greater prestige; the 'Normans' are allotted a merely secondary role and 'Normandy' is merely one of a number of subsidiary territories ruled over by the true 'Frenchman' Charlemagne.[33] The poem was probably written for a wider audience than just one French region, and no place in Ponthieu is mentioned in the text, but for political, historical and genealogical reasons Ponthieu, or one of its northern French neighbours, can hardly be ruled out as its place of composition or adaptation.

Nor is it impossible that the *Roland* is more or less contemporary with the Bayeux Tapestry, that is to say probably dating from the period between 1066 and about 1080 and perhaps more specifically from the early to mid-1070s. Various arguments have been advanced in favour of the *Roland* being significantly later in date than the tapestry, but none is persuasive.[34] While the thrust of the *Chanson de Roland* puts the 'Normans' very much in the shade of the 'French', there are nevertheless some oblique references to Duke William's recent conquest of England. Thus it is mentioned that Charlemagne 'crossed the salty sea to England and won the poll-tax for Rome's own use' and that 'England became his domain'.[35] Neither statement is true of Charlemagne but both are true of William the Conqueror. For this reason, if nothing else, the poem in its surviving form must date from after 1066. The widespread notion that the *Chanson de Roland* must, of necessity, have been written after a battle in Spain in 1086 (the Battle of Zalaca) is based on a series of false assumptions.[36] Arguably, so is the notion that the *Roland* reflects the time of the First Crusade (post 1096); there is no reference at all, either implicit or explicit, to the Crusade in the East. What the *Roland* reflects is rather the climate of opinion that made the First Crusade possible. This was a time, some twenty or so years earlier, when contingents of French knights were already fighting against the Muslims in Spain, just as we find them in the *Roland*. Moreover, there may well be a number of oblique references in the *Roland* to contemporary events in 1071 or 1072, forming a cluster of allusions that suggests that the poet was writing not long afterwards.[37] There is also no reference to the Norman conquest of Sicily, although the Norman successes in Calabria and Apulia are implicitly referred to. This suggests that the poet was writing before the conquest of Sicily was complete in 1091, and probably before it was substantially complete in the late 1070s. One place in Sicily is mentioned in passing by the poet – Palermo.[38] Palermo was captured by the Normans in January 1072. For all these reasons a date for the composition or adaptation of the work in the early 1070s seems to be entirely plausible.

Such general considerations are hardly much of an advance on the matter. What we need is some more precise clue that the *Chanson de Roland* was composed or at least adapted by a poet working in Ponthieu. There is at least one such clue. Among several holy relics mentioned by the poet, one stands out in particular. So important is it that Charlemagne (Charles) has it embedded in the pommel of his sword:

> We could speak for a long time about the lance
> With which our Lord was wounded on the cross.
> Charles has its point, thanks be to God,
> Which he has mounted in his golden pommel.[39]

The reference here is to the lance of the Roman centurion that pierced the side of Jesus as he lay hanging on the cross.[40] It is Charlemagne's ownership, 'thanks be to God', of the tip of the Holy Lance that gives his soldiers their assured sense of destiny, that they have a joyous and heavenly future which their unquestioned faith held was open to them as a result of the suffering and death of Jesus on the cross. The point of the Holy Lance is embedded in the sword of Charlemagne; the sword is thus named *Joyeuse*, 'the Joyful'; and it is from the name of the sword *Joyeuse* that seems to have been taken the battle cry that the poet puts into the mouths of Charlemagne's knights, *Monjoie*, 'My Joy'. The Holy Lance thus stands at the centre of a group of related concepts of great mystical significance to the poet.[41] And it turns out to be of the greatest interest in our quest to link the tapestry's Turold with the authorship of the poem. We must, therefore, narrow our focus on to this question.

The *Chanson de Roland* tells us that the point of the Holy Lance belonged to Charlemagne. The only place in the whole of eleventh-century France where a similar story has been found is the abbey of Saint-Riquier, the chief monastic centre of Ponthieu. The abbey of Saint-Riquier, it will be recalled, lies only a few miles from Count Guy's capital of Abbeville, in other words, only a short distance from where the dwarf-*jongleur* Turold would have composed and sung his songs. The Saint-Riquier story is given to us by Hariulf, the monk who completed his chronicle of Saint-Riquier in large part by 1088. Hariulf's interest in the matter arose because the precious lancepoint had, for several decades during the ninth century, been a prized possession of his own abbey. He tells us that Louis the Pious, son and successor to Charlemagne, gave the abbey a large number of holy relics, the most precious of which was 'the point of the lance with which a soldier pierced the side of that divine Master who died for our salvation (it is this wound which gives rise to the sacraments of the church)'.[42]

Hariulf did not know how the biblical lancepoint had come into Louis' possession. He merely reported that 'it is said' that Louis had acquired this relic on a visit to Constantinople. However, no such visit is known, and a later account states that Charlemagne himself had given the relic to the abbey of Saint-Riquier. Within some fifty years or so, however, the abbey of Saint-Riquier lost it. Around the year 880, under imminent danger of Viking pillage, it was moved for safe keeping to the town of Sens and it was never returned and has subsequently disappeared.[43]

Despite this relic being associated by Hariulf with Charle-

1 Turold

2 The meeting between
Duke William and
Earl Harold

3 'Where a priest
and Ælfgyva'

4 Mont-Saint-Michel and the crossing of the sands

5 Harold's oath to Duke William

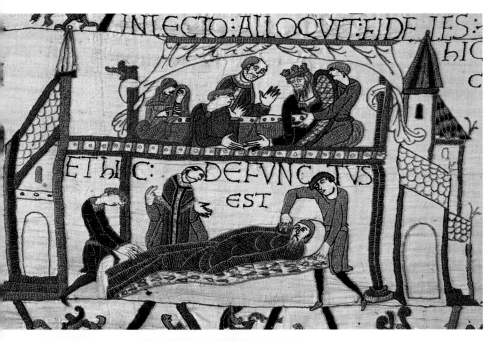

6 King Edward's
last bequest

7 Bishop Odo of Bayeux
presides over a banquet

8 Wadard

9 Vital

10 Bishop Odo encourages the young knights at the Battle of Hastings

11 Count Eustace II of Boulogne points out Duke William

12 The death of King Harold

magne's son Louis, rather than directly with the emperor, Hariulf's story remains of the greatest interest in our quest. There is no other contemporary report which so closely parallels what we read in the *Roland*. Both speak specifically of the point of the Holy Lance. Both say that the family of Charlemagne owned it. In the words of one scholar who investigated the matter in detail, the tradition found at Saint-Riquier and the similar story in the poem 'can hardly be unrelated'.[44] From this it seems distinctly possible that the poet of the *Chanson de Roland* was working within earshot of the traditions preserved at the abbey of Saint-Riquier and thus that he might well have been working in Abbeville as Count Guy of Ponthieu's *jongleur*.

There is one further piece of evidence. In 1982 Professor D. D. R. Owen published an article in which he showed that more than a dozen parallels and similarities can be identified between the famous Latin poem about the Battle of Hastings, *Carmen de Hastingae Proelio*, and the French *Chanson de Roland*.[45] Owen argued that these parallels strongly suggest that there is some direct relationship between the Latin and the French poems. He concluded that the poet of the *Carmen* was deeply familiar with the vernacular *Roland*, and that he drew upon it, 'deftly garnishing the historical facts as he had received them with epic turns of phrase, accentuating oppositions, adding picturesque touches to both characters and events'. Moreover, it would appear that the version of the *Roland* with which the *Carmen*-poet was familiar was more or less the one which has been transmitted down to us.

This conclusion is extremely important, but its importance has been obscured. At the time when Owen published his article it was widely considered that the *Carmen* was a twelfth-century work and that it could not have been written by Bishop

Guy of Amiens. But Guy's authorship of the poem has now been firmly re-established.[46] So if Owen is right that the author of the *Carmen* knew and used the *Roland*, then the *Chanson de Roland* must have been composed, in a form not dissimilar to what we know today, before Guy died, which was in either 1074 or 1075.[47] This is a dating remarkably consistent with what has been proposed above. Furthermore, if Bishop Guy was familiar with the *Chanson de Roland*, at a time so close to its presumed date of composition, the two poems could well have originated in broadly the same milieu. This cannot be proved; the *Chanson de Roland* might quickly have become popular. But the influence of the *Chanson de Roland* on Bishop Guy would be all the more understandable if he were working not far from where the *Roland* was composed. We know that when Guy wrote the *Carmen* he was the Bishop of Amiens. His episcopal seat lay only two dozen miles along the River Somme from Abbeville, where his nephew Count Guy ruled over Ponthieu. In his youth Bishop Guy had even been a student at Saint-Riquier. Once again our hypothesis that the *Chanson de Roland* might well have been composed in the region of Abbeville and Saint-Riquier, and by none other than Turold, Count Guy of Ponthieu's household *jongleur*, is remarkably consistent with the evidence. It is consistent, too, with the theory that Count Eustace II of Boulogne was the patron of the Bayeux Tapestry for it was Eustace, the noble heir of Charlemagne, who stood to gain most in prestige from the tapestry's implicit allusions to the *Chanson de Roland* and its talented author Turold.

The discussion in this chapter has ranged over a number of matters; no doubt a great deal more could be said. It would certainly be remarkable if we have an embroidered portrait of the author of the first great work of French literature. If that were true, the whole magnificent edifice – from Molière to Flaubert, from Corneille to Hugo, and all the other luminaries as well – would rest on the shoulders of this enigmatic dwarf. That there is considerable scope for caution is clear. The clues are slender; much mystery remains. But the possibility that the two Turolds are identical is distinctly more interesting than has hitherto been supposed.

19

The Scandal of Ælfgyva

The lady named as Ælfgyva in the Bayeux Tapestry intrigues and teases us in many ways [scene 17; plate 3]. She is clearly meant to be a focus of our attention. There are only three women depicted in the whole of the main frieze; by contrast, some 600 men strut and saunter across the embroidered stage. Out of the three women, Ælfgyva is the only one who is given a name and it is a name that was popular in the very highest echelons of Anglo-Saxon society. Who this Ælfgyva was and what she is doing in the tapestry are questions which have long baffled observers. With its hint of sex and scandal the Ælfgyva scene remains one of the most mysterious in the whole work.

The scene seems like a curious interjection into the flow of the story, with no obvious link to what occurs before or after. During his enforced stay in Normandy, Harold has been brought to Duke William's palace, probably at Rouen. Harold is seen in earnest discussion with William: we have seen how the artist is probably illustrating his attempt to negotiate the release of his brother Wulfnoth. Then follows Ælfgyva's scene.

She is shown being touched, perhaps stroked, on the cheek by a priest; and a bizarre naked figure in the lower border, gesturing up Ælfgyva's skirt, lewdly appears to mimic the action of the priest. Immediately after this scene, the story moves on. Harold and William depart together in order to campaign in Brittany; they are soon seen crossing the flat sands near Mont-Saint-Michel into Breton territory. The inscription above the Ælfgyva scene is enigmatically short. All it says is UBI UNUS CLERICUS ET ÆLFGYVA (Where a certain cleric and Ælfgyva). Dot, dot, dot, one can almost hear.

What is going on? Who is Ælfgyva? Who is the priest? Does the absence of a verb in the inscription hint at some sexual scandal, as we might suppose from the lewd figure in the lower border? Ælfgyva's identity and her role in the story have been given a great deal of attention by scholars, but there has been little agreement; much mystery remains. For one thing, the meaning of the priest's gesture is disputed. For another, there was no shortage of well-born ladies named Ælfgyva.

The name Ælfgyva (elf-gift) was the name of a family saint in the West Saxon royal dynasty. St Elfgiva, as she is also spelt, died in 944, having piously retired to an abbey. 'She was,' wrote William of Malmesbury in the 1120s, 'a saintly person to whom God granted many revelations.'[1] This lady was the wife of King Edmund of England and the mother of Kings Edwy and Edgar; and through her grandson, Æthelred the Unready, she was a great-grandmother of Edward the Confessor. A name with such connections was bound to appeal, and by the eleventh century it was a common name in the best circles of Anglo-Saxon England.

Many Ælfgyvas/Ælfgifus (the spelling is used interchangeably) have, over the years, been proposed as the tapestry's lady. In the very highest echelons of Anglo-Saxon society we know of three Ælfgyvas/Ælfgifus in particular; each held the status of a queen in the generation before 1066.[2]

A lady named Ælfgifu was the first wife of Edward the Confessor's father Æthelred the Unready. From her union with Æthelred descended the once-exiled and now returned branch of the Anglo-Saxon royal family represented in 1066 by Edgar Ætheling. Edgar's hereditary claim to the throne was strong. Could his great-grandmother Ælfgifu, who had died at the dawn of the millennium, be the lady in the tapestry? Is, perhaps, some point being made detrimental to Edgar's claim to the throne?

When this first Ælfgifu died, King Æthelred married Emma, the daughter of Duke Richard I of Normandy. Upon her marriage to Æthelred, Emma of Normandy abandoned her name of birth and obligingly took the same name as her husband's first wife, Ælfgifu. Their children were Edward, Alfred and Godgifu; and Edward, of course, was later to reign as Edward the Confessor. Æthelred died in 1016. Following the Danish conquest of England, and the flight of her children by Æthelred to Normandy, Ælfgifu-Emma retained her position as queen by marrying the new all-powerful King Canute. The vast empire of her Danish husband included at its height England, Denmark and Norway. She now despised Æthelred. By Canute, she had a son Harthacanute and a daughter Gunnhildr; Harthacanute would reign as king of Denmark (1035–42) and as king of England (1040–42). Ælfgifu-Emma's Norman parentage also provided the tenuous blood link that gave William the Conqueror part of his justification for invading the country in 1066; she was William's great-aunt. In these ways, Ælfgifu-Emma was a pivotal person in the great struggles for England, both Scandinavian and Norman, that marked the eleventh century.

When Ælfgifu-Emma married Canute in 1017 she found that he already had an English mistress, a mistress, moreover, who had already borne him two sons. The mistress turned out to be a strong-minded lady intent on following her own agenda. Her name – could it be anything else? – was Ælfgifu. 'The other Ælfgifu' is how the *Anglo-Saxon Chronicle* describes her. But in modern history books Canute's mistress is most commonly called Ælfgifu of Northampton. In the circumstances, Ælfgifu of Northampton and Emma were at odds from the start. Indeed, the next twenty-five years of English, Danish and Norwegian history were to be profoundly affected by the personal jealousy and bitter rivalry that existed between these two able and ambitious women. Ælfgifu of Northampton succeeded in placing one of her sons by Canute on the English throne, Harold Harefoot (king, 1037–40); and she was also the mother of Sveyn 'Alfifasson', who ruled as king of Norway under her own regency between 1030 and 1035. She died at some point after 1040, although exactly when is not known. Could she be the eponymous lady depicted in the Bayeux Tapestry?

Most commentators take sexual scandal to be the point of the Ælfgyva scene. Some, however, have argued that what is being represented is not a sexual scandal at all. We learn from William of Poitiers that in 1064/5 one of the undertakings made, and later repudiated, by the captive Harold was to marry one of Duke William's daughters (the fiancée may have been called either Agatha or Adelaide).[3] It has been suggested that the lady named as Ælfgyva in the tapestry is in fact this Norman lady; and that what we see is some ceremony of betrothal. Thus, according to this theory, there is no scandal; it is said that the priest is actually *placing a veil* over the bride-to-be's head, this apparently being part of the formalities of engagement.[4] (Alternatively, it is said that the priest is *removing* her veil, which, according to another theory, was what was involved in the formalities of engagement).[5] William's daughter is called by the English name Ælfgyva because, so the theory goes, she would have taken that name upon her marriage to Harold – just as her great-great-aunt Emma had done when she adopted the English name Ælfgifu in 1002 upon her own marriage to King Æthelred the Unready. This theory has the great advantage of allowing us to place the Ælfgyva scene not only in Rouen, but also neatly within the thread of the story line. It is suggested that in the immediately preceding panel Harold and William are meant to be discussing the planned marriage. The formal indication of betrothal thus follows; and there would otherwise be no mention of Harold's betrothal.

There are nonetheless considerable difficulties with this theory. For one thing, it is a matter of conjecture that William's daughter would have taken the name Ælfgyva on her marriage; Harold repudiated the engagement and it never took place. And can we really take the designer of the tapestry, working most probably in the 1070s, as referring to the king's very daughter by a purely hypothetical name, a name by which she was not known in the 1070s and indeed which she had never borne and which she would only have taken had the thoroughly discredited marriage to Harold taken place? For another thing, the marriage was deferred in 1064/5 because the girl in question was a mere child; but the lady we see in the tapestry is clearly an adult.

Most problematic of all, however, is the allusion to scandal. For it is very hard not to regard the Ælfgyva scene, with its teasingly incomplete inscription, as relating in some way to a sexual scandal. The naked figure in the lower border, gesturing up Ælfgyva's skirt, explicitly seems to mimic the action of the priest; and there is another partially clothed figure, a workman wielding a tool, in the immediately preceding lower compartment. This is not, it has to be said, the way one would naturally expect a royal princess, one still living and unmarried, and a half-niece of Bishop Odo, to be portrayed in the embroidery. Even if, as some would implausibly argue, the figure in the lower border is purely 'decorative', and nothing to do with the scene above, to juxtapose such lewd imagery with a portrait of the king's daughter would have been unbelievably negligent on the part of the designer. The contrasting buildings in which Ælfgyva stands and from which the priest strides are open to similar sexual innuendo.

A not dissimilar explanation of the Ælfgyva scene is that the eponymous lady is the sister of Harold whom Eadmer tells us (without giving her a name) was to be engaged to one of William's nobles.[6] This was part of the agreement Harold was constrained to enter into in order to secure his release from Normandy. Harold may have had a sister named Ælfgyfu; she is mentioned in the Domesday Book.[7] This Ælfgyfu's existence is otherwise unattested, and it is possible that the Domesday entry is a scribal error, but assuming she did indeed exist, she may be the sister of Harold whom Eadmer referred to and we have the beginnings, at least, of a more promising explanation. Given the tapestry's close association with Eadmer's account of Harold's visit to Normandy it cannot be without interest that the story of the betrothal of Harold's sister should also come from Eadmer. The appearance of Ælfgyva where we see her in the embroidery, just after Harold and William's discussions, is consistent with this explanation, although it is unlikely that she was actually in Normandy at the time. Thus there may just be an allusion in this scene to Harold's promise to wed his sister to a Norman noble; but even if true it cannot be the entire explanation. We have noted on many occasions the artist's ingenuity at teasing his audience with multiple meanings. Invariably, however, he has one underlying meaning which he wishes to convey. Failure to realise this has long bedevilled research into the Bayeux Tapestry; historians have too often assumed that there can only be one meaning and have thus been misled on to false trails by one of the more superficial interpretations. What suggests that the Ælfgyva scene has some further, deeper meaning is the sexual innuendo.

The gesture of the priest, using a single open hand, does not obviously amount to the placing or arranging, or even the removing, of a veil. On the contrary, the closest, if somewhat later, parallels in medieval art once again give the scene an erotic import. 'The face-fondling gesture,' writes J. Bard McNulty, 'was for centuries charged with sexual meaning. It continued to be used in the art of later centuries, where it was sometimes combined with gestures even more sexually explicit.'[8] The earliest example of such a gesture quoted by scholars is a sculptured scene of Salome dancing before Herod from a twelfth-century capital which originally decorated the church of Saint-Etienne in Toulouse (the capital is now to be found in the Musée des Augustins, Toulouse). Overall, the evidence for the view that the Ælfgyva scene relates to a sexual scandal appears to be pretty compelling.

Were there any important women named Ælfgyva/Ælfgifu who were known, or rumoured, to have had some scandalous involvement with a priest? Intriguingly, rumours of this nature circulated at various times about two of the Ælfgifus already mentioned: Canute's wife Ælfgifu-Emma (whom we shall henceforth refer to as Emma) and her bitter rival for her husband's affections, 'the other Ælfgifu', she of Northampton.

Both were long dead in 1064/5. If either of them is the tapestry's Ælfgyva we will be forced to conclude that the designer has used a 'flashback' to an earlier event in order to make some point about the present. The existence of rumours of clerical impropriety involving not one but two persons named Ælfgifu cannot fail to interest us.

According to a curious story that was circulating in the fourteenth century, the widowed Emma, Canute's former queen and mother of Edward the Confessor by her earlier marriage, was accused in 1043 or 1050 (the accounts differ) of a liaison of particularly scandalous proportions.[9] In short, she was supposed to have been on much more friendly terms than she ought to have been with one of England's foremost ecclesiastics, Ælfwine of Winchester. At first King Edward believed the stories, but protesting her innocence, and that of the bishop, Emma successfully endured a trial by ordeal by walking unscathed across nine red-hot ploughshares (the horizontal cutting blade of the plough). A penitent Edward begged forgiveness; but he was nonetheless beaten with a rod (so the fourteenth-century story goes) by both his mother and Bishop Ælfwine. Could it be that the tapestry's Ælfgyva scene is an allusion to this late-reported scandal involving Emma and the Bishop of Winchester?

The story is found in no contemporary source. It has every appearance of being purely legendary. Its relationship with known events is confused and no modern historian takes it seriously.[10] It also differs in key respects from what we see in the tapestry. For one thing, the alleged affair was with a bishop. If the Ælfgyva scene concerned Emma and an episcopal lover, the Tapestry would surely have called the tonsured character a bishop, 'UNUS EPISCOPUS', not simply a cleric, 'UNUS CLERICUS'. For another, according to the story,

Emma was widely believed to have proved her innocence by enduring hot iron: in other words by the miraculous intervention of God; and to the medieval mind that was the highest and most indisputable indication of the purest innocence. That the scandal was raised again in the 1070s by the artist of the Bayeux Tapestry, if indeed it was ever raised at all, seems pretty inconceivable. It is also hard to find a reason why Emma should be called out as a subject of special interest at this point in the Bayeux Tapestry. We must therefore turn to the story of scandal that involved her rival and namesake Ælfgifu of Northampton, Canute's mistress. To do so it is necessary to enter the turbulent world that threw these two forceful woman into bitter rivalry.[11]

At the tail-end of the tenth century successive waves of Danish attack and pillage had brought the country almost to its knees. King Æthelred was proving himself an ineffectual ruler, helpless to resist the Vikings. His attempts to buy them off only encouraged them to return; and in the north and east they had long settled in large numbers. It was into this violent world that Ælfgifu of Northampton was born. Her family were important landholders in Northamptonshire, coming from English or Anglo-Danish stock. In these dark and lawless days suspicion and treason were rife and violence was never far away. In 1006 Ælfgifu's father, Ælthelm, was tricked and murdered while hunting and around the same time her brothers Ufegeat and Wulfheah were blinded, apparently on King Æthelred's orders. The situation for the native dynasty worsened until at last it became untenable. In 1013 Swein Fork-Beard, the King of Denmark, invaded at the head of his own army and within a year he had conquered the whole of England. Æthelred and most of his family were forced to flee to exile in Normandy, the land of his wife Emma. Swein's sudden death on 3 February 1014 provided only a temporary respite from the Danish onslaught. Both Æthelred and Edmund Ironside, his son and heir, died in short succession of each other in 1016. Swein's son Canute, already in possession of much of the country and now without any serious rival in England, was accepted as undisputed king. Edmund's own sons narrowly escaped death by fleeing to the Hungarian exile from which one of them, Edward the Exile, was to return reluctantly with his young family in 1057.

At some time before 1016, and perhaps as early as 1013, Canute must have been introduced to Ælfgifu of Northampton and they became lovers. What we know of Ælfgifu indicates that she was probably a beautiful and certainly a manipulative young woman. One story, which may be fanciful, tells us that she was also a lover of Olaf, afterwards the king and saint of Norway, during one of his reputed stints as a fighter in England. The story goes on to say that Ælfgifu's affair with Canute was the main cause of the enmity that subsequently arose between Canute and Olaf. What is known with greater certainty is that during her affair with Canute two sons were born, Harold, nicknamed Harefoot, and Swein. Canute and Ælfgifu of Northampton never married; contemporaries euphemistically referred to their union as 'Danish' in style (*more danico*). Ælfgifu may have hoped that Canute would one day marry her but she must have been aware that this sort of arrangement was far from uncommon. It held out the advantage to Canute of allowing him to satisfy his amorous appetites with a prominent English beauty, whilst leaving open the option of negotiating a diplomatic marriage for reasons of state later.

The opportunity for such a marriage soon arose. In July 1017 Emma coldly abandoned her exiled sons in Normandy and crossed the Channel to accept Canute's hand in marriage.

The union had advantages for both sides. For Emma, the marriage to the Danish conqueror of her late husband's land meant that she could regain her high position as queen of England, and all the wealth, power and pomp that went with it. She had, moreover, grown to despise Æthelred and she no doubt hoped that the children she had borne him would with the new turn of events fade into insignificance. In a work of tendentious history which was written at her request in the early 1040s – the *Encomium Emmae Reginae* – the marriage to Æthelred is never mentioned; indeed it is implied that Edward and Alfred were the sons of Canute. For Canute the marriage was particularly useful in securing the goodwill of Emma's brother, Duke Richard II of Normandy, at a time when the exiles might have been championed by the Normans and thereby posed a threat to the new Danish rule.

A more immediate threat to Emma's position was the existence in England of the two bastard sons of Ælfgifu of Northampton. As part of her agreement to marry Canute, Emma insisted on an undertaking by him that the throne of England should pass to their progeny alone. By this requirement she sought to exclude Ælfgifu's bastards as well as her own children by Æthelred. In due course, Emma and Canute did have a son, Harthacanute by name, who was born in 1018. The chances of Ælfgifu of Northampton's boys ever inheriting the throne seemed to diminish still further when in succeeding years rumours were spread that they were not Canute's children at all – or even Ælfgifu of Northampton's. This sounds rather suspiciously like malicious gossip put about by a jealous wife in order to undermine the position of her husband's former lover and that of his bastards; but we are hardly in a position to judge the truth of the matter today. Whether true or not, these rumours about Ælfgifu of Northampton and her sons were widely reported and are of the highest interest in our investigation.

In the *Encomium Emmae Reginae* the allegation is made that Harold Harefoot, rather than being Ælfgifu of Northampton's child, was actually the son of a servant girl who, as a newborn baby, had been smuggled into Ælfgifu's bedchamber so that he could be passed off as a child of her union with Canute. The rumour about Harold Harefoot's lowly parentage was evidently widespread; it also found its way into three versions of the *Anglo-Saxon Chronicle*, compiled in different parts of the country, for the year 1035. In the next century the rumours were repeated in more detail by the apparently well-informed chronicler John of Worcester. Here, most interestingly, is what John of Worcester says of the other bastard, Swein: 'Several asserted that Swein was not the son of the king and that same Ælfgifu, but that Ælfgifu wanted to have a son by the king, and could not, and therefore ordered the new-born child of some priest's concubine to be brought to her, and made the King believe that she had borne him a son.'

And of Harold Harefoot he wrote this: 'Harold claimed to be the son of King Canute by Ælfgifu of Northampton, but that is quite untrue, for some say that he was the son of a certain *sutor* [a "cobbler" or "workman"], but that Ælfgifu acted in the same way as she had done with Swein. But because the matter is open to doubt, we have been unable to make a firm statement of the parentage of either.'[12]

Swein, then, is supposed to have been the son of a fornicating priest; Harefoot the offspring of a cobbler or other workman. It was only in 1980 that the American historian J. Bard McNulty drew full attention to the relevance of these stories to the Bayeux Tapestry, arguing that the Ælfgyva in the tapestry was Ælfgifu of Northampton.[13]

It was not alleged, it is true, that Ælfgifu of Northampton had actually had an affair with a priest. Rather it was said that, desperate to produce a child for Canute, she had connived with a fornicating priest so as to smuggle his child by an unknown mistress into her bedchamber and to pass him (Swein) off as a son of her relations with Canute. It appears, however, that the face-touching gesture did not necessarily imply sexual intercourse between the persons shown; it could merely imply connivance in a plot in which sex played an important part.[14] The case for Ælfgifu of Northampton as the tapestry's epony-mous lady appears to be becoming strong. Certainly the coinci-dence of the name and the hint of sexual scandal involving some priestly interest are suggestive. Some sort of workman was alleged to be the father of Harold Harefoot, and the depiction of a workman in the preceding lower compartment in the tap-estry is again intriguing. It may not be irrelevant either that the rumour about Harefoot is specifically found in the E version of the *Anglo-Saxon Chronicle*, which was being written at the time at St Augustine's Abbey in Canterbury, where the tapestry's artist appears from art historical evidence to have been connec-ted. Moreover, the rumour about Harefoot is also found in the *Encomium Emmae Reginae*, a work written by a monk from St-Omer, which survives in a single manuscript copy that is itself first heard of in the possession of St Augustine's Abbey in the later Middle Ages, but which may well have belonged to St Augustine's from the mid-eleventh century.[15]

What we lack at this juncture is a plausible reason why this fifty-year-old scandal should have been referred to, seemingly in quite another context, in the Bayeux Tapestry. There is no obvious solution to this difficult question. To attempt an answer we must trace the subsequent course of events, as the jealous rivalry between Emma and Ælfgifu of Northampton grew yet more bitter in emotion and tragic in its consequences.

If Canute ever heard any of the rumours concerning Swein and Harold Harefoot, there is no evidence that he believed them. His continuing attachment to Ælfgifu of Northampton and the two boys is evident from the positions he sought to give them within his empire. The death of Canute's brother in 1018/19 meant that Denmark fell under Canute's control and it seems that in the early 1020s he appointed the young Swein as his lieutenant in the Wendish region of Denmark. Because of the lad's youth – he cannot have been more than about ten years old – the ambitious Ælfgifu of Northampton accompanied her son to Denmark as his regent and protector. Herself of Anglo-Danish stock, and coming from a region of England where there had been substantial Danish settlement, she would have had little difficulty in passing from one part of Canute's empire to another.

By 1028 Canute was seeking to expand that empire by bringing Norway under his control. He sought to defeat the Norwegian King Olaf – Olaf apparently being, it will be recalled, himself a former lover of Ælfgifu of Northampton. Olaf was a Christian convert and he had sought to rule a still largely pagan Norway with a zealous bias towards his own religion. In the process he had become very unpopular and Canute realised that he could exploit this situation to his advantage. He travelled along the coast with a sizeable Anglo-Danish fleet, putting in here and there, offering bribes and promises of greater freedom to the disgruntled locals. It was enough. Powerful nobles submitted to Canute and Olaf was forced to flee. In 1030 Olaf was killed in battle attempting a comeback. Canute was now able to appoint the young bastard Swein as king of Norway; and once again, because of Swein's youth, his mother Ælfgifu of Northampton ruled as regent. At around the same time, in the delicate balancing act that was needed to keep the two women of his life contented, Canute placated Emma by naming her young son Harthacanute as King of Denmark.

As effective ruler of Norway, the lady from Northampton had reached what should have been the pinnacle of power, but her rule turned out to be an abysmal failure. She increased taxation, demanded greater services and made the Norwegians follow unpopular Danish laws. Those guilty of acts of violence – violence that, as one historian puts it, was 'characteristic of the fierce northern people'[16] – were subjected to severe and unexpected penalties. The Norwegians did not care for this new, brash foreign ruler, and she was a woman to boot; they found themselves longing for the days of Olaf. What is more, a succession of poor harvests, which spread hunger throughout the land, and bad luck were attributed to the Northampton-shire lady. Ælfgifu's rule of Norway was short-lived but long remembered. The expression 'Ælfgifu's time' was sub-sequently to become a synonym in Norway for any period of great poverty and repression. Norwegian resentment inevi-tably erupted into violence. The revolt was underpinned by a Christian cult which now began to develop around the memory of the late King Olaf. Realising the danger in this, Ælfgifu and her Danish bishop – Christians, of course, them-selves – urgently sought to dispel any suggestion that Olaf had been a martyr for the Christian faith. But tales of miracles concerning the slain Norwegian king continued to proliferate. The Christian religion was taking firmer root in the land of Odin and Thor; and politically, as a by-product, Ælfgifu of Northampton was losing out.

She and Olaf may once have embraced as lovers. As bitter enemies, he had been defeated and killed by her allies. Now in death Olaf returned to haunt Ælfgifu of Northampton and would ultimately bring about her downfall in Norway. In 1031 Bishop Grimkell, a Norwegian, located Olaf's grave at Nidaros and exhumed the body. It was reported that the corpse was miraculously as fresh as it had been on the day that Olaf was living. To the Norwegians, this was truly proof of his saintliness; and he was popularly canonised as a saint. It was later said that Ælfgifu of Northampton was herself at the graveside as the body was exhumed and that she frantically tried to explain away the state of the corpse on the basis of unusual soil conditions. Few would believe her. The revolt gathered fresh momentum when in 1035 Magnus, the young son of Olaf, returned to Norway. After an ineffectual period of struggle, Ælfgifu and Swein accepted the inevitable. Mother and son fled to Denmark, where Swein's half-brother Harthacanute ruled. With Magnus proclaimed king, Norway ceased to be part of the vast empire belonging to Canute and his complicated family. 'Ælfgifu's time' had ended with a humiliating retreat.

During all this period Canute, perhaps hampered by illness, had remained in England. On 12 November 1035 he died at Shaftesbury. With the passing of the great Danish monarch, who had entered into legend even in his own lifetime, the question of succession arose. His legitimate son by Emma, Harthacanute, was already ensconced as King of Denmark but the English succession remained outstanding. The death of the bastard Swein not long after his reputed father removed one of the potential claimants from the scene. Swein's mother Ælfgifu of Northampton now returned to England to make what she could of the new situation. The main contestants for Canute's crown were Emma's son, Harthacanute of Denmark, and Ælfgifu's younger son, Harold Harefoot. The conflict between the two women to win for their sons the crown of

England and for themselves the position of queen mother now entered its most bitter and tragic phase.

Emma could rightly point out that Canute had promised that only a son she bore him would succeed to England; but Harthacanute was now faced with an invasion in Denmark from a confident Magnus of Norway and he was unable to cross the North Sea to take up the English part of his inheritance. Two factions then emerged in England. Concentrated largely to the north of the Thames were the supporters of Harold Harefoot, energetically orchestrated by Ælfgifu of Northampton. In the south, supported by Emma and the powerful Earl Godwin of Wessex, were the advocates of the absent Harthacanute. From the beginning Harthacanute's case was hampered by his absence in Denmark. A compromise was reached. It was decided by the Witan, the assembly of the great and good of the nation, that Harold Harefoot should rule, but only temporarily as regent until the arrival of Harthacanute.

In the months that followed, however, Harefoot and his mother Ælfgifu of Northampton worked hard, travelling around the country, offering bribes and issuing threats, and winning leading men over to their cause. During the course of 1036 Harefoot gradually increased his powers so that he became effectively king of all England; and in the process Ælfgifu was regaining for herself the position of queen mother that she had once held in Norway, only this time on her home turf. With still no sign of Harthacanute, Earl Godwin and other important men in the south began to waver in their support for the young King of Denmark. Emma despaired; in this battle of the mothers, it seemed as if Ælfgifu of Northampton was going to be triumphant. At last she accepted that her favourite son Harthacanute was not going to be able to help her in her time of need. Emma's thoughts turned, as they had not done for many years, to the two sons by Æthelred whom she had long ago abandoned in their exile in Normandy.

Some time in 1036 an English messenger arrived in Normandy with an urgent and unexpected letter. It was a letter from the dowager Queen of England to her two long-forgotten sons, Edward and Alfred. 'Emma,' the letter began, 'queen in name only, imparts motherly salutation to her sons Edward and Alfred.' The letter then quickly turned to the question of the English succession, now that 'our lord' Canute had died. Disingenuously, Emma was silent about her earlier hopes that Harthacanute would reign; still less did she mention that the Danish dynasty of Canute had been responsible for Edward's and Alfred's exile in the first place. To her sons she now said:

> daily you are deprived more and more of the kingdom, your inheritance, and I wonder what plan you are adopting . . . your procrastination is becoming from day to day a support to the usurper of your rule [Harold Harefoot]. For he goes around hamlets and cities ceaselessly, and makes the chief men his friends by gifts, threats and prayers. But they would rather that one of you should rule over them . . . I entreat, therefore, that one of you come to me speedily and privately, to receive from me wholesome counsel, and to know in what manner this matter, which I desire, must be brought to pass.
>
> Send back word what you are going to do about these matters by the present messenger, whoever he may be. Farewell, beloved ones of my heart.[17]

Emma would later claim that the letter was a forgery concocted by Harold Harefoot in order to lure Edward and Alfred into a trap. Without further evidence (which is highly unlikely to surface at this distance in time) it is impossible to discern the truth; but many historians believe that Emma probably did write the letter and only later wished to disassociate herself in view of the tragedy that ensued from its delivery. If she did write the letter, appealing as a last-ditch measure to her sons by Æthelred in order to prevent the victory of Harefoot and his mother Ælfgifu of Northampton, it was a crass miscalculation of the situation. In 1036 England was simmering on the brink of civil war.

Edward sailed across the Channel with a band of Normans. A few years earlier he had attempted the same crossing, but storms had driven him only as far as the island of Jersey. This time he succeeded in raiding the Southampton area, but, faced with opposition, he retreated back to the continent with little loss and some booty. The king to be known in history books as Edward the Confessor would have to wait another six years before his own peaceful accession to the throne. The fate of Edward's younger brother Alfred, which has been alluded to earlier in this book, now took its dark and tragic course. Refusing aid from Flanders, Alfred came to Boulogne, where his sister Godgifu had recently entered into her marriage with the young Count Eustace II. Supported by Count Eustace I, who provided him with the assistance of 'a few men of Boulogne', Alfred crossed to England from the Boulonnais port of Wissant.[18] 'Few' is a relative term; the force was evidently large enough to be later billeted in separate groups of twenties, twelves and tens and John of Worcester, writing in the twelfth century, implies that it exceeded 600 soldiers.[19] Narrowly avoiding capture at their first attempted point of landing, Alfred's force made ground at 'another port' along the south coast. Believing they had evaded their enemies, they now sought to make their way across land to London. But the party was intercepted by Earl Godwin of Wessex.

Godwin, the foremost of the English earls, was in a delicate position. To preserve his power and wealth, he needed to back the right candidate for the throne; the wrong decision could be disastrous both for him and his family. He had been a supporter of the absent Harthacanute. Lately, however, the south had been swinging behind Harold Harefoot and Godwin knew this. The intervention, now, of a third royal claimant complicated an already complicated position. Godwin at first greeted Alfred as a friend and lord. He then diverted the English prince and his Boulonnais soldiers away from London and led them to Guildford. He was evidently seeking to curry favour with Harefoot and had decided to fall in with what Harefoot wanted. At Guildford, as evening fell, Godwin had the Boulonnais soldiers split up, billeting them in separate groups of twenties, twelves and tens. Only a small force was left behind to guard the young prince. The men of Boulogne were fed and given drink. Soon they took to their beds. They were now at their most vulnerable.

As they slept, the sound of quickening footsteps and low whispers would have broken the silence of the night. Earl Godwin, it seems, had washed his hands of the matter, leaving the sleeping soldiers to the mercy of Harold Harefoot's men, who had been secretly waiting in the dark. Godwin was always to deny any culpability for what followed; but at best he turned a blind eye. As the soldiers from Boulogne slept, Harefoot's men slipped on to the scene and robbed them of their weapons. Then they surprised them, securing them in fetters. When morning broke the helpless soldiers were taken out and, with their hands bound behind their backs, they were lined up and mocked. Then, in a cruel lottery, all but every tenth man was murdered in cold blood. 'They butchered innocent heroes,' the *Encomium Emmae Reginae* tells us,

> with blows from their spears, bound as they were like swine. Hence all ages will call such torturers worse than dogs, since they brought to condemnation the worthy person of so many soldiers, not by soldierly force but by treacherous snares. Some, as has been said, they slew, some they placed in slavery to themselves; others they sold, for they were in the grip of blind greed, but they kept a few loaded with bonds to be subject to greater mockery.[20]

Alfred fared perhaps the worst of all. He was bound and taken captive. He was then taken to Ely where he was mocked and tortured. At this point it was decreed that he should be blinded as a sign of contempt. No doubt Harefoot intended this as a warning designed to frighten Edward, and anyone else, from making any future intervention into English affairs. Two men were placed on Alfred's arms, and one each on his legs and chest. With his writhing body thus stilled, his eyes were put out. Horribly maimed, Alfred was then taken to Ely Abbey and in the care of the monks he died of his wounds not very long afterwards. The callous manner of Alfred's murder, and that of his Boulonnais entourage, was shocking even to those who lived in this shockingly violent age.

If nothing else, Harold Harefoot had stamped his authority on the land. In the following year, 1037, he was officially recognised as king of all England. Ælfgifu of Northampton had got what she wanted. Her son was now king; Emma's humiliation was complete and she was forced into exile in Flanders. But the saga of rivalry between the two women had further to run. Emma immediately set about plotting revenge on Harefoot and Ælfgifu. Her utter hatred of them both now rose to a new level of intensity. In a flailing gesture, she appealed once again to Edward to help her return to England. Edward wisely replied that such an enterprise would be fool-hardy. No men in England had sworn oaths in his favour; another disaster would surely ensue. On the other hand, he told her, his half-brother Harthacanute already had enough men and power in Denmark to invade England and overcome opposition. So Emma turned to her son by Canute. By 1039 Harthacanute had at long last made his peace with King Magnus of Norway and was free to turn his attention to England.

He journeyed first to Bruges to meet his mother and they agreed on a plan. Emma had finally found her champion – an eager son seeking to extend his own domain. Together they raised an army of invasion and sixty ships to carry it to England. But with the preparations in full flow, Harold Harefoot suddenly died at Oxford on 17 March 1040. So ended the short reign of one England's least respected kings. From the perspective of the island shores, it was clear that Harthacanute stood ready to invade; Edward's claim was forgotten. The crown was offered to Harthacanute, and shortly before mid-summer 1040 he and Emma arrived with their sixty ships, originally prepared for war but now peacefully received. After almost twenty-three years of bitter rivalry, Emma had finally emerged triumphant over Ælfgifu of Northampton. With the death of Harold Harefoot, Ælfgifu disappears from the old records. She probably fled and lived out her remaining years in obscure exile; but a more grisly fate cannot be excluded. One of Harthacanute's first acts as king was to have Harold Harefoot's body dug up from Westminster Abbey and ignom-iniously discarded in a fen.

Earl Godwin was left with the tricky task of explaining why he had switched to Harefoot's side in 1036. Most damagingly, he was accused of complicity in the death of Alfred. On trial he swore an oath that he had merely been obeying Harefoot's orders in delivering Alfred and his party to him. He swore that he had had no part in what followed; nor had he wished or counselled it. A number of men bore witness for him. To ease the matter through, he donated an enormously expensive ship with a gilded prow to Harthacanute. The ship was fully equipped with eighty hand-picked men and it gleamed with magnificent gold and gilt armaments and fittings. By dint of these manoeuvres, Godwin survived. The contemporary and later chronicles differ as to what degree of culpability was really to be ascribed to the Earl of Wessex. He would need to defend himself again against these charges during the reign of Edward the Confessor. Unfairly, the taint of guilt was to be inherited, in the eyes of some, by his son Earl Harold.

Obscurity surrounds the reason for Harthacanute's next move. In 1041 he appears to have called over Edward from Normandy in order to associate him in the rule of England. Perhaps he and Emma, faced with unpopularity, particularly as a result of Harthacanute's policy of harsh taxation, needed to bolster their position by bringing in a prince of the authentic Anglo-Saxon line. At any rate, Edward returned to his native shores after almost thirty years of exile in Normandy, French-speaking and French-educated. The first step had been taken in turning the face of England away from Scandinavia and towards France. The following year King Harthacanute, though he was no more than twenty-four years old, suddenly died at a Danish wedding feast by the Thames at Lambeth. It was said that he had been merry and in good spirits, but when he drank from a beaker he was suddenly seized with convulsions, lost the power of speech, collapsed and shortly expired. The whiff of poison hangs around his ending, though neither contemporaries nor modern historians have made any specific allegation. Certainly Harthacanute had quickly become unpopular. Now that he was dead Edward the Confessor ascended the throne as sole king. Godwin again protested his innocence in the murder of Alfred, apparently providing the new king with a ship as magnificent as the one he had given to Harthacanute. Much as he might have wished to banish the powerful Earl of Wessex, Edward needed Godwin as much as Godwin needed Edward. The two formed an uneasy alliance. It was to be another ten years before Edward was able to break away, and then only temporarily, from the influence of the Godwin family.

Edward's attitude to his mother was a different story. Smug, no doubt, at her ultimate triumph over Ælfgifu of Northampton, Emma must have hoped that she would retain her position as a wealthy and influential queen mother. Edward had different plans; he disliked and distrusted her. Harthacanute had been her favourite all along; wriggle as she might, it was probably her own foolhardiness that had led to the death of his full brother Alfred; and for Edward himself she had persistently done less than he wanted. As soon as he was in a position of sufficient power, Edward rode from Gloucester to Winchester with Earl Godwin and others, and taking Emma by surprise, seized her many treasures and disgraced her. She was allowed to live out the remainder of her days – which extended for another nine years – quietly at the palace in Winchester. She played no more active role in the affairs of England. Emma died in 1052, and was buried alongside her second husband Canute in old Winchester Cathedral.

So ended the story of bitter rivalry that engulfed two of the most powerful women of their age. The thrust of the argument of this chapter has been that the lady depicted in the Bayeux Tapestry is Ælfgifu of Northampton, whose eventful life in England, Denmark and Norway we have recalled. But why should the artist of the tapestry have broken off his tale of Harold and William in order to allude to an old scandal that had ceased to be relevant after 1040, when the last of Ælfgifu's bastards died? McNulty, who first proposed that the Northampton lady was Ælfgyva, argued that the reason for Ælfgifu of Northampton's portrayal at this point in the tapestry was to undermine the Norwegian claim to the English throne.[21] But the Norwegian claim to England rested upon a treaty that was said to have been entered into in the late 1030s between Harthacanute and King Magnus of Norway. Under the terms of this treaty each agreed that the other would inherit his kingdom should he die childless. Harthacanute was the legitimate son of Emma and Canute; the bastardy and low birth of his half-brothers Swein and Harold Harefoot would have had no bearing on this treaty and, therefore, no bearing on the Norwegian claim in 1066. Nor would the fact that the Norwegians had ousted Swein from their kingdom in 1035 affect the terms of Harthacanute's treaty with Magnus, which was made in or shortly before 1039. Moreover, at the time that the tapestry was made the Norwegian claim was not an issue. Harold's victory at Stamford Bridge had seen to that.

What, then, could be the true reason for making an allusion to the scandal of Ælfgifu of Northampton at this point in the Bayeux Tapestry? The import of the scene remains enigmatic; the answer can only be guessed. A principal contention of this book is that Count Eustace II of Boulogne is a much more important person in the tapestry than has conventionally been thought. He may even have been its patron. To depict the scandal of Ælfgifu is not simply to hold her up for vilification and amusement, it is to vilify the product of her illicit conniv-ances, Swein and Harold Harefoot. It is to remind those observers of the eleventh century who knew of the matter that Swein and Harefoot were of low and illicit birth (those who did not know would simply be amused by the enigma). Indeed, the most obvious way, and perhaps the only way, of illustrat-ing ignominious birth, purely pictorially, is to make an allusion to the parent. If the true point of the scene is to show up the bad blood of Swein and Harefoot, the chief point of that must have been to vilify Harold Harefoot in particular.[22] It was Harold Harefoot who was primarily responsible for the ter-rible murders of Alfred and so many men of Boulogne in 1036. This was something that directly affected Count Eustace. Whatever he thought of Earl Godwin, the vilification of Hare-foot would not have been inimical to his own viewpoint.

Nor would it be inimical to a point of view more favourable to the memory of Earl Godwin, for it singles out for vilifica-tion, not Godwin, but, by implication Harefoot. Harold, like his father, would presumably have argued that Harefoot alone was responsible for the crimes of 1036. At any rate, to show up Harefoot in the tapestry represents common ground between a Boulonnais and a more Godwinist point of view on the grisly matter of Alfred's murder and the slaughter of the men of Boulogne. Perhaps the artist's intention was to do no more than that.

20

Wadard and Vital

On 13 February 1932 a meeting of the Society of Genealogists took place at its assembly room in Bloomsbury Square, London. Geoffrey H. White, one of the most eminent genealogists of his time, rose to his feet to read a paper on 'The Companions of the Conqueror at the Battle of Hastings'.[1] White's paper had been eagerly anticipated. It had come to the society's attention that, following a considerable amount of research, a bronze plaque had been unveiled the previous June at Falaise Castle, the birthplace of William the Conqueror, recording the names of 315 knights who had fought by his side at the great battle. A similar, though not identical, list had been compiled in the 1860s for the church of Dives-sur-Mer. Already a note had been published in the society's journal concluding that the celebrations that had marked the unveiling of the Falaise Roll were 'socially delightful', 'admirable in their international effect', and even 'gastronomically laudable', but the list itself was 'of no value whatsoever' for serious historical purposes. If the Falaise Roll could not be trusted, many British persons, previously to be seen glowing with unusual pride at

272

the thought that one of their ancestors had invaded the country in 1066, would be summarily deprived of this distinction. Geoffrey White, Fellow of the Royal Historical Society, was now to give his learned opinion on the matter.

He approached the question with dry humour. White pointed out that an ancestor who came over with William the Conqueror was formerly regarded as an appendage that no English gentleman should be without. 'When a man rose in the world,' he continued, 'one of his first cares was to adopt an eligible ancestor. And the adoption of an ancestor was in many ways a much easier operation than the adoption of a child.' For instance, he surmised, it would be difficult to adopt a child who did not actually exist, but there was on the other hand no difficulty in adopting an imaginary ancestor. Again a child usually had relatives and their consent to the adoption had to be obtained; but a person who wished to adopt somebody else's ancestor never troubled about such formalities. 'Thus,' White went on, 'a really popular ancestor might accumulate quite a number of unconnected families as his descendants, much as a comet might develop a number of tails, or a Hollywood star a number of husbands, although I believe that the stars usually shed one husband before adopting the next.'

There were many in White's audience who were rather inclined to believe in the Falaise Roll. Disconcerted by the mocking tone with which White had begun his lecture, they listened edgily to what he had to say next. The compilers of the Falaise Roll and the list at Dives-sur-Mer had certainly undertaken a very great deal of work; but what divided them from serious researchers was the reliability of the sources used. To White and most historians, reliance could only be placed on the very earliest historical records, and unfortunately these mention only a handful of William's companions by name. White considered that the reliable sources were limited to William of Poitiers and the Bayeux Tapestry. On the basis of these two sources he came up with his own list comprising a meagre thirteen 'companions' who could be proved, in the strictest sense, to have been directly involved in the battle on the Norman side. Descent in the male line could not now be shown from any of these persons. Even our Wadard and Vital were not accorded the distinction of being proven warriors at Hastings, for the tapestry merely illustrates them in the run-up to the battle and they occur in no other historical account. Wadard is shown organising the plunder of food in the days beforehand [scene 37; plate 8] and Vital [scene 46; plate 9] is a scout shown speaking to Duke William shortly before the commencement of actual hostilities.

When White had concluded his paper, his colleague Dr T. R. Thomson rose to echo the same conclusions and even went so far as to imply that the compilers of the Falaise Roll were 'charlatans'. This now provoked an angry reaction from the floor. A Mr Townroe stood up to read out a letter from Professor Macary, the historian from Falaise who had worked extensively on the list. Macary had taken umbrage at the unfriendly attitude of the Society of Genealogists' previous note and now indicated that he was not prepared to enter into any further discussions on the matter. A Mr de Carteret gallantly rose to defend the probability that his eponym had been a 'Companion of the Conqueror'. Others made similar protests and the meeting concluded on a distinctly unfriendly note. In summing up the chairman, Lord Ferrer, likened the verbal sparring to another Battle of Hastings.

The compilers of the Falaise Roll included not only Wadard and Vital but hundreds of others as well. They used the poet

Wace extensively. Wace, writing an account of the battle a century after it had happened, gives us 116 additional names, but his lateness as a source has generally meant that he has been dismissed by modern historians as unreliable. More obviously unreliable are the various redactions of the 'Battle Roll', which purports to be a record of the principal knights who fought at Hastings preserved at Battle Abbey, the monastery that William founded on the spot where Harold fell. The 'Battle Roll' is nowadays considered to have been compiled only in the fourteenth century and to be worthless as evidence. Following the stormy meeting of the Society of Genealogists the matter rested for another decade. In the 1940s the question was re-examined by Professor David Douglas.[2] Using scattered charter evidence, the *Carmen de Hastingae Proelio* and Orderic Vitalis, Douglas was able to stretch the number of persons who were proven, or at least highly probable, companions-in-arms of Duke William up to twenty-seven identifiable individuals. On the basis of the Bayeux Tapestry, Wadard and Vital were now accorded the distinction of falling into the 'highly probable' category. This White was now prepared to concede. Although they are not actually shown taking part in the battle, it does indeed seem highly probable that both Wadard and Vital were present and fought at Hastings. The artist evidently had his own reasons for limiting the named warriors in the actual battle scenes to the trio of more important men – Odo, William and Eustace.

The latest interpretation of the *Carmen* adds a handful of further names to the small roster of proven or highly probable companions – the French baron Robert Gilfard, Hugh, brother of Count Guy of Ponthieu, and Taillefer. Robert Gilfard and Hugh of Ponthieu are named in the *Carmen* (along with Count Eustace and Duke William) as those who kill Harold. Taillefer juggles with his sword at the front line of the invading army. Although dismissed as a figure of romance, the early date now attributed to the *Carmen* suggests that Taillefer was a real person, though like Robert and Hugh he was very probably French rather than Norman. Dr Elisabeth van Houts has reassessed the evidence of the 116 predominantly Norman names given to us by Wace and also shown that, whilst it is not infallible, Wace's list should not be dismissed as cursorily as it has been in the past.[3]

Wadard and Vital, then, are part of a very select group of individuals – those whose presence at Hastings is evidenced by a strictly contemporary source. But why does the tapestry single out Wadard and Vital, two lesser-ranking Norman knights, from amongst others whose names are known and myriad more whose names have been lost? It is not that they are depicted performing any great feat of bravery; on the contrary, they seem deliberately to have been given secondary roles. The names of Wadard and Vital occur in no other account of the invasion. It seems that it is not what they did but who they were that commended them to the tapestry's artist. The first clue was discovered in the nineteenth century: both Wadard and Vital were knights attached to Bishop Odo of Bayeux and they received extensive lands from him in conquered England. Their precise significance, however, has remained an abiding mystery.

At first sight, it might seem that Wadard and Vital are merely names stitched in wool, persons too insignificant for any substantial evidence of their lives to have survived. We might, therefore, choose to pass over them without much comment or a second glance. This, however, would be wrong. The evidence of the Domesday Book that both were knights of Bishop Odo has proved to be only the starting point, and other information has come to light. As research into the Bayeux Tapestry progressed, scholars looked for evidence of Wadard and Vital in their native Normandy. It was noted that prior to 1066 both appeared side by side as witnesses to a land grant to the abbey of Saint-Pierre-de-Préaux, which is situated in the Risle valley in the central part of the duchy. They also appear severally in two other documents of that abbey. It has been deduced from this that, whatever their connection with Odo, they were tenants of the abbey of Préaux. What is also noteworthy is that Odo's father, Herluin of Conteville, is associated in documents with the abbey of Préaux and it was situated near to the abbey of Grestain, which had been founded by him. This may indicate an early connection between Wadard and Vital and the family of Odo's father. Vital additionally appears to be the owner of some houses in Caen, also held from Bishop Odo.[4]

The undoubted connections of Wadard and Vital with Odo have been interpreted by some as providing almost conclusive proof for the view that Odo was the tapestry's patron. The precise reason, however, why it should have been appropriate to depict these particular knights of Odo, among many others, has remained obscure. The tenor of this book has been to cast doubt on the idea, which has long reigned unquestioned, that Odo was the tapestry's patron. Rather it has been argued that Count Eustace II of Boulogne may have had a much closer involvement in the making of the tapestry than has hitherto been believed and that he may, in fact, have been its patron. Yet if Eustace was the tapestry's patron, why should he, or perhaps his designer, have wanted to depict men loyal to Odo so obscure as Wadard and Vital? Could either of them have had some connection with Count Eustace II of Boulogne? Or did either of them have some special connection with the designer of the work? Clearly, we need to investigate the lives of these two obscure men more closely, so far as the available evidence allows.

Knights such as Wadard and Vital would have been trained for knighthood from an early age.[5] A boy destined to become a knight was typically placed in the household of a superior lord between the ages of seven and twelve. Here he would be taught the skills of fighting, riding and hunting. Amid the forests of northern France he would practise with his companions, taking part in warlike games, wrestling, fighting with swords, galloping at targets, shooting with his bow and arrow. It was a dangerous life for a child. In the mid-eleventh century, two of the sons of a Norman lord named Giroie were both killed in separate accidents. One was thrown against a rock whilst wrestling; the other was struck by a misaimed lance while practising with his friends. As he grew older the young squire would take part in mock battles, which were beginning to take the form of tournaments. Not long before 1066, the technique of charging at the enemy on horseback, with the lance couched firmly underarm, had been developed in France; advances in saddle design had made it possible, but it was a manoeuvre that took much practice to perfect. Some knights are shown using this tactic in the Bayeux Tapestry; others use their lances in the more traditional thrown manner. The youngster might then accompany a fully-fledged knight to war, carrying his arms and armour, and taking his warhorse to battle; it would be in this capacity that he might first see action.

Finally, provided he had completed – and survived – his training the young man would be dubbed a knight by his lord. The equipment he now needed – weapons, armour and saddlery – was extremely expensive. Wadard and Vital both wear costly chain-mail armour, they carry a sword and a lance and ride the traditional Franco-Norman warhorse, the destrier. A destrier could cost up to eight times the price of a normal riding horse. The newly dubbed knight might now enter the service of the lord who had trained him, or he might venture further away in the hope of finding a new lord or with dreams of becoming a hero in battle and winning the hand of a rich and beautiful heiress. Life for the settled knight revolved around his lord's baronial hall. One account of the early life of a knight shows him attending the baronial court on a regular basis, sitting at his lord's table, giving counsel and daily practising his skill in arms.[6] After the Conquest, Orderic Vitalis gives us an account of the unruly court of Earl Hugh of Chester, where the principal occupations of a veritable swarm of knights and young squires seem to have been feasting, hunting and their own welfare, though additionally the earl's chaplains were at hand to instruct them on matters of religion.[7]

Nothing is known of the background of either Wadard or Vital, but we may guess that it proceeded something along these lines. It may be that they had been long attached to Odo's household, or that of his father Herluin of Conteville. By 1066 they seem to have attained the status of minor Norman landholders. When the call of war came, the knight was expected to fight for his superior lord, for war was his *raison d'être*. There was no call to arms more important than the one that resounded throughout Normandy during the first months of 1066. So it was that Bishop Odo of Bayeux must have called up his knights Wadard and Vital, and many others besides, to fight in Duke William's army against Harold of England. Whatever the natural trepidation a soldier might feel at the prospect of war in a foreign land, it offered the hope of loot and advancement in the world. To Wadard and Vital the cause must have seemed just and it would be fought under the protection of the papal banner.

It is impossible to know exactly what Wadard and Vital did on the battlefield of Hastings, what role they had, what feats they performed. Perhaps, however, the reason for their inclusion in the tapestry lies not in the events of 1066 but those involving Odo and Eustace a year later. It has been suggested in this book that the Bayeux Tapestry might have been commissioned by Count Eustace II of Boulogne as a gift of reconciliation to Bishop Odo following his abortive attack on Odo's castle at Dover in the autumn of 1067. If the 1067 rebellion forms the unspoken background to the explicit story told in the Bayeux Tapestry, then it will have determined how the story is presented and the choice of characters. Could it be that Odo's knights Wadard and Vital were also in some way involved in the 1067 incident? All the accounts of this incident agree that Eustace's attack was beaten back by a small number of knights who had been left in charge of Odo's castle. Could this be the answer to the riddle? Might the small number of Odo's unnamed defenders of Dover Castle against Eustace's attack have included Wadard and Vital? Wadard and Vital might easily have been among the remnant of Odo's knights defending Dover Castle after the bulk of his men had departed with him to the north of the Thames – indeed, perhaps they were the primary knights left in charge of the castle. On this scenario, Eustace would have crossed swords, perhaps literally, with one or other of them, and perhaps both. What is more, they might have been the knights who were responsible for capturing his *nepos*. If Eustace sought a reconciliation with Odo following his attack on Dover Castle, and the release of his *nepos*, it would have been entirely appropriate to acknowledge the skill and bravery of Odo's knights, Wadard and Vital, who had inflicted upon him so resounding a defeat against the odds.

There is some evidence to connect Wadard, in particular, with Dover and the defence of its castle. The Domesday Book, compiled in 1086, records that he held six houses in Dover as Odo's tenant (which is more than any other sole tenant mentioned). Wadard, then, clearly had an interest in Dover. There is some further, striking evidence to link Wadard with the defence of Dover Castle. The Domesday Book does not tell us how its defence was organised. But, strangely enough, surveys which date from two centuries later can be used to show that there is an obvious correlation between the defence of Dover Castle and the lands held by certain tenants of Odo, including Wadard. What is remarkable in the thirteenth-century surveys is that we find that various landholdings similar to those held by tenants of Odo (not only in Kent but elsewhere as well) carried with them the feudal duty to supply knights to defend Dover Castle. One of the most important of these landholdings was known in the thirteenth century as the barony of Arsic; Arsic corresponds to the core of the lands held by Wadard at the time of Domesday. The coincidence is slavish and must have been administratively very cumbersome. The implication is that the thirteenth-century arrangements simply followed, and can be used as evidence for the defence of Dover Castle established by Odo. Manors which were held by Wadard from Odo at the time of the Domesday Book in counties as far apart as Surrey, Dorset, Essex, Kent, Oxfordshire, Warwickshire, Wiltshire and Lincolnshire are all found to owe a duty of garrisoning Dover Castle in the thirteenth century, despite their geographical distance from the fortress. The Domesday Book does not generally deal with military service, but there are two entries regarding Wadard that particularly stand out: his lands held from Odo at Combe (in Kent) and at Thames Ditton (in Surrey) are both listed as owing 'the service of one knight'. It is not specified where or for what purpose the knight was owed. But in the later records both Combe and Thames Ditton owed one knight to the Arsic ward for the defence of Dover Castle.[8]

This does not, of course, prove that Wadard, and still less Vital, defended Dover Castle against Eustace's attack in 1067. What we have suggested is merely an interesting speculation. There is one further point, however, that can be made. It will be recalled that both Wadard and Vital carry lances in the tapestry. The tip of Wadard's lance points rather markedly at one particular letter in his name, a letter which is strangely detached from the rest: the letter 'D'. Vital, too, points to the letter 'D' in the inscription which runs above him. Could 'D' stand for Dover ('Dovere' in Latin documents) and thus be an allusion to their joint defence of Dover Castle?

The hypothesis suggested above offers, for the first time, the prospect of a precise reason for the inclusion of Wadard and Vital in the Bayeux Tapestry and an unexpected glimpse through the fog of history at the events of that autumn morning in 1067 when Count Eustace attacked Dover. Unfortunately, however, it is a hypothesis that can be taken only so far and no further. Like so much of eleventh-century history, we quickly run up against complete silence in the sources and a general paucity of evidence. There are some further known facts about Wadard and Vital, and these provide an alternative line of enquiry.

In the Domesday Book Wadard stands out clearly as a tenant of Bishop Odo of Bayeux, from whose patronage he benefited largely. For his loyalty and obedience to Odo, he was granted land in eight different English counties. One of the largest of Wadard's holdings was at Fringford, which lies just off the modern A421 between Oxford and Buckingham.

Wadard was assessed by the Domesday officials as holding ten and a half 'hides' here, which is about 1,260 acres. It is recorded that there were eighteen villagers at Fringford, twelve smallholders, four slaves and two mills. Something is known, too, about Wadard's family. In the Oxfordshire records of the Domesday Book there is mention of one Rainald Wadard, evidently one of Wadard's sons who accompanied him to England in the years after 1066. Rainald held two estates from Odo at Somerton and Fritwell, adjoining his father's estate at Fringford, and one holding each from the monastery of St Mary of Abingdon and Roger of Ivry respectively. It is also known that Wadard had two other sons who are mentioned in the cartulary of Préaux in Normandy, Martin and Simon.

In Wiltshire among Wadard's own holdings, courtesy again of Odo, was part of a larger area known as 'Swinedune', or 'Pig Hill'. Wadard's holding here was assessed at five 'hides', which is about 600 acres. There were five villagers, two smallholders with two ploughs, a mill, a meadow and some pasture land. Before the Battle of Hastings Wadard's Swinedune estate had been in the hands of an Anglo-Saxon thane named Leofgeat. At that time it was worth £2 annually. By the time of the Domesday survey of 1086 it seems that Wadard had been able to extract £4 per year from the English folk who toiled his land. Not that Wadard would recognise Swinedune today, for his little hamlet worth £4 has since grown and merged into the populous town of Swindon.

At Farningham in Kent Wadard's possession of the manor in 1086 is remembered by the Wadard Morris Men, a troop of traditional English country dancers founded in 1977. They remember Wadard as a knight of the Bayeux Tapestry and as 'the first lord of the manor of Farningham'. In a sense, this is rather unjust to the many previous holders of the land at

Farningham under Anglo-Saxon custom long before Wadard arrived in 1066. The name of the last of them, ousted by Wadard, is known, for he is mentioned in the Domesday Book: he was called Alstan. At any rate our Wadard, a battle-scarred veteran of Hastings, would be pleased to learn that his name lives on in the twenty-first century, not only in the Bayeux Tapestry, but in and around the country pubs of west Kent attached to the bells and colourful costumes of the hopping and dancing Wadard Morris Men. In total, Wadard's annual English income, as evidenced by the Domesday Book, was about £130. This sort of wealth, the spoil of conquest, made Wadard a rich man within the ranks of Norman knights. He must have been pleased with the way he had risen in the world. No longer an insignificant knight, he was a man of property who had acquired unaccustomed wealth.

So far we have only spoken of Wadard's holdings granted to him by Bishop Odo. This is natural enough for he was first and foremost, as the Lincolnshire entries tell us, 'Bishop Odo's man'. It was quite common, however, for a knight to hold lands from more than one lord. In the case of Wadard it has often been overlooked that he held additional land in Kent as a tenant of St Augustine's Abbey of Canterbury. This is of interest, of course, since the artistic evidence strongly connects the Bayeux Tapestry with St Augustine's Abbey. Wadard is recorded in the Domesday Book as holding two estates from St Augustine's. The first, assessed at some 300 acres, was at Northbourne, a few miles north of Dover; the second was a similar holding at nearby Mongeham. The Domesday Book records that Wadard needed to render no services to the abbot of St Augustine's for this land. Instead, he paid him 30 shillings (£1.50) annual rent, a sum which was considerably less than that merited by the value of the property (£9). William Thorne, a fourteenth-century chronicler of St Augustine's who had access to older material which is now lost, gives us slightly more information.[9] He tells us that Abbot Scolland, the Norman abbot who headed St Augustine's Abbey between 1070 and 1087, granted to a knight called Wadard certain land in Northbourne for life, on condition that he pay every year on the feast of Pentecost the sum of 30 shillings, together with a tenth part of everything he derived from the land. On Wadard's death the estate was to revert to the domain of St Augustine's. Exactly what lay behind this arrangement is lost to history. However, in the context of our quest to uncover the secrets of the Bayeux Tapestry, Wadard's overlooked connection with St Augustine's Abbey may be just as important as his connection with Odo. It raises the question whether Vital was also connected in some way with St Augustine's. Here chance has decreed that rather more evidence has survived.

Once again, because of the fixation with Bishop Odo, Vital's connections with St Augustine's have long been overlooked. Vital's lands as a whole were neither as valuable nor as widespread as those of his companion Wadard; but in addition to holding various estates from Odo in Kent, and also from Lanfranc, the Archbishop of Canterbury, Vital is recorded in the Domesday Book, like Wadard, as holding a small amount of land as a vassal of St Augustine's Abbey. The land in question was at the village of Preston near Canterbury. This, as it turns out, is merely a hint of the substantial ties that existed between Vital, Canterbury and St Augustine's Abbey, ties which by chance are discoverable in other surviving documents.[10]

In a survey of St Augustine's Abbey, preliminary to the Domesday Book, Vital is actually referred to as 'Vitalis of Canterbury' and is said to have possessed jointly with Ranulf of Colombières as many as forty-five houses in Canterbury, as a tenant of Bishop Odo, although for purposes of the Domesday survey only twenty-nine of these houses were acknowledged by them. Vital was also remembered as a benefactor of the church in his adopted city. For all his aggression, the typical Norman knight usually subscribed to a God-fearing piety and the weight of guilt for what he had done at Hastings may have soon begun to weigh heavily on Vital's mind. Early in William's reign, the papal legate, Bishop Erminfrid of Sion, had sought to cleanse the Church of guilt for supporting the slaughter at Hastings and had issued a series of regulations prescribing the penances that had to be undergone by those who had inflicted death or injury. Thus a knight was supposed to do a year's penance, of an unspecified nature, for each person he had slain. Where he had inflicted death and injury but was unsure of the exact number of his hapless victims, the regulations obliged him to do penance for one day per week for the rest of his life, or else to build a church. In the mayhem of Hastings, we can well imagine that Vital was unsure quite how many Englishmen he had injured or killed, with that lance and sword we see embroidered in the tapestry, for not long after 1066 we find that he established a church dedicated to St Edmund the Martyr at Ridingate in Canterbury. It is possible that this was in fulfilment of Bishop Erminfrid's ordinance. At any rate, Vital's choice of an English saint as the patron of his church seems to reveal a surprising degree of assimilation into the world of his new homeland. St Edmund was an Anglo-Saxon king martyred by Danish Vikings in 870, Danes who were distant kinsmen of Normans such as Vital himself. There were perhaps complexities in Vital's character that are not evident from his two-dimensional image in the embroidery.

Vital died soon after the Domesday Survey of 1086. Other documents reveal that his English lands were inherited by a son named Haimo. Like his father, Haimo was remembered as a pious benefactor, for he founded the church of St Mary's Bredin in Canterbury. Vital had another son who became a monk at Rochester and a daughter named Matilda, who married one William Calvellus. At an unknown date before 1086, this William founded a small nunnery dedicated to St Sepulchre just outside the city of Canterbury. Interestingly enough, the land on which the nunnery stood belonged to St Augustine's Abbey and the nuns, though only four in number, appear as the abbey's tenants in the Domesday Book. Theirs was a landholding of only four acres, for which they paid the abbot 'two shillings and one packload of flour'.[11] It is conceivable that it was here, at the nunnery founded by Vital's son-in-law, that the Bayeux Tapestry was embroidered, by and under the direction of these nuns, although there is, of course, no proof and the nunnery may have been established after the Tapestry was made.

These clues seem to bring Vital more to life; with each piece of new information, a little part of the fog of history clears. It is only by chance that by far the most intriguing information about Vital was recorded and has survived. We owe this to a monk named Goscelin. Some years before 1066 Goscelin left the Flemish monastery of Saint-Bertin in St-Omer, not far from Boulogne, and settled in England. At first he was attached to the household of Bishop Hermann of Sherborne, but after Hermann died in 1078 Goscelin decided to become an itinerant monk, journeying around the south of England from monastery to monastery, undertaking commissions to write the lives of English saints for the places he visited and winning renown as a talented musician. Finally, in the last decade of the century, he settled at Canterbury in St Augustine's Abbey where he died some time after 1107.[12]

Being not a Norman, but rather Flemish by origin and English by adoption, Goscelin was able to see the human tragedy of the Norman Conquest for what it was. Thus, around 1080, he wrote to a friend at Angers describing sadly how 'the sons of kings and nobles and proud ones of the land are fettered with manacles and irons . . . How many have lost their lives by the sword or disease, or have been deprived of their eyes, so that when released from prison the common light of the world is a prison for them!' Whilst he was at St Augustine's Goscelin turned his hand to writing an account of the miracles attributed to Saint Augustine himself (*De Miraculis Sancti Augustini*). Coincidentally he reveals in this work some further striking information about Vital. This is in connection with the rebuilding of the abbey, which had been begun in the early 1070s under the incoming Norman abbot Scolland.[13]

Everywhere the lordly Normans were tearing down old Anglo-Saxon churches and abbeys and rebuilding them in the grander continental style known as Romanesque. The new Norman abbott regarded the existing English buildings at St Augustine's as clumsy and inadequate. He journeyed to Rome in late 1071 and obtained Pope Alexander II's approval for his plans to rebuild St Augustine's. On his return, these plans were put into practice. The master mason was called Blitherus. Nothing is known of Blitherus (though the name suggests that he came from continental Europe and was perhaps Flemish or Lotharingian).[14] Goscelin describes Blitherus as 'the most eminent master of the craftsmen, the remarkable inaugurator of the church'. Large supplies of building material were, of course, required. The Normans favoured the malleable white limestone from the region of Caen, which is evident to this day in the White Tower at the Tower of London. Goscelin informs us that one Vital, who is surely the same man as the knight in the Bayeux Tapestry, was acting as King William's superintendent for the shipping of Caen stone to Westminster where the king's palace was being rebuilt. We also learn from Goscelin that this Vital's piety and efficiency were well known to Abbot Scolland and the monks of St Augustine's at Canterbury. What is more, at some stage, possibly later, Vital took the bold step of joining the confraternity of the abbey as a lay brother. At any rate, when Scolland needed to employ someone to arrange the shipment of Caen stone required at St Augustine's, he turned to Vital.

Goscelin records that Vital was particularly efficient in organising this task. A fleet of fifteen merchant ships had been requisitioned by him in Caen; these would have been ships not unlike the troop ships we see in the Bayeux Tapestry. Fourteen were destined for Westminster, but Vital employed the master of the fifteenth ship to carry a load of stone to Canterbury. The master agreed, and Vital handed him 'sealed letters' recording what was to be done.[15]

Goscelin's story of what happened next vividly illustrates the perils of cross-Channel shipping in the eleventh century, though his principal purpose was to relate what he perceived to be a miraculous event.[16] It was a fair dawn when the convoy of fifteen ships set sail. Vital must have watched from the shore as the ships departed into the distance with the cargo of stone he had consigned to them. All went well until the flotilla reached about a third of the way across the Channel. Then there was a change of wind; a violent gale blew up. The ships, overladen with their heavy cargoes, were tossed this way and that; great waves broke over the bows; and soon fourteen of them foundered and sank quickly in the deep sea, with the loss of many lives. Only one was left afloat and that was the ship destined for St Augustine's Abbey in Canterbury. Seeing the plight of their fellows, the desperate crew prepared to throw the stone overboard in order to save the vessel. But the master stopped them. He declared that their only hope was 'God and St Augustine', in whose service they could now claim to be sailing. It was their duty, he said, to carry the stone to Canterbury. The whole crew agreed and offered up suitable prayers. In addition, of course, they desperately bailed out; they stuffed tow into places where the seams had started; and where the gaps in the side of the ship had grown wide they packed them with cloth. It was a fearful struggle, but in the end the little ship lamely managed to reach the Sussex port of Bramber. Here, under unbearable strain, it finally broke up, splitting in half from end to end and disgorging its cargo of stone on to the sand.

To the master this appeared like a miraculous deliverance, caused by the intervention of St Augustine himself, and he was now more determined than ever to complete his mission. He managed to obtain a new ship, reloaded the stone and sailed round the coast and upriver to Canterbury. At St Augustine's Abbey he handed over the 'sealed letters', which had been given to him by Vital, and delivered the cargo. With a mixture of joy and weeping he retold to Abbot Scolland and his monks the whole story. Scolland rewarded the master not only with the amount stipulated in the letters but with a kindly bonus of some shillings as well. The master responded by giving the bonus back, requesting with tears that prayers should be offered up for his drowned mates.

At precisely what date this happened it is hard to say. The rebuilding programme was presumably commenced in earnest in 1072, after Scolland returned from Rome, and it might

well have been in that year that Vital was engaged to transport the stone from Caen. If this is so, he was already a friend
and colleague of Scolland, and a close associate of the abbey
in the early 1070s, when it is most likely that the tapestry
was made. At what stage he became a lay brother is also not
known. There is, however, one curious and so far unnoticed
aspect of his depiction in the tapestry that deserves comment
in this context. Vital is surrounded by four crosses, two in
the upper border, two in the lower border. No other figure
in the tapestry is portrayed in this way. It seems plausible
to suggest that the crosses were included round Vital by the
St Augustine's designer in recognition of Vital's piety and good
works, which were, of course, well known and acknowledged
by the monks of the abbey. It is also possible that when the
tapestry was made Vital was already a lay brother of the abbey
and that the crosses refer to this fact as well.

There is another intriguing fact that Goscelin tells us about
the rebuilding of St Augustine's Abbey. Not only was Caen
stone from Normandy used. Stone was also being ferried over
from the Marquise quarries in the county of Boulogne.[17] The
Marquise quarries lie some seven miles from Boulogne and
were still worked until well into modern times. The district of
Marquise was held by Arnulf of Ardres and later by his brother
Gonfrid, both of whom were companions and vassals of Count
Eustace II and may well have fought at Hastings under his
command.[18] Judging by his name, it is possible that the master
mason and architect of St Augustine's, Blitherus, himself came
from in or around Flanders as well. Vital was not involved in
the transport of the Marquise stone. Instead, we learn from
Goscelin that, during the abbacy of Scolland, the monks of
St Augustine's dispatched one of their own men in order to
assemble a team of quarrymen, to oversee the work and to

pay them weekly wages. Unlike the Caen material, the stone from Boulogne was cut and prepared at the quarries according to whether it was to be used for plain walling, columns, capitals, bases or other mouldings in accordance with Scolland's grand design. Goscelin's opportunity for telling us this information was provided by his desire to persuade us of further tales of the miraculous. Thus, at that time, writes Goscelin, Robert the Frisian, Count of Flanders (1071–93), had invaded Boulogne and the district around the quarries was being attacked and pillaged. One of the Marquise quarrymen, Burchard by name, managed to escape, taking with him for safe custody a cow, which was the sole possession in the world of his widowed mother. Burchard took cover with the cow in a thick wood but here he disturbed a flock of magpies and their noisy chattering threatened to give him away. Terrified at what might happen, Burchard prayed, as he had been instructed, to St Augustine for help. The flock of magpies flew off and the soldiers who might have found him turned away, too. This incident was reported back to the monks in Canterbury and it evidently impressed them. The date cannot be established with precision. Count Eustace II of Boulogne and Robert the Frisian were involved in outright hostility during the Flemish civil war in early 1071 and it is thus possible that the incident occurred in that year. However, relations between the two counts continued to be poor so a later date is also possible. At any rate, some time during the comital reign of Eustace II of Boulogne it appears likely that stone from his county was being shipped to Canterbury for the rebuilding of St Augustine's Abbey under Abbot Scolland. The supply of Marquise stone reveals a background of good relations between Eustace and St Augustine's Abbey, where the designer of the tapestry was evidently connected, and this fits in well with Eustace's grand appearance in the work.

There is one further piece to go in this jigsaw. Though his relationship with Lanfranc, the Archbishop of Canterbury from 1070, was notoriously bad, Bishop Odo was remembered as a friend of St Augustine's Abbey. He was, to be sure, involved in some disputes with the abbey over land rights but on the whole he figures in the records as a protector and benefactor of St Augustine's, according it several gifts and favours.[19] A pattern of relationships is beginning to be perceivable and it centres not around Odo but rather around St Augustine's Abbey: the artist had some strong connection there; Wadard and Vital were both tenants of the abbey; Vital had been employed to ship stone from Caen and became a member of the confraternity; stone was also being supplied to St Augustine's from Boulogne; and Odo was a friend and benefactor.

We have suggested that Count Eustace II may have been the Tapestry's patron and that it was intended as a gift of reconciliation to Odo. If this is so, Eustace evidently employed an artist with strong connections to St Augustine's; the designer might have been a long-standing monk of the abbey who had originally been a native of Eustace's own region. Perhaps, as suggested above, Wadard and Vital were included in the work because they were the defenders of Dover Castle in 1067. If not, perhaps the designer included them simply because they were two knights associated with Odo whom he knew personally and who both had strong ties to the abbey. It may be that they assisted in some way with the work, or gave the designer details of the battle and other events from their own personal experience. None of these reasons necessarily implies that Odo was the patron. We have learned a surprising amount about Wadard and Vital, the two minor Norman knights, but their exact significance in relation to the Bayeux Tapestry remains mysterious. As so often in medieval history, the surviving evidence is teasingly incomplete.

21

Bayeux Cathedral and the Mystery of Survival

The early history of the Bayeux Tapestry remains obscure. It is possible that the tapestry came into Odo's possession not long after it was made and that it was taken by him to Bayeux. This cannot be proven; but it is certainly not implausible. His early possession of the work is understandable if he were its patron and it is consistent, too, with the alternative theory that it was produced under the patronage of someone else, someone who wished to flatter Odo, like Eustace of Boulogne, and who presented it to him as a gift. When first recorded by history in 1476 we find that the tapestry is a possession of Bayeux Cathedral and that it was displayed on occasions around the nave. But was the work originally intended for an ecclesiastical setting?

The widespread notion that the tapestry was specifically made to be hung around the nave of Bayeux Cathedral is unlikely to be right. It was certainly the practice to do so in the late fifteenth century, but its original purpose was probably quite different. It was pointed out by the art historian Charles Dodwell as long ago as 1966 that the tapestry's tale is secular in tone, having much in common with the epic genre of *chansons de geste* in general and the *Chanson de Roland* in particular.[1] Although designed by someone connected with St Augustine's Abbey in England, the artist was not necessarily a life-long monk or even a monk at all; he could have been a layman attached to the abbey, of which there were often many. The tapestry's religious overtones are no more than would be expected in a secular work of its day intended to decorate the hall of some great lord. Had it been intended to be hung in an ecclesiastical setting the emphasis of the tale would probably have been quite different. Odo, for example, would surely have been depicted in his episcopal role, and in his episcopal robes, and Bayeux Cathedral itself would have been represented.

The last point is a telling one. Bayeux is shown on the embroidery but it is symbolised by a castle. Nowhere is the cathedral in sight. Bayeux cathedral could easily have been illustrated: William's army passes through Bayeux on its way back from the Breton campaign, and a passing glance at the cathedral could have been made, just as a glance is made in an earlier scene towards Mont-Saint-Michel. It seems that the artist simply did not conceive of Bayeux as a place with a cathedral. For this reason alone the idea that the tapestry was specifically made to be hung around the nave of Bayeux Cathedral on the occasion of its completion and rededication on 14 July 1077 is highly implausible. A great new church is shown in the tapestry in the course of completion; it is the largest building depicted in the whole of the work; and the hand of God even descends from the heavens in order to bless the new building. But this is not Bayeux Cathedral. It is Edward the Confessor's magnificent church at Westminster Abbey. The only other church depicted is the English church

at Bosham. If the Bayeux Tapestry was conceived and made
to celebrate the completion of Bayeux Cathedral, it does so
in a remarkably strange way. It is true that at the top of one
of the pillars in the nave of the cathedral is a little stone
rendering of Harold's oath scene. This, perhaps, confuses the
issue in the minds of some visitors; but the little frieze in
the cathedral is a nineteenth-century addition and it is of no
relevance to medieval history.[2] It is not even certain that the
tapestry shows the oath scene as taking place at Bayeux, let
alone that the relics over which Harold swore were those of
Bayeux Cathedral. The most that can be deduced from what
we see in the tapestry is that the oath (so far as the tapestry's
story goes) took place on open ground either at or near
Bayeux.

It is much more likely that the tapestry was made to be
hung around the walls of a large baronial hall, where it would
have provided the backdrop to feasting, drinking and the telling of epic tales. Odo could well have possessed such a hall;
perhaps he had more than one at his various abodes in Normandy and England. In this setting one can even imagine a
jongleur (a visiting Turold?) singing the tale of 1066 to a large
assembled company of knights and barons, while the story
itself lay illustrated for all to see along the interior walls. It
seems plausible to suggest that the tapestry (whether it was
the gift of others or a commission for himself) was made while
Odo was still in power, before his disgrace and imprisonment
in 1082. So much is generally agreed by specialists; but beyond
that the tapestry is difficult to date. William's army suffered
a humiliating defeat at Dol in Brittany during the autumn of
1076. The tapestry shows a Norman success at Dol in alliance
with Harold in 1064 or 1065. The depiction of this victory
would have been less appropriate in the eyes of the Normans

after their defeat at Dol in 1076. On the basis of this one can tentatively propose that the Bayeux Tapestry was made to be hung in a baronial hall at some time before the autumn of 1076. How, then, did it come into the possession of Bayeux Cathedral? And how did it survive for so long through the obscure Middle Ages before resurfacing in the written records of the cathedral in 1476? There is no certain answer to these questions. The following, though based on evidence, is a speculative reconstruction of what might have happened.

In November 1095 Bishop Odo of Bayeux journeyed to the centre of France in order to attend the Council of Clermont, the great gathering of the Church at which Pope Urban II pronounced the First Crusade. Perhaps the Bayeux Tapestry had not really been to Odo's taste; he might well have suspected it of anti-Norman bias from the start. Some historians have suggested that, even in its earliest days, the tapestry was not widely exposed. By 1095, however, almost thirty years had passed since the great events of 1066 and Odo had perhaps warmed again to the flattering way in which he is depicted in the embroidery – Odo, the second Archbishop Turpin, the indispensable right-hand man of William the Conqueror, Odo, the architect of the Norman victory. Did the old man perhaps cart the tapestry across France, with his sizeable baggage train, all the way to Clermont in order to display it to some of his more like-minded fellow ecclesiastics?

At some point before 1102 the poet Baudri of Bourgeuil saw the Bayeux Tapestry; his poem addressed to Countess Adela of Blois certainly bears the mark of its imprint, but quite when, or where, he saw the work is unknown. There is no record of his having ever visited Bayeux, nor that he ever met Bishop Odo. Their paths, however, crossed at least once for Baudri seems to have been present at the Council of Clermont as well. He later wrote a history of the Crusade – *Hieroslymitae Historiae* – in the course of which he gave a famous description of Urban's speech in such terms that it can hardly be doubted that he was reporting what he had heard with his own ears. Was it, perhaps, on this occasion that Baudri had a chance to see the Bayeux Tapestry? This is not inconceivable, for Baudri wrote his own poem only a few years later, some time between 1099 and 1102. There is something rather pleasing in supposing that Odo, the old rascal, decided to show off the exploits of his younger years as retold in the stitches of the English; and to that end he brought along the tapestry to display before the assembled grandees at Clermont on the eve of the First Crusade.

The poet Wace was born on the island of Jersey broadly around the time that Baudri wrote his poem *Adelae Comitissae*. He became a learned cleric at Caen, a few miles from Bayeux, and by the mid-1160s had been granted a prebend or stipend at Bayeux Cathedral by King Henry II. It was during this period that he devoted himself to writing one of his major works, a long history of the dukes of Normandy in rhymed French (or more specifically western Norman) verse called the *Roman de Rou*. A large section of the poem covers the events of the Norman Conquest of England. Wace researched assiduously; he travelled widely, trawled through documents and interviewed contemporaries. One might presume that he would have known of and used the evidence of the Bayeux Tapestry, especially if it was being held at Bayeux at the time. Strangely, however, there is no unequivocal evidence that he knew of the tapestry at all. There are, it is true, three striking points of similarity that are shared with no other surviving source: only Wace and the tapestry tell us where Harold was taken after he was captured by Count Guy of Ponthieu – the castle of Beaurain; only Wace and the tapestry site Harold's oath at (or at least near) Bayeux; and only Wace and the tapestry recount the story of Bishop Odo riding into the confusion of battle at Hastings, waving his baton to encourage the more faint-hearted knights. But the poem contains more points of divergence than it does of striking similarity.

Thus Wace makes no mention of the existence of the Bayeux Tapestry itself. Nor does he make any mention of Turold, Ælfgyva, Wadard, Stigand, Vital and Count Eustace of Boulogne. There are striking differences as regards Harold's oath scene. In the tapestry Harold swears the oath standing upright, touching two reliquary boxes with tremulously outstretched fingers [plate 5]; but Wace has Harold kneeling, not standing, and he swears the oath only upon one reliquary box.[3] The copper figurehead on Duke William's ship, on which he made the crossing to England in 1066, is described by Wace in the following terms:

> On the head of the ship at the front,
> Which sailors call the prow,
> He had a child made out of copper
> Carrying a strung bow and arrow.
> The child had his face turned towards England
> And looked as if he were firing in that direction
> So that, wherever the ship sailed,
> He looked as if he were firing in front of him.[4]

In the tapestry, however, the image is quite different; here the embroidered figurehead is situated at the back of the ship, not at the prow, and the child statue holds a horn to his lips rather than a bow in his hand [scene 35].[5] Moreover, although Wace has Odo riding in the battle encouraging the others with his baton, he describes him as riding a white horse and wearing chain-mail; Odo in the tapestry rides a blue horse and (more pertinently) does not wear chain mail.[6] Such differences are striking. They have led a number of historians to conclude that Wace probably did not see the tapestry, although at the same time he must have been living and working at Bayeux, or at least in nearby Caen, and he held a position at Bayeux Cathedral. How could he have not known of the tapestry when he trawled for his source material so widely? And if he did not see it, where could the tapestry have been during the time that Wace wrote?

A clue to the answer, or at least a possible answer, lies in Bayeux Cathedral itself.[7] In the central part of the nave lie some steps leading down to an old crypt that dates from the time of Bishop Odo. On the south side there is a window to the crypt and on the lintel of this window, facing out to the nave, there is a piece of french doggerel that was engraved in the fifteenth century. It tells us that on 3 April 1412 the then Bishop of Bayeux, Jean de Boissay, died and that as they were digging a grave for him in a prominent part of the church they made a surprising discovery.

> As this place was being dug
> In front of the great altar
> The lower chapel [the crypt] was discovered
> Which had previously been unknown.
> It was there that he was buried.
> May God care for his soul. Amen.[8]

It appears, therefore, that the old eleventh-century crypt had been blocked up and forgotten about and that it was unknown in the early fifteenth century until rediscovered in 1412.

Exactly when it became blocked cannot be stated for certain. A document in the thirteenth century implies that the crypt was inaccessible then, but nevertheless known about.[9] It does not seem impossible that the crypt was damaged and became inaccessible in 1105 when Henry I, at war with his brother Robert Curthose, attacked Bayeux Cathedral. Writers linked to Bayeux described this attack as devastating; Wace himself tells us that 'the church was entirely destroyed'.[10] That is a poetic exaggeration, since the building was not quite so badly affected as that; but there is no doubt that damage was done.

Just prior to his departure on Crusade, in September 1096, Odo might well have had the tapestry spread out before him for one last time and then placed it for safe custody in the safest place that there was, which was in the crypt of his cathedral at Bayeux. Less than ten years later, if this conjecture is right, the crypt would have become inaccessible and it was not opened up until 1412. If this is what happened we can now understand how in the 1160s Wace was unable to inspect the tapestry: for it lay concealed, presumably tightly-wound in a large chest, in the blocked-up crypt beneath his feet. Those points in his poem which are notably similar to the tapestry may be the result of written or oral traditions at Bayeux itself, traditions which, perhaps, recorded the distant memories of those who had seen the tapestry. Thus Bishop Odo was remembered riding in to the battle and waving his baton; but the details of the scene were not known to Wace and he described them quite differently.

As the grave was being dug for Bishop Jean in 1412, the crypt was rediscovered. Was it perhaps on this occasion that the Bayeux Tapestry itself came to light? The first time that the tapestry is mentioned in any surviving written document is in 1476, when it is recorded as among the possessions of the cathedral. An earlier note in the cathedral records states that repairs were effected to a certain tapestry in 1463, which may possibly be our embroidery. If anything like this is correct, we can understand how the Bayeux Tapestry survived through the long period between the 1070s and the fifteenth century, when so much else was lost. There is moreover no unequivocal evidence that any other writer of the twelfth century saw the Bayeux Tapestry; the speculation that it lay quiet and undisturbed for over 300 years in the collapsed crypt of Bayeux Cathedral would account for that as well.[11]

One further piece of intriguing evidence should be mentioned, though its import is unclear. There is a curious reference to a 'large high-loom tapestry without gold, the story of William of Normandy, how he conquered England' in an inventory dating from 1420 of the tapestries of Duke Philip the Good of Burgundy (1419–67).[12] In the context it seems unlikely that this 'tapestry', of which we have no other description, is the Bayeux Tapestry. But could the conjectured recent discovery of the Bayeux embroidery in 1412 have inspired a tapestry, in the strict sense, to be commissioned on the same theme by Duke Philip's immediate predecessor, Duke John the Fearless? Both dukes were noted as collectors of many and various tapestries of their day; news of the Bayeux discovery may have quickly been brought to Burgundy. Moreover, the 'William the Conqueror' tapestry does not appear in an earlier Burgundian inventory of 1404, and so it is not impossible that it was made in the years between 1412 and 1420. Clearly however, we are at the very limit of what is knowable. Sufficient evidence is simply not available to give anything like a definitive answer to these questions.

22

The Patronage of the Bayeux Tapestry

The view that Bishop Odo of Bayeux was the patron of the Bayeux Tapestry – because it flatters him and at least two of his knights – has remained unquestioned in over 100 years of study. It has, in short, become the settled orthodoxy on the matter. We have seen, however, how subtly and cleverly the work is shot through with an astonishing English undercurrent, undermining the Norman claim to the English throne at every turn. We have seen, too, that the tapestry highlights Odo's former adversary, the enigmatic Count Eustace II of Boulogne, and implicitly favours the French (and in particular Boulogne) over and above the Normans at the Battle of Hastings. This suggests, on the contrary, that Odo was not the patron. It is, of course, always possible that Odo commissioned a work which was, unbeknownst to him, secretly designed in a way that undermined and subverted Norman interests. While this theory cannot be disproved, it is surely likely that, if Odo commissioned the embroidery, he and his associates would have taken great interest in the work as it progressed and overseen the labours of the artist and embroiderers so as to ensure that no such mixed messages were promulgated.

The alternative hypothesis we have proposed that the forgotten Count Eustace of Boulogne was the patron, has several advantages. Eustace must have made considerable efforts to achieve his reconciliation with the Normans in the early 1070s. The idea that the tapestry was a peace offering to Odo accounts for the highlighting of both Odo and Eustace on either side of Duke William. It accounts, too, for what we have identified as a pro-French, rather than Norman, portrayal of the Battle of Hastings, for Eustace might well have wished this to be subtly recorded. We have seen that the appearances of Turold, Ælfgyva, Wadard and Vital can be understood in ways that are consistent with Eustace's patronage. The English undercurrent can also be understood. Eustace, as a non-Norman, would have been open to alternative views on the matter of Duke William's claim to the throne, such as may have been preserved at St Augustine's Abbey, and he did, in any event, form a mysterious alliance with the men of Kent in the autumn of 1067. Ultimately, however, the patronage of the Bayeux Tapestry is simply a matter which lies beyond the available evidence. The tapestry certainly flatters Odo but there could be several explanations for that aside from the idea that Odo commissioned the work. The desire of Eustace to reach a reconciliation with him is one such explanation. Might there not be others too?

We could even suggest a hypothesis which does away with the whole idea of an outside patron. The monks of St Augustine's could have themselves decided to commission the Bayeux Tapestry, as a gift, secular in tone, to Bishop Odo of Bayeux, Earl of Kent, in order to cultivate him as an ally. St Augustine's was certainly wealthy enough to cause such a work to be produced. Its income of £635 in 1086 made it one of the richest abbeys in England. As the oldest Abbey in England, dating from the time of St Augustine himself, it claimed freedom from the jurisdiction of the Archbishop of Canterbury. The monks of St Augustine's even produced a series of forged charters in the 1070s in an attempt to retain this privileged position.[1] Archbishop Lanfranc of Canterbury was not disposed to tolerate such an independently-minded monastery in his own back yard. Ill feeling between the monks of St Augustine's and the rival Christ Church Abbey over which Lanfranc presided, was already evident in the 1070s and this was to boil over into outright violence on the streets of Canterbury in the late 1080s.[2] Odo, too, had poor relations with Lanfranc and thus he may well have been perceived by the monks as a valuable potential ally able and willing to stand up for the Archbishop. If anything like this is right, the appearance of Wadard and Vital, both knights of Odo having strong ties to the abbey, is unremarkable. Furthermore, the monks may have also desired to flatter Eustace, whose stone from Marquise was helping rebuild their abbey, presumably around this same time. On the other hand, the more subtle and hidden ways that the Tapestry promotes Eustace and his Frenchmen suggest that the designer was already favourable to Eustace, perhaps being of Boulonnais origin himself, and that the Count of Boulogne was involved in some more direct capacity from the start, if not as patron, then at least as a supporter in some sense. Either way, he is a very much more central figure than has traditionally been believed.

If the question of patronage is less certain than it has previously been thought, it has become clear that the tapestry's content is far removed from the 'Norman propaganda' of conventional myth. Whoever was the patron and whatever the genesis of the idea, it is clear that the artist was playing a delicious and thoroughly dangerous game. The picture of the Bayeux Tapestry that has emerged in this book is one of an artistic masterpiece of intellectual brilliance, shot through with multiple layers of meaning. The purpose of Harold's voyage, the significance of Ælfgyva, Harold's oath, the meaning of the word 'French' in the battle scenes and the death of Harold are all treated by the artist in a way that deliberately teases the audience with ambiguity. At one level all of these scenes can be read as consistent with the Norman story. Ultimately, however, the artist's underlying meaning is revealed by subtle and persistent pictorial clues. He flattered Bishop Odo, but at the same time stitched ingeniously into the embroidered story are veiled statements of the English point of view and coded clues as to the role of Count Eustace and his men in the downfall of Harold, even an indication that Eustace himself struck the fatal blow that brought the last Anglo-Saxon king to his knees. The tapestry tells us that the Norman claim to the throne was built upon a lie. It was the lie that near the end of his reign King Edward sent Harold to Normandy in order to confirm William's status as the next king. In fact, Harold had journeyed to the continent on his own account but foolishly he swore an oath in William's favour in order to extract himself from his prolonged and dangerous stay in Normandy. When Harold himself ascended the throne in January 1066, in breach of this oath, God's judgement was not long in falling upon him and his country alike. Instrumental in the enforcement of God's will were not the Normans but rather Count Eustace II of Boulogne and his Frenchmen, Eustace the noble heir of Charlemagne whose merits were perhaps being regularly sung and vaunted by the dwarf *jongleur* Turold in the baronial halls of northern France. Elsewhere the English viewpoint was being silenced and censored, and the role of the non-Norman Frenchmen minimised, but Odo would be taking back to Normandy a work of art that, unbeknownst to him, subtly undermined Norman propaganda in almost every respect. The Bayeux Tapestry emerges from all this not as a Norman work or even a purely English one but as a truly Anglo-French production, foreshadowing the age that dawned with the Norman Conquest, but in ways quite unexpected.

It was at St Augustine's Abbey that one of the versions of the *Anglo-Saxon Chronicle* was kept up, nowadays called the E version. The E version of the *Chronicle* tends to be the most favourable towards Earl Godwin and his family, but it, like the other versions of the *Chronicle*, passes over in silence the whole matter of Harold Godwinson's fateful journey to the continent that was the catalyst of all that followed. The truth behind Harold's mission, and with it King Edward's crucial wishes towards the end of his reign, was recorded at St Augustine's not, on this occasion, in ink scratched upon parchment but with colourful stitches pierced through white linen cloth. In this sense, the Bayeux Tapestry can truly be described as the lost *Anglo-Saxon Chronicle* as well as the secret Chronicle of the House of Boulogne, a generation before the blood of Charlemagne achieved a new pinnacle of success in the Kingdom of Jerusalem.

As long ago as 1935 the French historian Henri Prentout wondered whether there was anything new that could be written about the Bayeux Tapestry, whether, in fact, everything that could be said had already been said.[3] The same sentiment is not infrequently expressed today. Such pessimistic notes have often quickly been followed by some fresh insight or intriguing argument. The secrets of this extraordinary work of genius continue to fascinate and beguile us. It is by no means impossible that further astonishing discoveries await to be made.

Notes

1 *In Search of the Bayeux Tapestry*

1 In a forthcoming study, David Hill and John McSween (*The Bayeux Tapestry: The Establishment of a Text*) will look closely at how the present appearance of the tapestry differs from the earliest eighteenth- and nineteenth-century drawings and (by the 1870s) photographs of the work. Almost 400 points of difference will be noted, showing either that the pre-1870 artists were inaccurate or that 'restorers' over the last 300 years have altered some of the details. The early artists were certainly not infallible. Only where a 'change' is supported by photographic and/or forensic evidence can it be accepted without demur. Rather than physically unpicking the work of restorers, the ultimate goal would presumably be to reproduce, in those places where an alteration can be proved, the original appearance of the tapestry in an electronic format for display in the museum next to the tapestry itself.

2 For the tapestry's subversive English point of view, this work is particularly indebted to the studies of Bernstein and Wissolik listed in the bibliography. The view that the tapestry is entirely pro-Norman (which it will be argued is incorrect) also has an academic pedigree and is represented by Grape, *Bayeux Tapestry*.

2 *A Tale of Consequence: The Impact of Conquest*

1 *Beowulf*, lines 994–6.
2 *Liber Eliensis*, II, 63, p. 136.
3 For general accounts of the Norman Conquest, see R. A. Brown, *The Normans and the Norman Conquest*; Williams, *The English and the Norman Conquest*; Douglas, *William the Conqueror*; Bates, *William the Conqueror*.
4 Simeon of Durham, *Opera Omnia*, II, p. 188.
5 Orderic Vitalis, *Ecclesiastical History*, II, p. 233.
6 For example, see Michel de Boüard, 'La chanson de Roland et la Normandie'; Rita Lejeune, 'Le caractère de l'archêveque Turpin'.
7 *Song of Roland*.
8 Loyd, *Origins of Some Anglo-Norman Families*; Keats-Rohan, *Domesday People*.

3 *Sources*

1 For a detailed survey, see Gransden, *Historical Writing in England*.
2 *Anglo-Saxon Chronicle*. Accounts of the Norman invasion are found in version 'E', which is considered to have been written at St Augustine's Abbey, Canterbury, and version 'D', which was probably written at Worcester. Manuscript 'C', from Abingdon, ends in 1066.
3 *Life of King Edward*.
4 William of Jumièges, *Gesta Normannorum*, ed. and tr. by E. M. C. van Houts.
5 William of Poitiers, *Gesta Guillelmi*. William of Poitiers was a Norman. The designation 'of Poitiers' refers to where he was educated.
6 *Carmen de Hastingae Proelio*, ed. and tr. by F. Barlow.
7 Eadmer, *Eadmer's History*, tr. by G. Bosanquet.
8 William of Malmesbury, *Gesta Regum Anglorum*; Henry of Huntingdon, *Historia Anglorum*; Orderic Vitalis, *Ecelesiasheal History*; Wace, *Roman de Rou*.
9 Orderic Vitalis, *Ecclesiastical History*, IV, p. 95.

Notes

4 Stitches in Time

1 The following account is indebted to S. A. Brown, *Bayeux Tapestry: History and Bibliography*, pp. 1–22.

2 Baudri, *Oeuvres poétiques*; the relevant section of the *Adelae Comitissae* is translated by Michael Herren in Brown, *Bayeux Tapestry: History and Bibliography*, Appendix III; on the probability of Baudri having seen the Bayeux Tapestry, see Brown and Herren, 'The *Adelae Comitissae* of Baudri de Bourgeuil'.

3 Quoted in Wilson, *Bayeux Tapestry*, p. 12.

4 Quoted in S. A. Brown, *Bayeux Tapestry: History and Bibliography*, p. 4.

5 Montfaucon, *Monuments*, II, p. 2.

6 Ducarel, *Anglo-Norman Antiquities*, pp. 79–80.

7 Hume, *History of England*.

8 Barré *et al.*, *La Tapisserie de la reine Mathilde, comédie, en un acte*

9 Stothard, 'Some Observations on the Bayeux Tapestry'.

10 Dubosq, *La Tapisserie de Bayeux: dix années tragiques*, p. 21.

11 Dibdin, *A Bibliographical, Antiquarian and Picturesque Tour*, I, p. 248.

12 Dubosq, *La Tapisserie de Bayeux: dix années tragiques*, and S. A. Brown, *Bayeux Tapestry: History and Bibliography*, pp. 17–20.

13 Nicholas, *Rape of Europa*, p. 285.

14 Von Choltitz, 'Pourquoi, en 1944, je n'ai pas détruit Paris'.

15 The attempt of the SS men to take the Bayeux Tapestry is briefly portrayed in the fact-based 1966 film *Is Paris Burning?* starring Jean-Paul Belmondo, Yves Montand and Orson Welles and based on a book by Larry Collins and Dominique Lapierre.

5 The Strange Journey of Harold Godwinson

1 On Edward and Harold, see Barlow, *Edward the Confessor*; Barlow, *The Godwins*; Walker, *Harold*.

2 *Anglo-Saxon Chronicle* (D), 1063.

3 Brooke, *The Saxon and Norman Kings*, pp. 25ff.

4 Harald Hardrada's claim was based on a treaty entered into in the 1030s between King Harthacanute of Denmark and Magnus, Harald Hardrada's predecessor as King of Norway. It was apparently agreed that if either died childless the survivor would inherit the deceased's

313

domain. Harthacanute was at that time not yet king in England, although he did become king in 1040. He died childless in 1042 and was succeeded in England by Edward the Confessor.

5 McLynn, *1066*, chapter 3.

6 For William the Conqueror, see the biographies of Bates, Douglas and de Boüard listed in the bibliography to this book.

7 *Anglo-Saxon Chronicle* (D), 1051 (literally 1052). William of Poitiers (*Gesta Guillelmi*, p. 121), writing after the Conquest, states that Archbishop Stigand and Earls Godwin, Leofric and Siward formally consented around this time to William succeeding. The several problems with this later contention are discussed by Barlow, *Edward the Confessor*, pp. 107–9.

8 *Anglo-Saxon Chronicle* (D), 1057.

9 Walker, *Harold*, pp. 81ff.

10 Barlow, *Edward the Confessor*, p. 58.

11 *Gesta Guillelmi*, p. 69.

12 Orderic Vitalis, *Ecclesiastical History*, II, p. 199.

13 *The Anglo-Saxon Chronicle* (E) 1052 states that Edward and Godwin both took hostages as part of the negotiations for their settlement in September 1052. Eadmer (*History*, p. 6) is quite clear that Wulfnoth and Hakon were handed over at this time and that they were merely transported to Normandy (presumably without Godwin's consent) for safekeeping. However, William of Poitiers (*Gesta Guillelmi*, pp. 21, 121) states that the hostages were specifically sent to Normandy as security for the supposed designation of Duke William as heir to the throne and that they were brought over by Robert of Jumièges, the Norman Archbishop of Canterbury. This latter contention suggests that they were taken to Normandy in the spring of 1051, when Robert passed through Normandy on his way to Rome, although in the autumn of 1052 he also returned from England to Normandy, in haste and never to return, when the Godwins were restored. The whole matter is rendered uncertain by these conflicting accounts but the evidence of Eadmer, both as to the purpose and date of Wulfnoth and Hakon's detention, tends to be overlooked by modern historians. For general commentary see Barlow, *Edward the Confessor*, pp. 107–9; Barlow, *The Godwins*, p. 48; Walker, *Harold*, chapter 3.

14 Eadmer, *History*, p. 6. Wace, *Roman de Rou*, Part III, lines 5585 ff.,

Notes

repeats both stories and confesses he does not know which to prefer. Of the other twelfth-century writers, William of Malmesbury, *Gesta Regum Anglorum*, p. 417, reports that Harold was simply on a fishing trip that went wrong. This cannot be the tapestry's view for the party departs with hawks and hounds. Later Henry of Huntingdon, *Historia Anglorum*, p. 381, baldly states that Harold was on his way to Flanders, not Normandy, and was driven by a storm southwards to Ponthieu.

15 The insight that the artist of the tapestry is telling a smilar story to Eadmer is made by Wissolik, 'Saxon Statement: Code in the Bayeux Tapestry', and by Bernstein, *Mystery of the Bayeux Tapestry*, especially pp. 115–17.

16 Barlow, *The Godwins*, p. 54.

17 Jenkins, *England's Thousand Best Churches*, pp. 685–6.

18 Musset, *La Tapisserie de Bayeux*, pp. 92–3; Taylor, 'Belrem'.

19 The story of Canute and the tide first appears in Henry of Huntingdon, *Historia Anglorum* (first half of twelfth century), p. 367.

20 Marwood, *The Stone Coffins of Bosham Church*. The story of Canute's daughter is, however, doubted by D. W. Peckham in 'The Bosham Myth of Canute's Daughter'.

21 The place where Harold landed is identified as the River Maye by Eadmer, *History*, p. 6. The Maye is a tiny river that flows into the sea on the north side of the Somme estuary.

22 Wace, *Roman de Rou*, Part III, lines 5623ff.

23 Morton and Muntz, *Carmen*, p. 5n.

24 William of Poitiers *Gesta Guillelmi*, p. 69.

25 On Harold's gifts to Waltham Holy Cross, see Barlow, *The Godwins*, pp. 78–9.

6 The Fox and the Crow

1 See Bernstein, *Mystery of the Bayeux Tapestry*, chapter 9 and in particular as regards the ambiguous import of the fox and the crow pp. 133–5. The relevance of the border imagery to the main drama is one of the most difficult and controversial aspects of the tapestry. See also Grape, *Bayeux Tapestry*; Albu, *The Normans in their Histories*.

2 The interpretation here follows Taylor, 'Belrem'. For alternative views, see the commentary in Foys, *Bayeux Tapestry Digital Edition*.

3 Hariulf, *Chronique de Saint-Riquier*, p. 250.

315

4 William of Malmesbury, *Gesta Regum Anglorum*, p. 419.

5 Grierson, 'A Visit of Earl Harold to Flanders'.

6 The memory, much garbled, of resistance against pagan incursions into Ponthieu in the ninth century was preserved through the heroic poem, *Gormont et Isembart*, of which unfortunately only part survives. See Hariulf, p. 149. *Gormont et Isembart* is quite possibly the very earliest surviving, albeit fragmentary, *chanson de geste*.

7 The 'Frenchness' of Ponthieu and Boulogne in implicit in the *Carmen*. See also Keats-Rohan, *Domesday People*, p. 14.

8 Orderic Vitalis, *Ecclesiastical History*, IV, p. 89.

9 William of Poitiers, *Gesta Guillelmi*, p. 71, states that William gave Guy lands and other gifts. The later twelfth-century source, Wace, *Roman de Rou*, Part III, line 5664, specifies that William gave Guy land on the River Aulne.

10 Bates, *William the Conqueror*, p. 115.

11 Eadmer, *History*, pp. 6–7.

12 In the tapestry's present condition this man has a beard. However, in the eighteenth-century reproduction made around 1730 by Antoine Benoît for Bernard de Montfaucon the figure in question has a moustache. In the present context the difference is immaterial; both scenarios strongly suggest that the figure is English. For commentary see Foys, *Bayeux Tapestry Digital Edition*.

13 The interpretation that Harold is here attempting to negotiate the release of the hostages was first suggested by Wissolik, 'The Saxon Statement: Code in the Bayeux Tapestry', but the force of his point has not been noted by others. Wissolik suggests the bearded figure is Harold's nephew Hakon but his reasons are not compelling. I suggest the figure is more likely to be the more senior of the two, Harold's brother Wulfnoth, but neither can this strictly be proved.

14 William of Poitiers, *Gesta Gullelmi*, p. 71.

15 Bertrand, 'Le Mont-Saint-Michel et la tapisserie de Bayeux'; Bates, *Regesta*, no. 213.

16 Suggestions for the identity of the figure are made in Bertrand, 'Le Mont-Saint-Michel et la tapisserie de Bayeux' (Ranulphe); McNulty, *Narrative Art*, p. 42 (Richard II); Messent, *The Bayeux Tapestry Embroiderer's Story*, p. 88 (Scolland/tapestry's artist).

17 Keynes, 'The Æthelings in Normandy'. The authenticity of the docu-

ment recording this gift has been questioned but it is regarded more favourably by Keynes. As to its relation to a later grant of St Michael's Mount to Mont-Saint-Michel by Count Robert of Mortain, see Bates, *Regesta*, p. 667. For Edward's charter see also Fauroux, *Recueil*, no. 76.

18 William of Poitiers (*Gesta Guillelmi*, p. 71) tells us that Duke William provided Harold and his men 'with knightly arms and the finest horses, and took them with him to the Breton war'.

19 Stenton (ed.), *Bayeux Tapestry*, p. 167 (Gibbs-Smith); Villion, *Visions secrètes*, p. 27. Villion suggests that the constellations are in the neighbourhood of the Milky Way and that an allusion is being made to the pilgrim route to Santiago de Compostela which would have passed through Mont-Saint-Michel and Dol.

20 William of Poitiers, *Gesta Guillelmi*, pp. 75–7.

21 Eadmer, *History*, p. 7.

22 Bernstein, *Mystery of the Bayeux Tapestry*, pp. 196–7; *Brevis Relatio*, p. 28; Wace, *Roman de Rou*, Part III, lines 5691–4.

23 Bernstein, *Mystery of the Bayeux Tapestry*, pp. 168–9.

24 William of Poitiers, *Gesta Guillelmi*, p. 71.

25 Quoted in Barlow, *The Godwins*, p. 118.

26 Eadmer, *History*, p. 8.

7 **The English Decision**

1 *The Life of King Edward*, p. 69.

2 *The Life of King Edward*, p. 111 (Sulcard addition).

3 *The Life of King Edward*, pp. 69–71; Barlow, *Edward the Confessor*, pp. 229–32.

4 *Ibid.*, p. 125.

5 *Ibid.*, p. 119.

6 *Ibid.*, pp. 117–19.

7 *Ibid.*, p. 121.

8 Smith, 'Archbishop Stigand and the Eye of the Needle'.

9 *The Life of King Edward*, p. 123.

10 William of Poitiers, *Gesta Guillelmi*, p. 119.

11 Foreville, 'Aux origines de la renaissance juridique'; Beckerman, 'Succession in Normandy, 1087, and in England, 1066'; Cowdrey, 'Death-bed Testaments', pp. 716ff.; Williams, 'Some Notes and

Considerations'; also, Tabuteau, 'The Role of Law in the Succession to Normandy and England, 1087'.

12 Walker, *Harold*, p. 136.

13 John of Worcester, *Chronicle*, p. 601.

14 Walker, *Harold*, pp. 36–8.

15 *The Life of King Edward*, p. 121. To portray Stigand in this light was not, therefore, an exclusively Norman view. It is true, however, that Stigand had been on good terms with St Augustine's Abbey (Gem, ed., *St Augustine's Abbey*, p. 50) where the art historical evidence suggests the tapestry was made. My interpretation assumes the poor view of Stigand to be the interpretation of the artist, who was influenced by The *Life of King Edward*.

16 Van Houts, 'The Norman Conquest through European Eyes'; E. A. Freeman, *Norman Conquest*, III, pp. 645–50.

17 William of Poitiers, *Gesta Guillelmi*, pp. 141–3.

18 *Ibid.*, p. 107.

8 *Invasion*

1 *Ibid.*, p. 109.

2 *Ibid.*, p. 105. Doubts as to the truth of Poitiers' statement that William obtained papal support have been raised (Morton, 'Pope Alexander II and the Norman Conquest'; Walker, *Harold*, pp. 148–9) but Poitiers is usually taken to be accurate on this point.

3 Van Houts, 'The Ship List'.

4 Orderic Vitalis, *Ecclesiastical History*, II, pp. 138–41, 142–5.

5 *Anglo-Saxon Chronicle* (D and E).

6 Barlow, *The Godwins*, p. 97; Walker, *Harold*, p. 145.

7 Churchill, *History of the English Speaking Peoples*, I, p. 128.

8 William of Poitiers, *Gesta Guillelmi*, p. 113.

9 These details are summarised in the *Carmen*, introduction by Barlow, pp. lxvii–lxviii.

10 Taylor, 'Belrem'; Bachrach, 'Some Observations on the Bayeux Tapestry'.

11 Whether Ulf's mother was Harold's mistress Edith Swan-Neck or his wife Ealdgyth is not clear from surviving documents. Walker, *Harold*, p. 197, argues that Ulf's mother is more likely to be Edith Swan-Neck.

12 Wace, *Roman de Rou*, III, lines 7541–2; Gaimar, *L'estoire des Engleis*, lines 6077–8.

9 *The Battle of Hastings*

1 Accounts of the Battle of Hastings are given in many of the secondary sources, including Barlow, *The Godwins*; Walker, *Harold*; and in most detail, Lawson, *The Battle of Hastings*.
2 William of Poitiers, *Gesta Guillelmi*, p. 129.
3 *Ibid.*, p. 129.
4 *Ibid.*, p. 125.
5 Tanner, 'Counts of Boulogne'.
6 William of Poitiers, *Gesta Guillelmi*, pp. 133–5. Wace, writing 100 years after the event, extensively supplements the list of combatants but his list has not been considered wholly reliable.
7 *Carmen*, introduction by Barlow, p. xxx.
8 William of Poitiers, *Gesta Guillelmi*, p. 143.
9 The terminological opposition of *Francia* and Normandy is implicit throughout William of Poitiers' work as well in other Norman writers. That Guy of Amiens does not include the Normans within the meaning of 'French' is shown by his reference to the ducal army being arranged with the Bretons on one flank, the Normans in the centre and the French on the other flank (*Carmen*, p. 25). Implicitly 'French' in the *Carmen* includes Ponthieu and Boulogne. For the 'Frenchness' of Boulogne, see also, Tanner, 'Between Scylla and Charybdis', pp. 248–9.
10 Gibbs-Smith, in Stenton (ed.), *Bayeux Tapestry*, p. 188.
11 Brooks and Walker, 'The Authority and Interpretation of the Bayeux Tapestry'.
12 Amatus of Montecassino, *Storia de' Normanni*, pp. 11–12.
13 William of Malmesbury, *Gesta Regum Anglorum*, p. 455.
14 Henry of Huntingdon, *Historia Anglorum*, p. 395.
15 Baudri, in S. A. Brown, *The Bayeux Tapesry: History and Bibliography*, p. 174.
16 Lawson, *Battle of Hastings*, pp. 231ff.
17 Bernstein, *Mystery of the Bayeux Tapestry*, pp. 152ff.
18 *Carmen*, p. 33.
19 *Ibid.*, introduction by Barlow, p. lxxxii.
20 William of Poitiers, *Gesta Guillelmi*, p. 141.

21 Eadmer, *History*, p. 9.

22 William of Poitiers, *Gesta Guillelmi*, p. 141; *Waltham Chronicle*, pp. 54–5.

23 Pollock, *Harold Rex: Is King Harold II Buried in Bosham Church?* The positive evidence being non-existent, an application to exhume the bones for analysis was rejected by the consistory court in 2003: In re Holy Trinity, Bosham [2004] 2 WLR 833.

24 Barlow, *The Godwins*, p. 113.

25 For example, see Messent, *The Bayeux Tapestry Embroiderer's Story*.

26 Baudri, in S. A. Brown, *Bayeux Tapestry: History and Bibliography*, pp. 175–7.

27 William of Malmesbury, *Gesta Guillelmi*, pp. 417, 467.

28 Tanner, 'Counts of Boulogne', p. 272.

10 English Art and Embroidery

1 Montfaucon, *Monuments de la monarchie françoise*, II, p. 2.

2 See generally Brooks and Walker, 'The Authority and Interpretation of the Bayeux Tapestry'; Gameson, 'The Origin, Art, and Message of the Bayeux Tapestry'; Bernstein, *Mystery of the Bayeux Tapestry*, chapter 2.

3 Dodwell, *Anglo-Saxon Art*.

4 *The Life of King Edward*, p. 23; William of Malmesbury, *Gesta Regum Anglorum*, p. 405.

5 William of Poitiers, *Gesta Guillelmi*, p. 177.

6 On Goscelin see *The Life of King Edward*, introduction by Barlow.

7 *Liber Eliensis*, II, 63, p. 136.

8 *Domesday Book*, p. 410, p. 195.

9 *Les actes de Guillaume*, no. 16.

10 Wormald, 'Style and Design'.

11 Hart, 'The Canterbury Contribution to the Bayeux Tapestry' and 'The Bayeux Tapestry and Schools of Illumination at Canterbury'; Gameson, 'The Origin, Art, and Message of the Bayeux Tapestry'.

12 Hart, 'The Canterbury Contribution to the Bayeux Tapestry', p. 7.

11 A Connection with Bishop Odo of Bayeux

1 See Bernstein, *Mystery of the Bayeux Tapestry*, Chapter 1, and the sources referred to therein.

Notes

2 William of Poitiers, *Gesta Guillelmi*, p. 71; Orderic Vitalis, *Ecclesiastical History*, II, p. 135.

3 See Bernstein, *Mystery of the Bayeux Tapestry*, p. 30 and the sources referred to therein.

4 Stothard, 'Some Observations on the Bayeux Tapestry'.

12 The Bayeux Tapestry and the Babylonian Conquest of the Jews

1 The biblical accounts are in 2 Chr. 36:17–21; 2 Kings 25:1–21; Jer. 41–2.

2 Ezek. 17:13–21.

3 Biblical references implicitly likening the Norman Conquest to the Babylonian Conquest of the Jews are made in *The Life of King Edward* (pp. 117–21) but no reference is explicitly made to Zedekiah's breach of oath, just as the author of the *Life* avoids explicitly mentioning Harold's perjury.

4 Bernstein, *Mystery of the Bayeux Tapestry*, Part III.

5 Dan. 7:17.

6 Bernstein, *Mystery of the Bayeux Tapestry*, p. 170.

7 *Ibid.*, pp. 174ff. However, Hart, 'The Bayeux Tapestry and Schools of Illumination at Canterbury', also finds exemplars in Canterbury manuscripts.

8 Jer. 22:24, 22:28 and 37:1. However, the nickname does not appear to be used in the Vulgate Bible which would have been known to the artist and may also have been known only in Jewish writings.

9 However, Hart, 'The Bayeux Tapestry and Schools of Illumination at Canterbury', notes an exemplar for this scene in a Canterbury manuscript that illustrates a different biblical escape (*OE Hexateuch*; Joshua 2: 7–15).

10 William of Poitiers, *Gesta Guillelmi*, p. 171.

11 Short, 'The Language of the Bayeux Tapestry Inscriptions'.

13 The Tanner's Grandsons

1 Bates, 'The Character and Career of Odo, Bishop of Bayeux'; biographies of William the Conqueror by Douglas, Bates and de Boüard.

2 Benoît, *Chronique des ducs de Normandie*, II, lines 33445ff.; Wace, *Roman de Roy*, III, lines 2824ff.

3 Benoît and Wace have the tree cast its shade over Normandy; William

of Malmesbury, *Gesta Regum Anglorum*, p. 427, has it cover England as well.

4 William of Jumièges, *Gesta Normannorum*, p. 125; Orderic Vitalis, *Ecclesiastical History*, IV, p. 102.

5 Bates, *William the Conqueror*, p. 124, notes that the bones in her grave were despoiled in the sixteenth century and, therefore, it is not certain that they are hers.

6 Bates, *William the Conqueror*, p. 53.

14 *The Scion of Charlemagne*

1 Tanner, 'Counts of Boulogne' 'Between Scylla and Charybdis'.

2 *Genealogia Comitum Boloniensium*.

3 Platts, *Origins of Heraldry* (p. 28) also notes a descent from Charlemagne through the emperor's favourite daughter Bertha and the poet-courtier Angilbert. A quite different lineage in the male line for Count Eustace II of Boulogne is given by Baigent *et al.*, *The Holy Blood and the Holy Grail*, linking him to the so-called Grail family and the curious story of Rennes-le-Château. This makes Eustace II's paternal grandfather, not Count Baldwin I of Boulogne, but one Hughes de Plantard. Although this is dubious and not supported by any contemporary documentary evidence, it has been taken up by a number of other writers of the 'alternative' history genre. Strangely the Bayeux Tapestry, for all its suggestive imagery, has remained an untapped resource for such writers.

4 William of Poitiers, *Gesta Guillelmi*, p. 185; *Carmen*, p. 31; Orderic Vitalis, *Ecclesiastical History*, II, p. 206.

5 Chiefly Tanner, 'Counts of Boulogne'. Her book on the subject, *Families, Friends and Allies: Boulogne and Politics in Northern France and England c. 879–c. 1162*, had not yet been published at the time of writing this book.

6 The episode and its sources are fully discussed in Barlow, *Edward the Confessor*, pp. 45ff. For Eustace's marriages, see also pp. 307ff.

7 Barlow, *Edward the Confessor*, pp. 307ff, suggests that there may, after all, have been issue.

8 Barlow, *The Godwins*, pp. 40ff.

9 Tanner, 'Counts of Boulogne', p. 268.

10 Morton and Muntz, *Carmen*, p. xxxix.

Notes

11 From charter evidence; Bates, *William the Conqueror*, p. 82.
12 William of Poitiers, *Gesta Guillelmi*, p. 139.
13 *Ibid.*, p. 183.

15 Count Eustace and the Death of King Harold

1 Stothard, 'Some Observations'.
2 For example, Grape, *Bayeux Tapestry*, p. 23; discussed in Bridgeford, 'Was Count Eustace the Patron?' pp. 180ff.
3 The earliest reference to Count Eustace's whiskers I have found comes from the late twelfth century: Lambert of Ardres, *History*, p. 142, refers to Eustace II as 'Eustace the Whiskered of Boulogne'. Late as this is, there seems no reason seriously to doubt the historicity of the name. My statement in Bridgeford, 'Was Count Eustace the Patron?', that the nickname is found in the Old French Crusade Cycle appears to be incorrect.
4 Although omitted in print in Montfaucon's book, the moustache properly appears in Benoît's original drawing. This was shown by Dr David Hill at the conference on the Bayeux Tapestry in October 1999 at Cerisy-la-Salle. The theory that the moustache is a later 'improvement' by nineteenth-century repairers is, therefore, wrong.
5 *Carmen*, pp. 31–2.
6 Eustace's banner is sometimes said to be the papal banner given by Pope Alexander II to Duke William's expedition. Other sources, however, say that this was borne by one Thurstan, son of Rollo: Orderic Vitalis, *Ecclesiastical History*, II, p. 172. Nor has it been conclusively identified as an emblem of Boulogne.
7 Platts, *Origins of Heraldry*, p. 41.
8 The identification of the other three apart from Eustace is not entirely certain. The interpretation here follows *Carmen*, introduction by Barlow, p. lxxxii, where the issue is fully discussed.
9 *Carmen*, p. 32.

16 Eustace and the Attack on Dover

1 William of Jumièges, *Gesta Normannorum*, pp. 177–9; William of Poitiers, *Gesta Guillelmi*, pp. 183–5; Orderic Vitalis, *Ecclesiastical History*, II, pp. 205–7.

2 For both suggestions, Tanner, 'Counts of Boulogne', pp. 272–4.

3 *Ibid.*, p. 266.

4 Barlow, *Edward the Confessor*, pp. 307ff.

5 The date of the reconciliation is often given as 1077 on the basis that William of Poitiers implies that it had taken place not long before he was writing and he may possibly have completed his work after 13 September 1077. However, the date of William's *Gesta Guillelmi* is subject to conflicting evidence and may well be earlier; see William of Poitiers, *Gesta Guillelmi*, introduction, p. xx. Thus Barlow, *Edward the Confessor*, p. 308, suggests a date for the reconciliation of shortly before 1074.

17 *The Downfall of Bishop Odo*

1 On Odo, Bates, 'The Character and Career of Odo, Bishop of Bayeux'; Bernstein, *Mystery of the Bayeux Tapestry*, pp. 31ff.

2 F. du Boulay, quoted in Bernstein, *Mystery of the Bayeux Tapestry*, p. 32.

3 The start date for the list was 1066, presumably reflecting the curiously common assumption that English history only begins in 1066. It should have been possible to include some Anglo-Saxon fortunes on the basis of Domesday evidence alone.

4 Orderic Vitalis, *Ecclesiastical History*, II, p. 203.

5 *Ibid.*, II, p. 265.

6 *Ibid.*, IV, p. 117.

7 Bates, 'The Character and Career of Odo, Bishop of Bayeux', p. 12.

8 William of Malmesbury, *Gesta Regum Anglorum*, p. 507.

9 Orderic Vitalis, *Ecclesiastical History*, IV, pp. 40–44; William of Malmesbury, *Gesta Regum Anglorum*, p. 277; *Hyde Chronicle*, p. 296.

10 Wace, *Roman de Rou*, III, lines 9185ff.

11 Harold's brother Wulfnoth was taken by William Rufus to England but placed under restraint in Winchester.

12 Orderic Vitalis, *Ecclesiastical History*, IV, p. 99.

13 Bates, 'The Character and Career of Odo, Bishop of Bayeux'.

14 See Orderic Vitalis, *Ecclesiastical History*, IV, p. 189.

15 *Ibid.*, IV, p. 129.

16 *Ibid.*, IV, 133ff.

17 With only one exception, the sheer anomaly of Eustace's appearance

has simply not been noticed in studies of the Bayeux Tapestry. Only one attempt has been made to address the point: Shirley A. Brown, 'Why Eustace, Odo and William?' Brown suggested that Odo commissioned the tapestry after his fall-out with William and that the purpose of highlighting Eustace, already forgiven for his revolt, was to encourage William to forgive Odo as well. On balance this seems unlikely, both as to date and purpose. Odo and Eustace had specifically fallen out themselves, and highlighting the role of another adversary of William would be an odd and rather oblique way to encourage his forgiveness.

18 Bridgeford, 'Was Count Eustace the Patron?'.

18 Turold the Dwarf

1 For the contention that it is the adjacent knight, not the dwarf, who is the Turold, see Lejeune, 'Turold dans la tapisserie de Bayeux'.

2 This is suggested by Bennett, 'Encore Turold dans la tapisserie de Bayeux'. If the knight is also called Turold, a prime candidate would be Turold of Rochester, another knight of Bishop Odo with land in Kent. He was also accused of encroachments by Archbishop Lanfranc. But the name was common.

3 For the view that Turold is not a dwarf, see Bennett, 'Encore Turold dans la tapisserie de Bayeux'.

4 I am grateful for information in this respect to Dr S. Pavan.

5 Keats-Rohan, *Domesday People*, pp. 430–32.

6 Adigard des Gautries, *Les Noms des personnes scandinaves en Normandie de 911 à 1066*, pp. 171–3 and 342–7.

7 Wilson, *Bayeux Tapestry*, p. 176, alludes to this theory. Whether the dwarf is Turold and whether the dwarf designed the tapestry are clearly two different questions but they seem to be conflated by Gibbs-Smith in Stenton (ed.), *Bayeux Tapestry*, p. 165.

8 J. J. G. Alexander, *Medieval Illuminators and Their Methods of Work*, pp. 9–16.

9 *Ibid.*, pp. 12–16.

10 Rita Lejeune (herself a noted scholar of the *Chanson de Roland*), 'Turold dans la tapisserie de Bayeux'. Lejeune, however, thought that the name Turold did not apply to the dwarf-*jongleur*.

11 Faral, *Les Jongleurs en France au Moyen Age*.

12 *Domesday Book*, p. 92. The land of Adelina *Joculatrix* lay in Upper Catford; *Domesday People*, p. 124.

13 *Domesday Book*, p. 445 (*Berdic joculator regis*).

14 Lomenec'h, *Chantres et ménéstrels à la cour de Bretagne*, p. 24.

15 The suggestion that the *jongleur* accompanied the two Norman knights is made by Lejeune, 'Turold dans la tapisserie de Bayeux', but it simply does not conform to what we see in the tapestry.

16 For Count Guy's family connections, *Carmen*, introduction. For monkish opinion of him, Hariulf, *Chronique de Saint-Riquier*, p. 250; William of Malmesbury, *Gesta Regum Anglorum*, p. 419.

17 For medieval dwarfs generally, Johnson, 'Medieval German Dwarfs'; Harward, *The Dwarfs of Arthurian Romance and Celtic Myth*; Verchère, 'Périphérie et croisement'.

18 Johnson, 'Medieval German Dwarfs', p. 212. Johnson's statement that William the Conqueror had a dwarf and that dwarfs held horses in state processions may be a confusion based upon Turold in the Bayeux Tapestry.

19 Runciman, *History of the Crusades*, III, p. 93.

20 Orderic Vitalis, *Ecclesiastical History*, III, p. 319.

21 Hariulf, *Chronique de Saint-Riquier*, p. 149.

22 *Song of Roland*, tr. Burgess.

23 Le Gentil, *La Chanson de Roland*, chapter 3. There is much debate as to whether the poem is the result of successive versions over a long period of time or the product of a single poet. Burgess, *Song of Roland*, p. 14, concludes: 'My own preference is to see Turoldus as the author, relating his own version of a heroic poem which would have existed in a variety of earlier states.'

24 Moignet, *La Chanson de Roland*, p. 16.

25 Some specialists (but not all) consider this subsequent episode to be the work of another poet.

26 For example, Maclagan, *Bayeux Tapestry*, p. 25; S. R. Brown, 'The Bayeux Tapestry and the Song of Roland'. It is often also said that Taillefer, a 'Norman' knight, sang the *Chanson de Roland* as the Normans advanced at Hastings. A *jongleur* called Taillefer is mentioned juggling with his sword by the *Carmen* but there is no mention of him singing the *Roland*. William of Malmesbury (*Gesta Regum Anglorum*, 1120s) states that the Normans sang of Roland and Charlemagne as they advanced but does not mention any Taillefer.

Notes

In the 1160s Wace amalgamated the two traditions. The earliest surviving version of the *Roland* refers obliquely to the Norman victory (and certain later events) and, therefore, this cannot have been sung at Hastings. It is not impossible that an earlier version than this was sung but the evidence of Malmesbury is relatively late. The name Taillefer has not been found in Normandy. It is most strongly associated with the nobility of Aquitaine and the Languedoc. Given the French tenor of the *Carmen*, it is most likely that the Taillefer at Hastings was a non-Norman Frenchman of some description.

27 *Song of Roland*, tr. Burgess, lines 1515ff. See also 1490ff. for the interesting description of Turpin's horse which in some respects is similar to Odo's.

28 As argued by Short, 'The Language of the Bayeux Tapestry Inscriptions'.

29 A belligerent Norman monk Turold of Fécamp, afterwards of Malmesbury and then Peterborough, is sometimes proposed as the author (for example, de Boüard, 'La Chanson de Roland et la Normandie'). A Peterborough record speaks of him as a *'nepos'* of King William and on the basis of this it is often said that he is either a son or nephew of Bishop Odo. However, *'nepos'* could denote other relationships besides nephew and Turold of Fécamp was probably a more distant kinsman of Duke William.

30 Joseph Bédier, quoted in Douglas, 'The Song of Roland and the Norman Conquest', p. 105; Moignet, *La Chanson de Roland*, pp. 278ff.

31 Bender, *König und Vasall*, pp. 26ff.

32 Hariulf, clearly a late source, states (*Chronique de Saint-Riquier*, p. 61) that Charlemagne gave Angilbert 'the whole maritime region'. But even in his known capacity as Abbot of Saint-Riquier, Angilbert was undoubtedly one of the most important men in Ponthieu.

33 It is tempting to try to make something of the fact that Angilbert's nickname was Homer and the Greek Homer is mentioned in passing in the *Roland* (line 2616). It is at least possible that the name Homer was familiar to the poet because of Angilbert.

34 This point was not addressed by Douglas, 'The Song of Roland and the Norman Conquest'. See also F. Lot, 'Etudes sur les légendes épiques françaises', who concluded (p. 376) that 'Historically and psychologically, it is impossible that the *Chanson de Roland* is by a Norman.' It should also be mentioned in passing that Normandy did not exist

at the time of Charlemagne and the references to Normandy and the Normans in the *Roland* are anachronistic.

35 The suggestion that the *Roland* is later than the tapestry because the tapestry shows lances both couched and thrown whereas the *Roland* only speaks of them as couched (a later technique) tries to deduce too much from what are, after all, specific and very different works of art. Moreover, lances are also thrown in the *Roland*, by the Saracens, and the preference for describing the couched lance on the Christian side may be aesthetic or ideological rather than realistic.

36 *Song of Roland*, tr. Burgess, lines 372, 2332.

37 Bridgeford, 'Camels, Drums and the Song of Roland'.

38 The possible allusions are: King William's advance into Scotland in the autumn of 1072 (line 2331); the capture of Jerusalem by Atsiz ibn Abaq in 1071 (line 1566); the devaluation of the Byzantine currency in or after 1071 (line 132); the Battle of Manzikert in 1071 (Baligant episode); the capture of Palermo in January 1072 (line 2923).

39 *Song of Roland*, tr. Burgess, line 2923. From the context Sezile (line 200) must be a town in Spain, not the island of Sicily.

40 *Song of Roland*, tr. Burgess, lines 2503ff. The mention of the Holy Lance has been used by some specialists to date the poem after 1098, when a Holy Lance was discovered by a crusader, Peter Bartholomew, at Antioch. The idea that the poet was reacting to news of the Antioch discovery, whose authenticity was 'disproved' when Bartholomew perished undergoing an ordeal by fire a year later, is not in itself particularly persuasive and the argument is made redundant by the prior existence of the Saint-Riquier tradition.

41 John 19:31–5.

42 Loomis, 'The Passion Lance Relics and the War Cry Monjoie'.

43 Hariulf, *Chronique de Saint-Riquier*, p. 150.

44 It may have been among the gifts given to King Althelstan of England by Hugh the Great of France in 926, subsequently ending in Exeter Cathedral where it is last referred to in the eleventh century. Of course, the Holy Lance was far too important a relic to be inconvenienced by a mere singular existence. Many Holy Lances have been venerated. The point is that the Saint-Riquier lance is the only one of its time to be associated with Charlemagne, apart from the one mentioned in the *Chanson de Roland*.

Notes

45 Loomis, 'The Holy Relics of Charlemagne', p. 443.
46 Owen, 'Epic and History'.
47 *Carmen*, introduction by Barlow, pp. xxiv–xl.
48 For Bishop Guy, *ibid.*, pp. xlii–liii.

19 *The Scandal of Ælfgyva*

1 Hill, 'The Bayeux Tapestry and its Commentators'; William of Malmesbury, *Gesta Regum Anglorum*, p. 253.
2 E. A. Freeman, *Norman Conquest*, III, pp. 708–11, discusses several candidates; reprinted in Gameson (ed.), *Study of the Bayeux Tapestry*.
3 William of Poitiers, *Gesta Guillelmi*, p. 157. The same point is made by Eadmer, *History*, p. 7.
4 Hill, 'The Bayeux Tapestry and its Commentators', p. 26. Hill denies the sexual content of the scene.
5 Grape, *Bayeux Tapestry*, p. 40.
6 Eadmer, *History*, p. 7.
7 *Domesday Book*, p. 307, 'Ælfgyfu, sister of Earl Harold' (Buckinghamshire Waldridge).
8 McNulty, 'Ælfgyva in the Bayeux Tapestry', p. 665; Kurder, *Der Teppich von Bayeux*, p. 73.
9 Eric Freeman, 'The Identity of Aelfgyva in the Bayeux Tapestry'.
10 E. A. Freeman, *Norman Conquest*, II, pp. 568–71.
11 The account of the two lives that follows is indebted to Campbell, 'Queen Emma and Ælfgifu of Northampton'.
12 John of Worcester, *Chronicle*, p. 521.
13 McNulty, 'Æflgyva in the Bayeux Tapestry'.
14 *Ibid.*, p. 665 n. 8.
15 *Encomium Emmae Reginae*, introduction to 1998 reprint, p. xlv.
16 Campbell, 'Queen Emma and Ælfgifu of Northampton', p. 74.
17 *Encomium Emmae Reginae*, pp. 41–3.
18 *Ibid.*, p. 43; William of Jumièges, *Gesta Normannorum*, p. 107.
19 John of Worcester, *Chronicle*, p. 523.
20 *Encomium Emmae Reginae*, p. 45.
21 McNulty, 'Ælfgyva in the Bayeux Tapestry', pp. 667–8.
22 Swein does not appear to have had any issue but, interestingly enough, Harefoot seems to have had a son called Ælfwine (by a wife or mistress who, confusingly, was named Ælfgifu). Ælfwine is heard of only once.

It is recorded in a document in the cartulary of the abbey of Conques, in central France, that not long before 1060 a wandering Englishman on pilgrimage through the county of Rouergue one day presented himself to the lords of Panat as being the son of one 'King Harold' of England. In the context this can only mean Harold Harefoot (king, 1037–40). Ælfwine impressed the locals with his piety and he became the abbot of a nearby monastery: W. H. Stevenson, 'An Alleged Son of King Harold Harefoot'. In theory, one might take the Ælfgyva scene in the tapestry as undermining any lingering pretension to the English throne that Harefoot's progeny may have had. In practice, Ælfwine would not have had any real expectation of succeeding, nor any supporters in England, and he appears to have become a monk in France long before 1066. This, therefore, cannot be the answer to the Ælfgyva enigma.

20 *Wadard and Vital*

1 An account of the meeting was published in *The Genealogists Magazine* and is reprinted with other copious information on the subject in Camp, *My Ancestors Came with the Conqueror.*
2 Douglas, 'Companions of the Conqueror'.
3 Van Houts, 'Wace as Historian'.
4 Prentout, 'An Attempt to Identify Some Unknown Characters in the Bayeux Tapestry'.
5 Chibnall, *The World of Orderic Vitalis*; Gravett, *Norman Knight.*
6 *La Crépin, vie de Saint Herluin.*
7 Chibnall, *The World of Orderic Vitalis*, pp. 15, 119.
8 Bridgeford, 'Was Count Eustace II of Boulogne the Patron?'.
9 Urry, 'The Normans in Canterbury'.
10 *Ibid.*; Gem (ed.), *St Augustine's Abbey*, pp. 60–61.
11 *Domesday Book*, p. 30.
12 On Goscelin's life, *The Life of King Edward*, introduction by Barlow.
13 Gem, 'Canterbury and the Cushion Capital'; Gem (ed.), *St Augustine's Abbey.*
14 Gem, 'Canterbury and the Cushion Capital', pp. 88–9.
15 The mention of commercial documents at this early date is said to be unusual.
16 Translated by Gem in 'Canterbury and the Cushion Capital'.

17 Gem, 'Canterbury and the Cushion Capital', pp. 86–7, commentary and discussion pp. 88ff.
18 Lambert of Ardres, *The History of the Counts of Guines and the Lords of Ardres*, pp. 141–2.
19 Gem (ed.), *St Augustine's Abbey*, chapter 3 (Ann Williams); Bernstein, *Mystery of the Bayeux Tapestry*, p. 54.

21 Bayeux Cathedral and the Mystery of Survival

1 Dodwell, 'The Bayeux Tapestry and the French Secular Epic'.
2 Vallery-Radot, *La Cathédrale de Bayeux*, p. 41. The scene dates from 1857. There seems no evidence of any pre-existing similar sculpture linking the tapestry with the cathedral.
3 Wace, *Roman de Rou*, III, lines 5685ff.
4 *Ibid.*, III, lines 6453ff.
5 Interestingly, the image depicted in the tapestry seems identical to how William's ship is described in the *Ship List of William the Conqueror*, except that for some curious and as yet unexplained reason the embroidered version is a mirror image of that in the *Ship List*. Van Houts, 'The Echo of the Conquest in the Latin Sources'.
6 Wace, *Roman de Rou*, III, lines 8115ff.
7 The conjectures which follow are indebted to H. Prentout, 'Les Sources de la conquête de l'Angleterre' (who put them forward only as conjectures).
8 Vallery-Radot, *La Cathédrale de Bayeux*, pp. 68ff.
9 *Ibid.*, p. 69.
10 Wace, *Roman de Rou*, III, line 11121.
11 Although William of Malmesbury has Harold die in a manner which is reminiscent of the tapestry, his account of Harold's voyage is completely at odds with what we see in the tapestry. Malmesbury has him depart only on a fishing expedition, which is blown off-course to France. Marjorie Chibnall has examined the relationship between the Bayeux Tapestry and Orderic Vitalis and concluded that Orderic either did not know of the tapestry or chose not to use it: Chibnall, 'Orderic Vital et la tapisserie de Bayeux'.
12 Thomson, *A History of Tapestry*, p. 91; Thomson also reproduces the inventory.

22 *The Patronage of the Bayeux Tapestry*

1 Gem (ed.), *St Augustine's Abbey* (Ann Williams), Chapter 3.
2 Gem (ed.), *St Augustine's Abbey* (Ann Williams), Chapter 3.
3 Prentout, 'An Attempt to Identify Some Unknown Characters in the Bayeux Tapestry'.

Bibliography

Les Actes de Guillaume le Conquérant et de la reine Mathilde pour les abbayes caennaises, ed. L. Musset (Caen, 1967)

Adigard des Gautries, J Les Noms des personnes scandinaves en Normandie de 911 à 1066 (Lund, 1954)

Albu, Emily, The Normans in Their Histories: Propaganda, Myth and Subversion (Woodbridge, 2001)

Alexander, J. J. G., Medieval Illuminators and Their Methods of Work (Newhaven and London, 1992)

Amatus of Montecassino, Storia de' Normanni di Amato di Montecassino (Rome, 1935)

The Anglo-Saxon Chronicle, tr. and ed. Michael Swanton (London, 1996)

Bachrach, B., 'Some Observations on the Bayeux Tapestry', Cithara 27.1 (1987), pp. 5–28

Baigent, R., Leigh, R. and Lincoln, H., The Holy Blood and the Holy Grail (London, 1984)

Barlow, Frank, Edward the Confessor (New Haven, CT, 1997)

——, The Godwins (London, 2002)

Barré, Pierre-Yves, et al., La tapisserie de la reine Mathilde, comédie, en un acte, en prose, mêlée de vaudevilles (Paris, 1804)

Bates, David, 'The Character and Career of Odo, Bishop of Bayeux (1049/50–1097)', Speculum 50 (1975), pp. 1–20

——, *Regesta Regum Anglo-Normannorum: The Acta of William I 1066–1087* (Oxford, 1998)

——, *William the Conqueror* (London, 2001)

Baudri de Bourgeuil, *Les Œuvres poétiques de Baudri de Bourgeuil 1046–1130*, ed. P. Abrahams (Paris, 1926)

Beckermann, John S., 'Succession in Normandy, 1087, and England, 1066: The Role of Testamentary Custom', *Speculum* 47 (1972), pp. 258–60

Bender, Karl-Heinz, *König und Vasall: Untersuchungen zur Chanson de Geste des XII Jahrhunderts* (Heidelberg, 1967)

Benedictines de Bayeux, *Ide de Lorraine* (Bayeux, 1978)

Bennett, Mathew, *Campaigns of the Norman Conquest* (Oxford, 2001)

Bennett, P. E., 'Encore Turold dans la tapisserie de Bayeux', *Annales de Normandie* 30 (1980), pp. 3–13

Benoît, *Chronique des ducs de Normandie*, ed. C. Fahlin, 3 vols. (Lund, 1951–67)

Beowulf, ed. F. Klaeber (3rd edn, New York, 1941)

Bernstein, David, *The Mystery of the Bayeux Tapestry* (London, 1986)

Bertrand, Simone, 'Le Mont-Saint-Michel et la tapisserie de Bayeux', in *La Normandie bénédictine au temps de Guillaume le Conquérant* (Lille, 1967), pp. 137–40

Boüard, Michel de, 'La Chanson de Roland et la Normandie', *Annales de Normandie* 3 (1952), pp. 34–8

——, *Guillaume le Conquérant* (Paris, 1984)

The Brevis Relatio de Guillelmo Nobilissimo Comite Normanorrum Written by a Monk of Battle Abbey, ed. Elisabeth M. C. van Houts, Camden Miscellany 5th series 10 (Cambridge, 1997); reprinted with translation in van Houts, *History and Family Traditions*, chapter 7

Bridgeford, Andrew, 'Was Count Eustace II of Boulogne the Patron of the Bayeux Tapestry?' *Journal of Medieval History* 25 (1999), pp. 155–85

——, 'Camels, Drums and the Song of Roland', *Medieval Life*, Spring 2001, pp. 26–8

Brooke, Christopher, *The Saxon and the Norman Kings* (London, 1986)

Brooks, N. P. and Walker, H. E., 'The Authority and Interpretation of the Bayeux Tapestry', *Proceedings of the Battle Conference on Anglo-Norman Studies* 1 (1979), pp. 1–34 and 191–9

Bibliography

Brown, R. Allen, *The Normans and the Norman Conquest* (2nd edn, Woodbridge, 1985)

Brown, S. A., 'The Bayeux Tapestry and the Song of Roland', *Olifant* 6 (1979), pp. 339–50

——, *The Bayeux Tapestry: History and Bibliography* (Woodbridge, 1988)

——, 'The Bayeux Tapestry: Why Eustace, Odo and William?' *Anglo-Norman Studies* 12 (1990), pp. 7–28

Brown, S. A. and Herren, M. W., 'The *Adelae Comitissae* of Baudri de Bourgeuil', *Anglo-Norman Studies* 16 (1994), pp. 55–73; reprinted in Gameson (ed.), *Study of the Bayeux Tapestry*

Camp, Antony J., *My Ancestors Came with the Conqueror* (London, 1990)

Campbell, M. W., 'Queen Emma and Ælfgifu of Northampton: Canute the Great's Women', *Mediaeval Scandinavia* 4 (1971), pp. 66–79

The Carmen de Hastingae Proelio of Guy Bishop of Amiens, ed. and tr. Frank Barlow (Oxford, 1999)

Chibnall, Marjorie, *The World of Orderic Vitalis* (Woodbridge, 1984)

——, 'Orderic Vital et la tapisserie de Bayeux', forthcoming in B. Levy and F. Neveux (eds.), *La Tapisserie de Bayeux/The Bayeux Tapestry*, (Caen)

Churchill, Winston S., *The History of the English Speaking Peoples* (London, 1956)

Cowdrey, Herbert, 'Death-bed Testaments', in *Schriften der Monumenta Germaniae Historica* 33 IV (Hanover, 1988)

Crépin, Gilbert, *La Vie de Saint Herluin (Vita Herlewini)* (Bec, n.d.)

Dibdin, Thomas Frognall, *A Bibliographical, Antiquarian and Picturesque Tour in France and Germany*, 3 vols. (2nd edn, London, 1829)

Dodwell, C. R., 'The Bayeux Tapestry and the French Secular Epic', *Burlington Magazine* 108 (1966), pp. 549–60; reprinted in Gameson (ed.), *Study of the Bayeux Tapestry*

——, *Anglo-Saxon Art* (London, 1982)

Domesday Book, ed. Ann Williams and G. H. Martin (London, 2002)

Douglas, David, 'The Companions of the Conqueror', *History* 28 (1943), pp. 129–47

——, 'The Song of Roland and the Norman Conquest', *French Studies* 14 (1960), pp. 99–116

——, *William the Conqueror* (London, 1964)

Dubosq, René, *La Tapisserie de Bayeux dite de la reine Mathilde: dix années tragiques de sa longue histoire 1939–48* (Caen, 1951)

Ducarel, Andrew, *Anglo-Norman Antiquities, Considered in a Tour through Part of Normandy* (London, 1767)

Eadmer, *Eadmer's History of Recent Events in England*, Books I–IV, tr. G. Bosanquet (London, 1964)

Encomium Emmae Reginae, ed. Alistair Campbell with a supplementary introduction by Simon Keynes (Cambridge, 1998)

Faral, E., *Les Jongleurs en France au Moyen Age* (2nd edn, Paris, 1964)

Fauroux, M., *Recueil des actes des ducs de Normandie de 911 à 1066* (Caen, 1961)

Favier, Jean, *Charlemagne* (Paris, 1999)

Foreville, Raymonde, 'Aux origins de la renaissance juridique', *Le Moyen Age* 58 (n.d.), pp. 43–83

Foys, Martin K., *The Bayeux Tapestry Digital Edition* CD-Rom (Scholarly Digital Editions, 2003)

Freeman, Eric, 'The Identity of Aelfgyva in the Bayeux Tapestry', *Annales de Normandie* 41 (1991), pp. 117–34

Freeman, E. A., *The Norman Conquest*, 6 vols. (London, 1867–79)

Gaimar, *L'Estoire des Engleis*, ed. Alexander Bell (Oxford, 1960)

Gameson, Richard, 'The Origin, Art, and Message of the Bayeux Tapestry', in Gameson (ed.), *The Study of the Bayeux Tapestry*

Gameson, Richard (ed.), *The Study of the Bayeux Tapestry* (Woodbridge, 1997)

Gem, Richard, 'Canterbury and the Cushion Capital: A Commentary on Passages from Goscelin's *De Miraculis Sancti Augustini*', in N. Stratford (ed.), *Romanesque and Gothic: Essays for George Zarnecki* (Woodbridge, 1987)

Gem, Richard (ed.), *St Augustine's Abbey Canterbury* (London, 1997)

Genealogia Comitum Boloniensium, ed. L. C. Bethman, *Monumenta Germaniae Historica Scriptores* 9 (Stuttgart, 1963), pp. 299–301

Gibbs-Smith, C., 'Notes on the Plates', in Stenton (ed.), *Bayeux Tapestry*

Gormont et Isembart, ed. A. Bayot (3rd edn, Paris, 1969)

Gransden, Antonia, *Historical Writing in England c. 550–c. 1307* (London, 1974)

Grape, Wolfgang, *The Bayeux Tapestry* (Munich, 1994)

Bibliography

Gravett, Christopher, *Norman Knight* (Oxford, 1993)

Grierson, 'A Visit of Earl Harold to Flanders in 1056', *English Historical Review* 51 (1936), pp. 90–97

Hariulf, *Chronicon Cenulense ou chronique de l'abbaye de Saint-Riquier*, tr. Marquis le Ver (Abbeville, 1899)

Hart, Cyril, 'The Canterbury Contribution to the Bayeux Tapestry', in *Art and Symbolism in Medieval Europe: Papers of the Medieval Europe Brugge Conference 1997*, vol. V, ed. G. de Boe and F. Verhaeghe (Zellick, 1997), pp. 7–15

——, 'The Bayeux Tapestry and Schools of Illumination at Canterbury', *Anglo-Norman Studies* 22 (1999), pp. 117–67

Harward, Vernon J., *The Dwarfs of Arthurian Romance and Celtic Myth* (Leiden, 1958)

Henry of Huntingdon, *Henry, Archdeacon of Huntingdon, Historia Anglorum*, ed. and tr. Diana Greenway (Oxford, 1996)

Hill, David, 'The Bayeux Tapestry and its Commentators', *Medieval Life* 11 (1999), pp. 24–6

Hume, David, *The History of England* (many editions)

Hyde Chronicle, Liber Monasterii de Hyda, ed. E. Edwards (London, 1886)

Jenkins, Simon, *England's Thousand Best Churches* (London, 1999)

John of Worcester, *The Chronicle of John of Worcester*, ed. R. R. Darlington and P. McGurk, tr. Jennifer Bray and P. McGurk, vol. II (Oxford, 1995)

Johnson, S., 'Medieval German Dwarfs: A Footnote to Gottfried's Merlot', in *Gottfried von Strassburg and the Medieval Tristan Legend* (Cambridge, 1990)

Keats-Rohan, K. S. B., *Domesday People: A Prosopography of Persons Occurring in English Documents 1066–1166*, vol. I, *Domesday Book* (Woodbridge, 1999)

Keynes, Simon, 'The Æthelings in Normandy', *Anglo-Norman Studies* 13 (1991), pp. 173–205

Kuder, Ulrich, *Der Teppich von Bayeux* (Frankfurt, 1994)

La Chanson de Roland, ed. and tr. into modern French by Ian Short (2nd edn, Paris, 1990)

Lambert of Ardres, *The History of the Counts of Guines and the Lords of Ardres*, tr. Leah Shopkow (Philadelphia, 2001)

Lawson, M. K., *The Battle of Hastings* (Stroud, 2002)

Le Chevalier au Cygne, *The Old French Crusade Cycle*, Vols. I and II, ed Jan A. Nelson (Alabama, 1985)

Le Gentil, P., *La Chanson de Roland* (Paris, 1967)

Lejeune, Rita, 'Le Caractère de l'archêveque Turpin et les événements contemporains de la Chanson de Roland (version d'Oxford)', *Société Rencesvals IVe Congrès International* (1967), pp. 9–21

——, 'Turold dans la tapisserie de Bayeux', in *Melanges offerts à René Crozet* (Poitiers, 1966), pp. 419–25

Liber Eliensis, ed. E. O. Blake (London, 1962)

The Life of King Edward Who Rests at Westminster, ed. and tr. Frank Barlow (2nd edn, Oxford, 1992)

Lomenec'h, Gerard, *Chantres et ménéstrels à la cour de Bretagne* (Rennes, 1993)

Loomis, Laura Hibbard, 'The Holy Relics of Charlemagne and King Athelstan: The Lances of Longinus and St Mauricius', *Speculum* 25 (1950), pp. 437–56

——, 'The Passion Lance Relics and the War Cry Monjoie in the *Chanson de Roland* and Related Texts', *Romanic Review* 40 (1950), pp. 241–60

Lot, Ferdinand, 'Etudes sur les légendes épiques françaises', *Romania* (1928), pp. 357–79

Loyd, L. C., *The Origins of Some Anglo-Norman Families* (Leeds, 1951)

Maclagan, E., *The Bayeux Tapestry* (London, 1945)

Marwood, Geoffrey W., *The Stone Coffins of Bosham Church* (Chichester, 1974)

McLynn, Frank, *1066: The Year of Three Battles* (London, 1998)

McNulty, J. Bard, 'The Lady Ælfgyva in the Bayeux Tapestry', *Speculum* 55 (1980), pp. 659–68

——, *The Narrative Art of the Bayeux Tapestry Master* (New York, 1989)

Messent, Jan, *The Bayeux Tapestry Embroiderer's Story* (Thirsk, 1999)

Moignet, G., *La Chanson de Roland* (Paris, 1972)

Montfaucon, Bernard de, *Les Monuments de la monarchie française*, vol. II (Paris, 1730)

Morton, Catherine, 'Pope Alexander II and the Norman Conquest', *Latomus* 34 (1975), pp. 362–82

Morton, Catherine and Muntz, Hope, *The Carmen de Hastingae Proelio of Guy Bishop of Amiens* (Oxford, 1972)

Musset, Lucien, *La Tapisserie de Bayeux* (Paris, 2002)

Bibliography

Nicholas, Lynn, *The Rape of Europa: The Fate of Europe's Treasures in the Third Reich and the Second World War* (London, 1995)

Orderic Vitalis, *The Ecclesiastical History of Orderic Vitalis*, ed. and tr. Marjorie Chibnall, 6 vols. (Oxford, 1969–80)

Owen, D. D. R. 'The Epic and History: *Chanson de Roland* and *Carmen de Hastingae Proelio*', *Medium Ævum* 11 (1982), pp. 18–34

Peckham, D. W., 'The Bosham Myth of Canute's Daughter', *Sussex Notes and Queries* XVII 6, pp. 179–84

Platts, Beryl, *Origins of Heraldry* (London, 1980)

Pollock, John, *Harold Rex: Is King Harold II Buried in Bosham Church?* (Bosham, 1996)

Prentout, H., 'Les Sources de la conquête de l'Angleterre', *Bulletin Annuel de la Société Jersiaise*, 1923, pp. 27–8

——, 'Essai d'identification des personnages inconnus de la tapisserie de Bayeux', *Revue Historique* 176 (1935), pp. 14–23; translated and reprinted as 'An Attempt to Identify Some Unknown Characters in the Bayeux Tapestry', in Gameson (ed.), *The Study of the Bayeux Tapestry*

Runciman, Steven, *A History of the Crusades*, 3 vols. (London, 1990)

Short, Ian, 'The Language of the Bayeux Tapestry Inscription', *Anglo-Norman Studies* 23 (2001), pp. 267–80

Simeon of Durham, *Opera Omnia*, ed. T. Arnold, 2 vols. (London, 1882, 1885)

Smith, Mary F., 'Archbishop Stigand and the Eye of the Needle', *Anglo-Norman Studies* 16 (1994), pp. 199–219

Song of Roland, tr. Glyn Burgess (London, 1990)

Stenton, Frank (ed.), *The Bayeux Tapestry: A Comprehensive Survey* (2nd edn, London, 1965)

Stevenson, W. H., 'An Alleged Son of King Harold Harefoot', *English Historical Review* 28 (1913), pp. 112–17

Stothard, C. A., 'Some Observations on the Bayeux Tapestry', *Archaeologia* (1821), pp. 184–91; reprinted in Gameson (ed.), *The Study of the Bayeux Tapestry*

Tabuteau, Emily Zack, 'The Role of Law in the Succession to Normandy and England, 1087', *The Haskins Society Journal* 3 (1991), pp. 141–9

Tanner, Heather J., 'The Expansion of the Power and Influence of the Counts of Boulogne under Count Eustace II', *Anglo-Norman Studies* 14 (1992), pp. 251–86

339

——, 'Between Scylla and Charybdis: The Political Role of the Comital Family of Boulogne in Northern France and England (879–1159)', unpublished Ph.D. thesis (1993)

Taylor, Arnold J., 'Belrem', *Anglo-Norman Studies* 14 (1992), pp. 1–23

Thomson, W. G., *A History of Tapestry* (3rd edn, London, 1973)

Urry, W., 'The Normans in Canterbury', *Annales de Normandie* 8 (1958), pp. 119–36

Vallery-Radot, Jean, *La Cathédrale de Bayeux* (Paris, n.d., c. 1926)

Van Houts, Elisabeth, M. C., 'The Ship List of William the Conqueror', *Anglo-Norman Studies* 10 (1988), pp. 159–83; reprinted in van Houts, *History and Family Traditions*, chapter 6

——, 'The Norman Conquest Through European Eyes', *English Historical Review* 110 (1995), pp. 832–53; reprinted in van Houts, *History and Family Traditions*, chapter 8

——, 'Wace as Historian', in K. S. B. Keats-Rohan (ed.), *Family Trees and the Roots of Politics* (Woodbridge, 1997); reprinted in van Houts, *History and Family Traditions*, chapter 10

——, *History and Family Traditions in England and the Continent, 1000–1200* (Aldershot, 1999)

——, 'The Echo of the Conqest in Latin Sources: Duchess Matilda, Her Daughters and the Enigma of the Golden Child', forthcoming in *La Tapisserie de Bayeux/The Bayeux Tapestry*, ed. B. Levy and F. Neveux (Caen)

Verchère, Chantal, 'Périphérie et croisement: aspect du nain dans la littérature médiévale', in *Exclus et systèmes d'exclusions dans la littérature médiévale* (Aix-en-Provence, 1978)

Villion, Pierre, *Visions secrètes de la tapisserie de Bayeux* (Caen, 1987)

Von Choltitz, Dietrich, 'Pouquoi, en 1944, je n'ai pas détruit Paris', *Le Figaro*, 12 October 1949

Wace, *The Roman de Rou*, ed. and tr. Glyn Burgess (Jersey, 2002)

Walker, Ian W., *Harold: The Last Anglo-Saxon King* (Stroud, 1997)

The Waltham Chronicle, ed. and tr. L. Watkins and Marjorie Chibnall (Oxford, 1994)

William of Jumièges, *The Gesta Normannorum Ducem of William of Jumièges, Orderic Vitalis, and Robert of Torigni*, Vol. I, ed. and tr. Elisabeth M. C. van Houts (Oxford, 1995)

William of Malmesbury, *Gesta Regum Anglorum*, vol. I, ed. and tr.

Bibliography

R. A. B. Mynors, R. M. Thomson and M. Winterbottom (Oxford, 1998)

William of Poitiers, *The Gesta Guillelmi of William of Poitiers*, ed. and tr. R. H. C. Davis and Marjorie Chibnall (Oxford, 1998)

Williams, Ann, 'Some Notes and Considerations on Problems Connected with the English Royal Succession 860–1066', *Battle* 7 (1978), pp. 144–233

——, 'Land and Power in the Eleventh Century: The Estates of Harold Godwinson', *Proceedings of the Battle Conference on Anglo-Norman Studies* 3 (1981), pp. 171–87

——, *The English and the Norman Conquest* (Woodbridge, 1995)

Wilson, David, *The Bayeux Tapestry* (London, 1985)

Wissolik, Richard D., 'The Saxon Statement: Code in the Bayeux Tapestry', *Annuale Mediaevale* 19 (1979), pp. 69–97

——, 'The Monk Eadmer as Historian of the Norman Succession: Körner and Freeman Examined', *The American Benedictine Review*, 30.1 (1979), 32–43

Wormald, Francis, 'Style and Design', in Stenton (ed.), *Bayeux Tapestry*

Index

Abbaye aux Dames, Caen 217
Abbaye aux Hommes, Caen 210,
    217
Académie Royale des Inscriptions
    et Belles-Lettres 29
Adalbero of Rheims, Archbishop
    183
Adela of Blois, Countess 26, 27,
    147, 152–3, 298
Adelae Comitissae (Baudri) 299
Adelina 230
Æflgyd 158
Ælfflaed 157
Ælfgifu 248–51, 252, 254, 255,
    256–62 *see also* lfgyva and
    Emma
Ælfgyva 5, 81, 83, 110, 132, 163,
    246, 247, 250, 251, 252, 253,
    257, 270, 300, 305, 307
    see also lfgifu and Emma
Ælfwine of Winchester 253
Aesop's fables 67

Æthelred the Unready 247, 248,
    250, 254, 255, 256, 264
Æthelric of Selsey, Bishop 211
Ahnenerbe (Ancestral Heritage)
    (SS) 39, 40
Alençon 42, 175
Alexander II, Pope 119, 120, 288
Alfonso of Spain 134
Alfred, Prince 185, 256, 263, 264,
    265, 266, 267–8, 269, 271
Alfred the Great, King 67, 203
Alstan 284
Angilbert 239
Anglo-Saxon Chronicle 8, 19–20,
    53, 55, 108, 114, 126, 187,
    211, 218–19, 249, 257 258,
    308
Apulia 240
Ark of the Covenant 92
Arnulf III 205
Arnulf of Ardres 291
Arnulf of Choques 222

343

Arsic 281–2
Askericus 231
Aubert 84
Aulne, River 75

Baldwin I of Flanders, Count
    70–1, 178, 179, 181, 188
Baldwin II of Flanders, Count 203
Baldwin V of Flanders, Count 205
Baldwin VI of Flanders, Count 205
Baldwin of Bologne 222
Baldwin of Le Bourg 207
Barlow, Professor 204
Battle Abbey 275
Baudri of Bourgeuil 26–7, 33, 147,
    148, 152, 153, 220, 298, 299
Bayeux, town of 1–4
Bayeux Cathedral 1, 2, 17, 27–8,
    30, 33, 35, 295, 296, 297,
    298, 299, 301, 302, 303
Bayeux Tapestry 1–10, 17–18
    Ælfgyva, scandal of 246–71;
    artist 7–8, 9–10; Edward's
    death, depicts 103–17
    Eustace, role in 9, 57, 140, 144,
    145, 150, 151, 155, 171, 172,
    191–208, 226, 270, 275, 303;
    fox and the crow, importance
    of 66–97; Harold, depiction
    of life 56–65, 99 see also
    Harold, King; historical
    journey 26–47, 100; invasion
    of England, depicts 118–54;
    named characters 5–6;
    opening 50–1; origin 155–61,
    295–303; patron 162–72,
    295, 304–9; sources 19–25,

100–17; title 8, 156; Turold
    the Dwarf, role in 225;
    Wadard and Vital, role in
    272–93
Beaurain 68–9, 73, 300
Becket, Thomas 31
Benedict X, Pope 107, 113
Benoît, Antoine 30, 147, 148,
    192–3
Beowulf 11, 15, 233
Berdic 230
Berlin 45, 46
Bernstein, David 148, 167, 168,
    170
Béroul 226
Bible, The 166
Bibliothèque du Roi, Paris 29
Bibliothèque Nationale, Paris 24
Biota, Countess 58, 180, 189
Blitherus 288, 291
Boissay, Bishop Jean de 301, 302
Bonaparte, Napoleon 33, 34
Bonneville 163
Bosham church 60–1, 66, 152,
    297
Boulogne 62, 142, 154, 171, 183,
    184, 185, 186, 188, 194, 195,
    200, 202, 223, 239, 291
Bourgeuil monastry 26
British War Cemetery 43–4
Bull's Eye 92
Byrhtnoth 11

Caen 76, 158, 176, 178, 277, 288,
    289, 290, 291, 293, 299, 301
Caesar, Julius 169
Calabria 240

Index

Calvellus, William 287
Canterbury Miscellany 159
Canute, King 49, 51–2, 53, 57, 61, 62, 107, 152, 185, 248–9, 253, 254, 255, 256 257, 258, 259, 261, 263, 267, 270
Canute IV, King 215
Capet, Hugh 183, 239
Carmen de Hastingae Proelio (the Song of the Battle of Hastings) (Bishop Guy of Amiens) 23, 128, 142, 143, 149, 182, 190, 193, 194, 195, 197, 198, 239, 243, 244, 275, 276
Catherine of Bar 207
Centre Guillaume le Conquérant 47
Cervotti, Monsieur 41–2
Chanson de Roland 16, 182, 183, 233–45, 296
Chansons de geste 233
Charlemagne, Emperor 63–4, 141, 181, 182–3, 186, 194, 203, 223, 233, 234, 235, 238 239, 240, 241–2, 243, 307, 308
Charles of Lorraine 181, 183
Charles the Simple, King 22
Château de Sourches 40, 42–3, 46
Choltitz, General von 44, 45, 46
Christ Church Abbey, Canterbury 23, 306
Churchill, Winston 38, 125
Commentary on Daniel (Jerome) 168
Conan II 230
Conan of Brittany, Duke 82, 87, 89, 169

Coniah 168
Constantinople 52
Corney, Bolton 163
Council of Clermont 220, 298–9
Curthose, Robert 215, 216, 217, 218, 219, 220, 221, 302
Cynesige, Archbishop of York 113

Dagobert, King 184
de Gaulle, General 44
Deireóil, Cnú 231
Delauney, François 162–3
Denmark 51–2, 54, 57, 185, 216, 254, 259, 261
Dibdin, Reverend Thomas Frognall 36–7
Dinan, Battle of 87–90
Dives 124, 125, 272, 273
Dodeman, Monsieur 40
Dodwell, Charles 295–6
Dol 82, 87, 89, 169, 215, 230, 297, 298
Domesday Book 12, 111, 133, 154, 158, 163, 206, 209, 215–16, 227, 230, 251, 276, 281 282, 283, 284, 285, 286, 287
Douglas, Professor David 275
Dover Castle 141, 165, 172, 199, 200, 201, 202–3, 204, 205, 209, 218, 223, 280, 282 284, 293
Drogo, Count of the Vexin 58, 186, 216
Ducarel, Andrew 30–1

Eadmer 23, 58, 59, 76–7, 80, 90–1, 95, 161, 251

Ealdgyth 133
Ealdred, Archbishop of York 113, 154
Ecclesiastical History (William of Jumièges) 24
Edgar (theling) 55, 56, 65, 108, 154, 204, 247, 248
Edith the Fair 65
Edith, Queen 20, 48, 50, 54, 55, 65, 80, 105, 108–9, 132–3, 154, 156, 157
Edmund, King 247
Edward the Confessor, King 40, 65, 95, 97, 122, 180, 186, 187, 247, 248, 268
  accession 49, 269, 308; death 20, 40, 101–12; Duke William, attitude towards 116, 118, 188, 203, 308; exile 52–3, 85–6, 264, 266; parentage 253, 256, 263; reign 48 ; succession 5, 6, 50, 51, 53–4, 55, 56–60; Westminster Abbey, role in creation of 98–101, 115, 296
Edward the Exile 54–5, 102, 255
Edwin, Earl 133
Edwy, King 247
Eisenhower, General 44
Ely Cathedral 11, 13, 157, 185, 266
Emma 248, 252–6, 259, 261–2, 266, 267, 268, 269, 270 *see also* lfgifu *and* lfgyva
Encomium Emmae Reginae 258, 265
Enguerrand of Ponthieu, Count 72, 179

Erec et Enide (de Troyes) 231–2
Erminfrid of Sion, Bishop 286
Estrithsson, King Swein 56–7
Eu 77
Eustace I, Count 185, 207, 264
Eustace II of Boulogne, Count 72, 154, 180, 183–5, 231, 292, 306, 307
  ancestry 141, 181–2, 238; attacked in Dover 187–8; Battle of Hastings, role in 141–3, 145, 149–50, 165, 195–6, 197; Dover Castle, attacks 200–7, 212, 282; family 23, 58, 71; Godwin, grudge against 185–6, 271; Harold, relationship with 188–9; heraldry, introduces into England 194; marriage 186–7, 264; patronage of tapestry 223, 244, 277, 280, 293, 295, 305; tapestry depictions of 57, 140, 144, 145, 150, 151, 155, 171, 172, 191, 192, 193, 198, 208, 226, 270, 275, 306; wealth 209; William, relationship with 9–10, 22, 120, 190
Eustace III, Count 206, 207, 218, 219, 220, 222
Eustace IV, Count 207
Ezekiel 167

Falaise Castle 272
Falaise Roll 272, 274
Falue, Monsieur 41–2
Fécamp abbey 125

Index

First World War 38
Fitz-Osbern, Earl William 141,
    200, 211–12
Flanders 70–1, 171, 183, 184, 185
Flers 41
Fork-Beard, Swein 51, 254, 255,
    257, 258, 259, 261, 270, 271
Foucault, Anne 29
Foucault, Nicolas-Joseph 29, 30
Franco-Prussian War (1870–1) 38
Franks 182, 183
French Revolution 32, 207
Fulbert 173, 174

Ganelon 235–7, 238
Geoffrey of Anjou, Count 179
Geoffrey of Cambrai 94
Geoffrey of Coutances, Bishop
    211, 218
Gerberoi 215
German Academy, Stettin 40
Gesta Guillelmi Ducis (the Deeds
    of Duke William) (William of
    Poitiers) 21, 24
Giffard, Walter 134, 141
Gilbert of Evreux 222
Gilfard, Robert 149, 196–7, 275,
    276
Giroie 278
Godfrey of Bouillon 206, 207, 222
Godgifu 58, 185, 186, 202, 204,
    264
Godwin, Earl 20, 49–50, 53, 54,
    56, 58, 59, 61–2, 102, 107,
    185, 186, 187, 188, 189, 195
    210, 262, 264, 265, 267, 269,
    271, 308

Godwinson, Harold see Harold,
    King
Godwinson, Wulfnoth 58, 59, 65,
    80, 94, 246–7, 271
Gonfried 291
Gormont et Isembart 233
Goscelin 157, 287–8, 289, 291,
    292
Gota 52
Gregory VII, Pope 214
Grestain Abbey 277
Grimkell, Bishop 260–1
Gruffydd, King 50, 133
Guiscard, Robert 222
Gunter of Bamberg, Bishop 231
Guy of Amiens, Bishop 23, 142,
    193, 243, 244
Guy of Ponthieu, Count 22, 23,
    63, 64, 67, 68–70, 71–3,
    74–5, 76, 77–8, 97, 142, 179
    188, 196, 225, 231, 232, 238,
    239, 275, 299
Gyrth, Earl 50, 65, 80, 138
Gytha 132, 151

Haimo 286–7
Hakon 58, 59, 65, 94, 271
Halley, Edmond 114
Halley's Comet 34, 114–15
Harald of Norway 55
Hardrada, King Harald 123,
    125–6
Harefoot, Harold 185, 186, 249,
    255, 256–7, 258–9, 261, 262,
    263, 264, 265, 266, 267–8
    270–1
Hariulf 233, 242

Harold II, King 111
Harold of Wessex, Earl *see*
  Harold, King
Harold, King 5, 17, 38, 48, 57,
  71, 115, 122, 125, 161, 166,
  167, 180, 186, 279
  accession 50, 56, 108, 109–13,
  189; ancestry 55–6, 203, 268,
  270; death 13, 144–52, 170,
  195, 196, 275; Edward,
  relationship with 56, 58;
  Hastings, role in Battle 137,
  138, 141, 145, 146–7, 148–9,
  150–3, 154, 156; Stamford
  Bridge, role in Battle 126–7;
  tapestry depictions of 20–2,
  51, 62–5, 66–70, 73–88, 104,
  105, 124, 144–52, 163, 168,
  170, 198, 297, 300, 307, 308;
  William, relationship with
  6–7, 47, 59–50, 67, 68, 74,
  77, 78–80, 81, 83, 84, 86, 88,
  90–7, 103, 108, 109, 119,
  246, 250–1, 270, 271;
  William's invasion, receives
  news of 131–5
Harthacanute 53, 186, 248, 256,
  259, 261, 262, 265, 267, 269,
  270
Hastings, Battle of 7, 15, 17, 22,
  23, 57, 79, 84, 104, 106, 131,
  139, 140, 142, 150, 151 153,
  155, 163, 164, 165, 172, 192,
  195, 200, 205, 206, 210, 221,
  223, 243, 272, 274, 275, 276,
  280, 283, 286, 291, 298, 304,
  305

Heaney, Seamus 15
Henry I of France, King 177,
  178–9, 216, 217, 302
Henry II of Champagne, Count
  231, 299
Henry IV, King 16
Henry of Huntingdon 23, 147
Henry VIII, King 152
Hereford, Earl of 186, 188
Herleva 173, 174, 176
Herluin of Conteville 173, 175,
  176, 277, 279
Hermann of Sherborne, Bishop
  287
Hill, Arthur 38
Himmler, Heinrich 39, 40, 43, 45,
  46
Historia Novorum in Anglia (*the
  History of Recent Events in
  England*) (Eadmer) 23, 58
  76–7, 90–1, 95–6, 161, 251
Hitler, Adolf 44, 46
Honors of Autun 232
Houts, Dr Elisabeth van 276
Hugh of Chester 279
Hugh of Montfort 141, 200, 201
Hugh of Ponthieu 149, 196, 197,
  275
Huguenots 28
Hume, David 31
Hundred Years War 15
Hungary 54

Ida of Lorraine, Countess 186,
  206, 207, 208
Ironside, Edmund 255
Isle of Wight 125, 214

Index

Jankuhn, Dr Herbert 40
Jehoiachim 168
Jehoiakim 168, 169
Jerusalem 166, 169, 206, 221, 222, 231, 308
John of Bayeux 217
John of Worcester 23, 257, 264
jongleur 229–30, 232–3, 234, 235, 243, 244, 297, 307
Juaye-Mondaye 39–40
Jumièges monastery 21

LaFarge, Bancel 46
Lancelot, Antoine 29, 30
Lanfranc, Archbishop 107, 210, 211, 214–15, 218, 285, 293, 306
Last Supper, The 130–1
Lejeune, Rita 229
Leo III, Pope 182
Leofgeat 283
Leofgyd 158
Leofwine, Earl 50, 65, 80, 138
Léonard-Leforestier, Lambert 32–3
Lillebonne 119
Louis the Pious 242
Louis V, King 183
Louvre 33, 45, 47

Magnus of Norway 261, 262, 267, 270
Maine, Walter, Count of 186, 189
Malcolm, King 123
Maldon, Battle of 11, 15, 157
Matilda of Boulogne 207
Matilda, Queen 2, 8, 30, 32, 34, 155, 157, 158, 162, 164, 178, 181, 186, 187, 215, 217

Maye, River 63
McNulty, J. Bard 252, 257, 270
Moignet, Gerard 235
Montfaucon, Bernard de 30, 155
Mont-Saint-Michel abbey 83–6, 89, 296
Monuments de la monarchie française (Montfaucon) 30
Mora 127
Morcar of Mercia, Earl 122, 133
Mortemer 179
Moses 92

Nebuchadnezzar 166, 168, 169
Normannorum Ducem (the Deeds of the Norman Dukes) (William) 21
Norway 52

Odin 71, 260
Odo of Bayeux, Bishop 177, 178, 180, 181, 190, 251, 275, 276, 279, 280, 281, 293, 297
Dover Castle, defends 200, 201, 203, 204–5; downfall 209–24; Hastings, role in Battle 140, 141, 145, 154; landlord 280, 281, 282, 283, 284, 285; patron of the tapestry 164–5, 295, 298, 299, 300, 301, 302, 304, 305, 306, 307, 308; tapestry depictions of 9, 90, 129–31, 140, 141, 145, 154, 162–3, 172, 173, 198–9, 237–8, 280, 295; William, relationship with 6, 7, 121–2, 129–31, 176, 181

Olaf 255, 259, 260, 261
Old English Illustrated Hexateuch 159
Old Testament 9, 167, 169, 183
Origins of Heraldry (Platts) 194
Osbern the Seneschal 176
Owen, D. D. R. 243

Palermo Cathedral 222–3
Paris 45, 46, 47, 179
Penenden Heath 211
Peter, Saint 99, 112
Pevensey 128, 163, 218, 219
Philip I, King 179, 205
Philip the Good of Burgundy, Duke 303
Picardy 68, 171, 230
Plantagenet, Henry 14–15, 17
Ponthieu 62–3, 64, 72, 74, 75, 76–8, 127, 225, 228, 230, 233, 238, 239, 241, 244
Prentout, Henri 308
Priam of Troy 181, 203

Queen Matilda's Tapestry (*la tapisserie de la reine Mathilde*) 8, 30, 33, 156

Ralf the Staller 212
Ranulphe, Abbot 84–5
Reading Museum 38
Rennes 87, 89–90
Richard I of Normandy, Duke 84, 248
Richard II of Normandy, Duke 84, 256
Richard III, King 175

Richilde 205
Rivallon of Dol 82, 87, 89
Robert of Beaumont 141
Robert of Hiésmois 173–4, 175
Robert of Jumièges 107
Robert of Mortain 84, 131, 176, 177, 181, 210, 213, 217, 226
Robert of Normandy, Duke 222
Robert the Frisian 205, 215, 292
Rodbert 104
Roger of Ivry 283
Roger of Montgomery, Earl 219, 230
Roger the Great, Count 222
Rollo 22, 181
Roman de Rou 299
Roncevaux 235
Rouen 22, 31, 78, 163, 179, 215, 216, 246, 250
Royal Historical Society 273
Royal Library in Brussels 23

Saint-Aubin-sur-Scie 72
Saint-Bertin monastry 287
Saint-Denis Cathedral 36
Saint-Evroul monastry 24
Saint-Pierre-de Préaux, abbey of 277
Saint-Riquier, abbey of 239, 242, 243, 244
Saint-Vigor, abbey of 30
Scolland, Abbot 284–5, 288, 289, 290, 291, 292
Scollandus, Abbot 85
Scott, Sir Walter 16
Second World War 38–47
Seine, River 175

Sens 242
*Ship List of William the
    Conqueror* 122, 127, 190
Short, Ian 170–1
Shrewsbury, Earl of 230
Sicily 240
Simeon of Durham 14
Society of Antiquaries, London 35
Society of Genealogists 272, 274,
    275
Somme, River 22, 124, 128, 244
Southawk 153
SS 39–40, 43, 44–5, 46
St Augustine's Abbey, Canterbury
    85, 108, 109, 159–61, 171,
    228, 258, 284, 285, 287
    288–90, 291, 292–3, 296,
    305, 306, 308
St Augustine's Gospels, The 159
St Edmund the Martyr 286
St Mary of Abingdon 283
Stamford Bridge, Battle of 126–7,
    135, 270
Stephen of Blois 207
Stephen, King 14
Stigand, Archbishop 104, 105,
    107, 110, 113, 114, 115, 116,
    154, 300
St-Omer 71, 104, 258
Stothard, Charles 35–6, 191, 192,
    207
Straits of Dover 201
Swan Knight 207–8
Swan-Neck, Edith 133, 151

Taillefer 275–6
Thomson, Dr T. R. 274

Thor 71,260
Thorne, William 284–5
Tofig the Proud 65
Tostig, Earl 20, 50, 122, 123, 125,
    126
Turold 5, 74, 81, 163, 225, 226,
    227–8, 229, 231, 232, 233,
    234, 235, 244, 245, 300, 305
    307, 308
Turpin, Archbishop 235, 237, 238,
    298

Ufegeat 254
Ulf 133
Urban II, Pope 220, 222, 298

Val-ès-Dunes, Battle of 176
Victoria and Albert Museum 36
Vikings 22, 52, 53–4, 62, 123,
    126, 227, 242, 254, 286
*Vita dward Regis (the Life of King
    Edward)* 20, 98–9, 100–2,
    104, 105–8, 113, 156–7
Vital 5, 163, 164, 274, 275, 276,
    277, 278, 279, 280, 282, 285,
    286, 287, 288, 289, 290–1
    293, 300, 306
Vitalis, Orderic 14, 23–4, 58, 123,
    132, 182, 200, 212, 216–17,
    219, 232, 275, 279

Wace 24, 174, 215, 274, 276, 299,
    300, 301, 302
Wadard 5, 163, 164, 274, 276,
    277, 278, 279, 280–2, 283,
    284, 285, 293, 300, 306
Wadard Morris Men 283–4

Walcher of Durham, Bishop 212
Walter of Mame 180
Waltham Abbey 152
Waltham's Holy Cross 65, 113
Waltheof, Earl 212
Wardle, Elizabeth 37
Wast 207
Westminster Abbey 98–9, 100,
    103, 112, 114, 115, 154, 267,
    289, 296
White, Geoffrey H. 272, 273
Wigalois 231
William (monk) 21
William of Arques 178, 179, 188
William of Jumièges 24, 200
William of Malmesbury 23, 70,
    147, 157, 214, 247
William of Normandy, Duke *see*
    William the Conqueror
William of Poitiers 21, 23, 24, 56,
    57, 64, 67, 77, 79, 94, 96,
    108–9, 110, 111, 112–13
    115, 118, 121, 124, 132, 135,
    136, 137–8, 140, 142–3, 149,
    151, 157, 190, 193, 201, 274
William of Warenne 141, 210
William Rufus, King 94, 216, 218,
    219–20, 221
William the Bastard 174
William the Conqueror 1, 2, 5, 6,
    7, 8, 9, 18, 21, 28, 85–7,
    169, 192, 213, 214, 246,
    275 286, 289, 296, 297,
    298, 303
  ancestry and family 22, 26, 30,
    162, 163, 164, 173, 178, 179,

181, 186–90, 215, 217, 218,
    238, 273; birthplace 272;
    Breton campaign 82–90;
    claim to throne 52–5, 57, 58,
    59, 60, 67, 96–7, 104, 108,
    109, 110–12, 116–17, 165,
    308; Count Guy of Ponthieu,
    relationship with 71, 72–7;
    death 215; Domesday, role in
    12, 158; English language,
    knowledge of 16; Eustace II,
    relationship with 196, 197,
    202–3, 204, 205, 206, 223–4;
    Harold, relationship with 47,
    67, 78–84, 88, 90–1, 92, 93,
    94, 102, 108, 251, 270, 271;
    Hastings, role in Battle 15,
    139, 140, 144, 145, 149, 150,
    153, 165, 196, 197, 198, 279;
    invasion of England 34, 38,
    118–35, 299
  law, execution of 210–11;
    tapestry depictions of 31, 44,
    67, 68, 78–9, 88, 139, 140,
    144, 145, 149, 150, 153, 165,
    167, 225, 226, 230, 300, 302,
    305
William, King *see* William the
    Conqueror
Wimarch, Robert fitz 105, 109
Winchester Cathedral 94, 269
Witan 51, 109
Wormald, Francis 158, 159
Wulfheah 254

Zedekiah 166–8

Acknowledgements

During my research for this book both the British Library in London and the Bibliothèque Nationale in Paris moved from their famous, older buildings to equally splendid new homes. What has been lost in historic atmosphere has been readily gained in efficiency and my thanks are due to all the library staff who have assisted me there, as well as to the librarians of Cambridge University Library, the Société Jersisaise, the Jersey Public Library and several other institutions. I have had the advantage of corresponding with, and sometimes meeting, many of the leading scholars of the Norman Conquest. Too numerous to mention by name, many of their works are listed in the Bibliography. It has certainly been an exciting time to research this period. Many of the leading sources have been republished in authoritative new English editions; researching in libraries, always a pleasure, has been made immeasurably easier with the advent of computerised indexes; and more and more material is becoming freely available on the Internet. My thanks cannot but be due to all the scholars whose expert work I have consulted. Inevitably, however, many questions are left without certain answer; the light of history shines only sporadically on the eleventh century. This remains a personal book, which argues for a new vision of the Bayeux Tapestry.

The passage from the *Roman de Rou* by Wace quoted at the beginning of this book is rendered in my own interpretation. Where the *Roman de Rou* is quoted elsewhere, I have used Professor Glyn Burgess' recent prose translation. I am grateful to the Société Jersiaise for permission to quote from that translation; to Oxford University Press for permission to quote from translations of the various Latin sources published in the Oxford Medieval Texts series; to Everyman's Library for permission to quote from the translation of the *Anglo-Saxon Chronicle* by Professor Michael Swanton; to Penguin Books for permission to quote from Professor Burgess's translation of the *Chanson de Roland*. Further details of these books may be found in the Bibliography. The Bayeux Tapestry has been reproduced by kind permission of the City of Bayeux.

My correspondence with Beryl Platts has been long and (for me) fruitful. Valentine Fallan of W.A.C.E. has kept me abreast on matters pertaining to Wace and has been a source of much information and encouragement. My gratitude is also due to many other people who have volunteered information or helped in various ways, including Catherine Cooper, Nicholas Falla, Rod McLoughlin, Dr S. Pavan and Mark and Julie Temple. I am grateful to the Fellows of Churchill College, Cambridge, for affording me the facilities of the Senior Combination Room during 2000; to the partners of Crills for allowing me a six-month sabbatical in 1998; to them and latterly the partners of Carey Olsen for their continued interest and encouragement; to my agent A. M. Heath & Co. Limited; and to Fourth Estate for seeing this book through to publication. Finally I must thank my wife who, when she married me, little knew that she was marrying this book as well and has suffered many of its attendant tribulations. To her and our daughter this book is offered as an imperfect tribute.

For the paperback edition I have taken the opportunity to make some minor corrections and changes. I am also grateful for further information provided by Richard Knowles F.S.A. and Richard Michel.